ENDER'S GAME
AND PHILOSOPHY

The Blackwell Philosophy and Pop Culture Series
Series Editor: William Irwin

A spoonful of sugar helps the medicine go down, and a healthy helping of popular culture clears the cobwebs from Kant. Philosophy has had a public relations problem for a few centuries now. This series aims to change that, showing that philosophy is relevant to your life—and not just for answering the big questions like "To be or not to be?" but for answering the little questions: "To watch or not to watch *South Park?*" Thinking deeply about TV, movies, and music doesn't make you a "complete idiot." In fact it might make you a philosopher, someone who believes the unexamined life is not worth living and the unexamined cartoon is not worth watching.

ENDER'S GAME AND PHILOSOPHY

The Logic Gate Is *Down*

Edited by Kevin S. Decker

WILEY Blackwell

This edition first published 2013
© 2013 John Wiley & Sons, Inc

Wiley-Blackwell is an imprint of John Wiley & Sons, formed by the merger of Wiley's global
Scientific, Technical and Medical business with Blackwell Publishing.

Registered Office
John Wiley & Sons, Ltd, The Atrium, Southern Gate, Chichester, West Sussex,
PO19 8SQ, UK

Editorial Offices
350 Main Street, Malden, MA 02148-5020, USA
9600 Garsington Road, Oxford, OX4 2DQ, UK
The Atrium, Southern Gate, Chichester, West Sussex, PO19 8SQ, UK

For details of our global editorial offices, for customer services, and for information about how
to apply for permission to reuse the copyright material in this book please see our website at
www.wiley.com/wiley-blackwell.

The right of Kevin S. Decker to be identified as the author of the editorial material in this work
has been asserted in accordance with the UK Copyright, Designs and Patents Act 1988.

Library of Congress Cataloging-in-Publication Data

Ender's Game and Philosophy : the Logic Gate is Down / edited by Kevin S. Decker.
    pages   cm. – (The Blackwell Philosophy and PopCulture Series)
  Includes bibliographical references and index.
  ISBN 978-1-118-38657-6 (pbk. : alk. paper)
1. Card, Orson Scott. Ender's game.   2. Science fiction, American–History and criticism.
3. Wiggin, Ender (Fictitious character)   4. Philosophy in literature.   I. Decker, Kevin S.,
editor of compilation.
  PS3553.A655Z59 2013
  813'.54–dc23
                                    2013006641

A catalogue record for this book is available from the British Library.

Cover image: Background © Roman Okopny; spacecraft © Sven Herrmann;
city © Murat Giray Kaya (all istockphoto); Boy © Tim Kitchen/Getty Images.
Cover design by: http://www.simonlevy.co.uk/

Set in 10.5/13pt Sabon by SPi Publisher Services, Pondicherry, India

1   2013

Contents

Introduction

What *Is* Ender's Game?

In his introduction to *Ender's Game* written six years after the book was originally published, author Orson Scott Card goes both backwards and forwards in time to talk about the inspiration for the story and its public reception. One of the most interesting things about Card's novel is the diversity of its audiences. Now with the 2013 film adaptation of *Ender's Game*, starring Asa Butterfield as Andrew "Ender" Wiggin and Harrison Ford as Colonel Hyrum Graff, the story of a young boy under siege from all quarters in a not-too-distant future will get its widest reception yet, and never at a better time.

Card tells us in his introduction that he was fascinated by the underlying premise of Isaac Asimov's original *Foundation* series, the epitome of Golden Age science fiction, celebrating the marriage of reason and technological progress. Granted a one-time-only Hugo Award in 1966 for "Best All-Time Series," Asimov's *Foundation* (1951), *Foundation and Empire* (1952), and *Second Foundation* (1953) use the conceit of "psychohistory," an incredibly advanced form of mathematical sociology, to plot the decline, fall, and rise of a Galactic Empire and the secret "Foundation" colonies of scientists whose job it is to make sure that the cosmos doesn't descend into a new dark age. About *Foundation*, Card writes:

> The novel set me, not to dreaming, but to *thinking*, which is Asimov's most extraordinary ability as a fiction writer. What *would* the future be like? How would things change? What would remain the same?

Ender's Game and Philosophy: The Logic Gate Is Down, First Edition. Edited by Kevin S. Decker.
© 2013 John Wiley & Sons, Inc. Published 2013 by John Wiley & Sons, Inc.

The premise of *Foundation* seemed to be that even though you might change the props and the actors, the play of human history is always the same. And yet that fundamentally pessimistic premise (you mean we'll *never* change?) was tempered by Asimov's idea of a group of human beings who, not through genetic change, but through learned skills, are able to understand and heal the minds of other people.[1]

This idea had immense appeal to Card when he read of Asimov in the late sixties, near the peak of American entanglement in Vietnam and social unrest tied to the war and the civil rights movement. It's no surprise, then, that as a young person Card turned to sci-fi for healing rather than mere entertainment.

Like Asimov's predictions about the distant future, Card's (although centered closer to the present) concern things that haven't happened yet and some things that may never happen. This doesn't make them wholly fantastical, though, as Card's uncanny predictions of the Internet, the use of child soldiers, and biological warfare (in *Speaker for the Dead*) show. Like Card, philosophers often pose questions about the intersection of time, change, and human nature: can we ever change? What resources from our past have we forgotten? Is human nature inherently violent and disruptive, does society or some malevolent force guide us to be so, or can we ever transcend our temptation to cruelty and the use of brute force?

As Card himself admits, *Ender's Game* is a disturbing novel. It's unrelenting in the degree to which its protagonist is oppressed in social, military, and ethical ways. In the chapters in the first part of this book, "Third: The Making of an Impossible Child," four philosophers and educators consider how Ender's character and moral development are affected by the system of monitoring children on Earth for the correct temperament and abilities to become a child soldier. Ender's existence as a "Third" is a rarity in an overpopulated world in which parents are restricted to two children. So not only is Ender's very birth a consequence of the policies of the military regime that both protects and controls the Earth, but his education and socialization—at least after Colonel Graff spirits him away to Battle School—are carefully controlled to produce the result Earth needs. But is this any way to treat a child?

In one of the letters Card received after the publication of *Ender's Game*, an army helicopter pilot confesses:

> I read *Ender's Game* during flight school four years ago. I'm a warrant officer, and our school, at least the first six weeks, is very different from the commissioned officers'. I was eighteen years old when I arrived at Ft. Rucker to start flight training, and the first six weeks almost beat me. Ender gave me courage then and many times after that. I've experienced the tiredness Ender felt, the kind that goes deep to your soul. It would be interesting to know what caused you to feel the same way.[2]

Of the many audiences that have appreciated Card's book, the men and women in uniform are the most surprising in their identification with the main character. As in the case of the army aviator, their sympathy mainly has to do with the shared experience of training and combat and the resultant transformation of a person's entire worldview. In the second section of this book, "Game: Cooperation or Confrontation?" four authors take on the philosophical connections between war and games that make up the bulk of the novel's adventures. These chapters show that empathy as well as strategy, and the ability to commit oneself to something for its own sake, are all vital needs of space commanders.

And what about the poor buggers? The hive-queens and their drones are portrayed by the International Fleet Command of Ender's time as merciless and predatory. All they care about is eliminating every human from the face of the galaxy. Only a select few—Mazer Rackham, and eventually Ender—can understand what they might do next. But Leon Perniciaro, who wrote a master's thesis entitled "Shifting Understandings of Imperialism: A Collision of Cultures in *Starship Troopers* and *Ender's Game*," points out how different the portrayal of giant, insect-like alien invaders appears in Robert Heinlein's 1959 shoot-em-up *Starship Troopers* versus *Ender's Game*, with Card's surprising use of the buggers, or Formics, as foils but not enemies.[3] Card's sympathetic portrayal of the aliens opens up the possibility that philosophy can assist us in understanding, rather than demonizing, those who seem to present themselves as our enemies. So in the third section of this book, "Hive-Queen: All Together Now," three philosophers discuss all things Formic and philotic, showing how "others" from different cultures have contributed to the development of humanity's image of itself.

"We're saving the world, after all. Take him," says one of Graff's colleagues when the decision is made to recruit and train Ender Wiggin. Some of Ender's most peculiar and incompatible traits—his ability to empathize with and even love his enemy as well as his violent streak—have emerged in the I.F.'s analyses as "the right stuff" for a commander who will lead a strike at the bugger homeworld. From the very beginning—as a number of the authors in these pages point out—Ender knows what he's being trained for, and the logical limit of what he's being asked to do is complete destruction of the buggers—xenocide. So why does he continue to play along? In the fourth section of this book, "War: Kill or Be Killed," four authors—including an Air Force colonel—scrutinize ethics in times of war to assess the degree to which Ender, Graff, the International Fleet Command, and humanity as a whole are responsible for the "evil that men do" in times of conflict.

Ender's Game may be unique in science fiction in that it has at least two sets of sequels. On the one hand, three books, beginning with *Speaker for the Dead* (1986), continue the sociocultural prophecies as Ender travels the universe and gets married on the planet Lusitania. On the other hand, the "Shadow" series, beginning with *Ender's Shadow* (1999), tells the story of *Ender's Game* from Bean's perspective and then dives into the fate of Earth after the Third Invasion. No one can fault Orson Scott Card for the "big picture" thinking of his Enderverse, with developments that are both shocking and challenging to our sense of what's good and true. In the final section of this book, "Hegemon: The Terrible Things are Only About to Begin," four philosophers sketch the world that war and invasion have created—a future Earth in which the experience of every child is electronically overseen by the military and in which anonymous personalities on the nets determine international relations.

So it's time to begin the exercise. The battleroom door is opening. Your reactions will be monitored. Don't settle for anything less than victory, and remember: *the enemy's gate is down.*

Notes

1.   Orson Scott Card, "Introduction" to *Ender's Game, Author's Definitive Edition* (New York: TOR Books, 1991), xii.

2. Ibid., xxii.
3. Leon Perniciaro, "Shifting Understandings of Imperialism: A Clash of Cultures in *Starship Troopers* and *Ender's Game*," MA Thesis, University of New Orleans, May 2011, http://scholarworks.uno.edu/cgi/viewcontent.cgi?article=2322&context=td, accessed October 1, 2012.

Part One

THIRD
THE MAKING OF
AN IMPOSSIBLE CHILD

CHAPTER 1

"The Teachers Got Me Into This"

Educational Skirmishes ... with a Pinch of Freedom

Cam Cobb

What does *Ender's Game* tell us about the art of education, or pedagogy? And what on Earth does this have to do with freedom? To answer these questions, we need to step back in time. For thousands of years, people have debated the structure learning should take. For Socrates (469–399 BC), education was an interactive experience involving critical inquiry, dialogue, and a collaborative process that encouraged people to question the world around them by reasoning things out. Socrates left quite an impression on his students, most notably Plato (429–347 BC). Intermingling his own views with Socrates' in a long dialogue called the *Republic*, Plato envisioned education as the identification of natural skills of children with the aim of preparing them to take on roles in society that corresponded to their perceived abilities. Children gifted in the use of reasoning, for instance, would join the "guardians" and rule the state. For Plato, then, education would be highly selective, and would also train the young for their future work. In this regard, Plato emphasizes his own kind of vocational education, centering on training in a skill or trade to prepare for a career. While Socratic critical inquiry and Platonic "vocational prep" aren't exactly opposing philosophies of education, they do at times conflict with one another.

And this conflict returns us to Ender. In this chapter we'll consider what Ender's experiences tell us about the differences between liberal

Ender's Game and Philosophy: The Logic Gate Is Down, First Edition. Edited by Kevin S. Decker.
© 2013 John Wiley & Sons, Inc. Published 2013 by John Wiley & Sons, Inc.

education, vocational training, critical inquiry, and that elusive matter of freedom *in*, and as a result *of* education. Specifically, we'll address the following questions: Does everyone need a liberal education? Are schools training grounds for the workplace? And finally, is critical inquiry essential to being an educated person?

Liberal Education Is Paideia's Game

A liberal education is one that is meant to free or "liberate" a person's mind. It has nothing to do with being liberal or conservative in the way those terms are used in contemporary politics. A liberal education involves studying subjects such as mathematics, logic, ethics, aesthetics, music, poetry, rhetoric, and biology. In Plato's Athens, these subjects were known collectively as *paideia*, which, in a very general sense, means to educate. Yet *Ender's Game* devotes so much attention to non-liberal topics—the social life of Ender and his schoolmates, the interactive learning of the war games in the battleroom, and the individual problem solving in the virtual reality of the Giant's Drink—that it's easy to believe that Ender had very little liberal education at all.

Plato felt that vocational learning was important, but he also saw liberal education as complementing it. True education was a matter of balancing one's body and mind. When sketching the details of his ideal city-state in the *Republic*, Plato carefully described the military training of the rulers of the city: "The person who achieves the finest blend of music and physical training and impresses it on his soul in the most measured way is the one we'd most correctly call completely harmonious."[1] Plato reasoned that learning music and poetry would inspire a more harmonious soul in soldiers, enhancing their courage and lessening their tendencies toward cruelty. Ultimately, for Plato, a well-balanced curriculum helps foster harmony in individuals and societies.

Support for liberal education has fluctuated over the years. Mortimer Adler (1902–2001) reasoned that everyone is owed a liberal education because "the best education for the best is the best education for all."[2] Yet public schooling in the United States in the late twentieth century was riddled with problems in Adler's view, mainly due to low expectations. In his words, "A part of our population—and much too large a part—has harbored the opinion that many of the nation's children are not fully educable."[3] Unimpressed with the prevalent practice of "tracking" learners according to their abilities, Adler argued that we have not "always been honest in our commitment to democracy and its promise of equality."[4] *The Paideia Proposal*, Adler's 1982 manifesto, mapped out an alternative system in which every learner would study a blend of classically oriented courses for 12 years.

Alas, the future society of *Ender's Game* does not follow *The Paideia Proposal*. Still, Ender does get a kind of liberal education with three core aspects. First, in terms of comprehension and performance, Ender learns about military history, military tactics, and strategic-oriented mathematical calculations in the classroom. Second, he develops problem-solving skills in the cyber-reality of the computer game, the Giant's Drink. Third, in terms of interactive performance and cognition, Ender learns about hand-to-hand combat and command in the simulated war games of the battleroom. Though these three pieces of Ender's education lend variety to the content and delivery of the Battle School curriculum, the variety is admittedly limited.

For Ender and his fellow trainees, Battle School is an intense, emotionally draining experience. Anderson warns Graff after Ender is promoted to the rank of Commander, "We want to teach him, not give him a nervous breakdown."[5] Anderson's fear is well-founded. Competition is fierce and the pace is demanding. Children's performances in the battleroom are ranked on a daily basis, and rankings are circulated for all to see. Battle School isn't a place where children feel free to show or talk about their emotions. Dink observes, "That's right, we never cry. I never thought of that. Nobody ever cries."[6] In this unforgiving setting, Ender has a series of violent entanglements with his peers, fights and arguments that he deeply regrets. "I'm doing it again, thought Ender. I'm hurting people again, just to save myself. Why don't they leave me alone, so I don't have to hurt them?"[7] While Wiggin doesn't initiate any of these conflicts, his lashing out often has fatal consequences.

Plato would likely chide Colonel Graff, saying that Battle and Command School fail to offer the sort of balanced curriculum called for in the *Republic*. Nowhere in Ender's learning is there any poetry, music, or visual arts. Nowhere is there any learning about grammar, rhetoric, or biology. Graff would perhaps counter that education is a matter of *realpolitik*, pointing out that Ender didn't need liberal education to lead Earth to victory.[8] In response, Plato would counter that educating an army of soldiers who aren't harmonious souls would lead to cruelty, which has wider social implications.

Vocational Prep: A Heaping Tablespoon, or the Main Dish?

Philosophers of education have argued that vocational training is an important part of education, but they're also conflicted about *how much* of a part it should be. If these thinkers were chefs, we might say that some call for a pinch of trade preparation while others believe it should be the main dish itself.

So where does this leave Ender? Wasn't his education entirely vocational? Certainly, Battle School is designed to select, stream, and ultimately train different types of soldiers for Earth's army. But, looking more closely, further questions spring to mind: What sort of vocational education did Ender experience? Was Ender's occupational training balanced with other subject areas? Was Ender simply compelled to follow orders and forego critical inquiry, or was he educated to develop his own strategies when faced with complex problems? In reaching for answers, we need to consider two versions of vocational learning, one put forward by Plato and another set out by thinkers concerned with what's called a "Taylorist" view of increasing social efficiency.

For Plato, a balanced education would mix vocational learning with a broad-based liberal education. On the vocational side, schools should identify the aptitudes of learners and sort them into different streams, which would eventually lead to different occupations. Curriculum—the content, depth, length, and method of one's studies— would be designed to match an individual's aptitudes and career path. Plato's choices for career paths are rather limited. He worked from the idea that children are predisposed by their natural proficiencies to enter one of three general classes, all of which are necessary to a har- monious society. These are the guardians, "auxiliaries" (or peace- keepers), and skilled producers of crafts. Some children are bound to become carpenters, others to become retailers, and still others—but only a select few—to become rulers. To sell this idea to the public we are given the "myth of the metals," a story told in Book III of the *Republic*. According to this myth, the natural aptitudes of children are spelled out by their souls, which contain different mixtures of gold, silver, and bronze. Each person is either dominantly gold (rulers), silver (auxiliaries), or bronze (artisans). Because the divine creator made every citizen's soul out of alloys of all these substances, it's possible for families to include members of different classes. Plato felt that this myth should be told to people as a "noble lie," because some people would be dissatisfied with their place in society. But people aren't always the best judge of their own interests. Plato thus favored a fairly rigid class system in which people are trained according to their merit. This class system would lead to a society in which people are trained to do better what they can already do. Of course, the drawback is that Plato's state is one in which individuals can't *choose* their careers, and class mobility is severely limited.

Since the *Republic* first appeared over two millennia ago, Plato's ideas have been crucially influential on the way we think about schooling. "Plato laid down the fundamental principle of a philosophy of education," American educator John Dewey (1859–1952) observed, "when he asserted that it was the business of education to discover what each person is good for, and to train him to mastery of that mode of excellence."[9]

But some educators didn't think Plato's "heaping tablespoon" model for vocational learning went far enough. As public schools sprang up in the United States in the late nineteenth and early twentieth centuries, a heated debate arose between those who favored vocational training, those who supported a liberal education, and those who championed critical inquiry. In the first camp, a collective—or, perhaps "cartel" is a better word—of thinkers argued that the purpose of education is to enhance worker productivity.[10] They felt that public schools should be designed to prepare children for the specific tasks of an industrial society.

Before delving further into this vocational-oriented view of education, we need to take a step back and consider "Taylorism." In the late nineteenth century, mechanical engineer F.W. Taylor looked at the manufacturing industry through a scientific lens. To enhance labor productivity he called for a greater degree of managerial control, tighter standardizations of practice, and more prescriptive forms of training.[11] Drawing from the ideas of "Taylorism," educators like W.W. Charters, Franklin Bobbitt, and David Snedden unleashed a flurry of rules, guidelines, and procedures to steer schooling away from a liberal curriculum's perceived frivolity.[12] Snedden argued that a vocational school must "reproduce practical processes, must give the pupil many hours of each working day in actual practical work, and must closely correlate theoretical instruction to this practical work."[13] Like the budding soldiers in Battle School, children would listen to instructions, follow them, and memorize a range of workplace-oriented tasks through repetition. What children would *not* learn in this setting is how to critically question the world around them.

Is Battle School Just Trade School?

Does the I.F.'s Battle School aim to prepare its students for specific occupations? To increase their efficiency as soldiers, or to make them "well-rounded persons"? To answer these questions, let's consider the purposes and organizational design of Battle School.

We'll begin with the purpose of Battle School. Colonel Graff, the principal of the school, offers some useful remarks. While recruiting Ender, Graff says, "Battle School is for training future starship captains and commodores of flotillas and admirals of the fleet."[14] Later, when strolling with Ender from the shuttle to the school, Graff elaborates on this point, "My job is to produce the best soldiers in the world. In the whole history of the world."[15] Here, Graff provides us with the first part of Battle School's mission statement: the school aims to train soldiers and produce an effective army.

But with a new phase of an interplanetary war looming on Earth's horizon, there's a second, more urgent, aspect to the mission. Graff later adds, "We need a Napoleon. An Alexander.... My job is to produce such a creature, and all the men and women he'll need to help him."[16] Clearly, the Battle School aims to identify and develop a general who will be able to lead Earth to victory. And this aspect of the mission is personally significant for Ender, whom Graff expects to fulfill this very role. If we were to judge Battle School strictly by Graff's mission statement, we'd say that it is specifically aimed at producing skills and, as such, is highly vocational in focus.

But does the design of Battle School correspond to its vocationally driven core purpose? Let's begin with streaming, the process of directing learners along pathways: children enter Battle School when they're five or six years old. They're chosen based on observations gleaned from a vast surveillance network and a series of tests. Very few children are actually invited to attend Battle School, so in a sense streaming begins at birth. But further streaming occurs inside the school itself. In terms of career pathways, Battle School is designed to continually assess and challenge learners, guiding them toward different occupations within Earth's army, all based on their perceived abilities. As Colonel Graff abrasively tells a group of incoming children, "Most of you are going to ice out. Get used to that, little boys. Most of you are going to end up in Combat School, because you don't have the brains to handle deep-space piloting."[17] This statement hearkens back to Plato's "myth of the metals." Maybe Graff had a copy of the *Republic* in his back pocket as he dressed down that group of newbies.

Ender advanced through the Battle School levels at a brisk pace, and was promoted from Launchie to Salamander Army at age six, two years ahead of any of his peers. Petra described the Salamander program as follows: "School for us isn't like it is for the Launchies. History and strategies and tactics and buggers and math and stars, things you'll need as a pilot or a commander."[18] At this higher level, school is about military history, tactical-oriented mathematics, and strategizing. So it would seem that the army platoon curriculum of Battle School is entirely vocational in nature.

Should Critical Inquiry Be Socratic or Social?

As we've seen, Ender's education was, for the most part, vocational. It involved an unhealthy dose of deception and surveillance, as Colonel Graff constantly manipulated Ender's social settings, friendships, and competitive interactions. But what sort of critical inquiry, if any, was involved in Battle and Command Schools, and how important was it for Ender's learning? Critical thinking encourages thought processes rooted in rigorous and reliable procedures of inquiry.[19] When the critical inquirer encounters ideas, she poses questions that help her to "identify faulty arguments, hasty generalizations, assertions lacking evidence, truth claims based on unreliable authority, ambiguous or obscure concepts, and so forth."[20] Let's consider two versions of critical inquiry.

As we've seen, Socrates treated thoughtful verbal exchange as integral to critical inquiry. Believing himself to be ignorant, he went about ancient Athens asking questions of others in an attempt to collaboratively reason things out. He examined a wide variety of important topics: justice, courage, love, piety, wisdom, and friendship. The technique of posing questions to test the validity of others' claims to know the truth is still today known as the "Socratic method." The version of critical inquiry demonstrated by Socrates' dialogues could be defined as an interactive, question-driven process of reasoning things out.

Critical inquiry can also be the key to *freedom* in the eyes of Brazilian educator Paulo Freire (1921–1997). In a schoolroom dominated by a teacher's agenda, students are treated as though they're empty containers to be filled with knowledge. Freire called this the "banking" view of education, where teachers provide, lead, and control while students receive, follow, and are controlled. To liberate people from this "teacher–student contradiction," Freire called for students as well as teachers to pose and investigate *real problems*. Through problem posing, "the teacher is no longer merely the-one-who-teaches, but one who is himself taught in dialogue with the students, who in turn while being taught also teach."[21] Problem posing, in Freire's view, also leads students to become "critical co-investigators in dialogue with the teacher. The teacher presents the material to the students for their consideration, and re-considers her earlier considerations as the students express their own."[22] For Freire, critical inquiry is both a result of, and an essential component of liberation.

Critical Inquirer for the Dead

While attending Battle and Command School, Ender faced a variety of complex open-ended tasks that required some critical thinking. These critical inquiries center on the Giant's Drink game and the battleroom.

During his free time, Ender often played a virtual reality game that presented him with a series of puzzles. Because of Ender's actions, the Giant's Drink initially transformed into Fairyland and later into the End of the World. The parameters and objectives of the game regularly shifted as the computer responded to Ender's strategies. As Major Imbu described it, "The mind game is a relationship between the child and the computer. Together they create stories. The stories are true, in the sense that they reflect the reality of the child's life."[23]

This way of developing both the learner and the curriculum at the same time would certainly appeal to Socrates. But over time, the perplexing nature of the game confounded Ender:

> Ender did not understand how the game functioned anymore. In the old days, before he had first gone to the End of the World, everything was combat and puzzles to solve—defeat the enemy before he kills you, or figure out how to get past the obstacle. Now, though, no one attacked, there was no war, and wherever he went, there was no obstacle at all.[24]

The individualized design of the Giant's Drink game invites multiple and varied experiences of critical inquiry. The open-endedness of the game invites Ender to solve complex problems through unconventional means. Unfortunately, the solitary nature of the game contrasts with the interactive and social emphasis placed on learning by both Socrates and Freire.

The rules of the battleroom may also inspire critical inquiry. They exist in a state of flux, and so reflect the unpredictable nature of life. When Ender is promoted to commander, for instance, his team's schedule is accelerated dramatically. Sometimes they face multiple challenges in a day, something unheard of at Battle School. Additionally, the challenges intensified, as Ender's opponents sometimes outnumbered his own team significantly. The teachers' flippant disregard for battleroom routines angered Ender, who "didn't like games where the rules could be anything and the objective was known to them alone."[25]

Although the constantly shifting parameters prompted Ender to further develop his skills as a soldier and commander, his feelings of frustration grew. When he was offered a space at Command School, these feelings motivated him to take a leave of absence and return to Earth. When Valentine, his trusted sister, encouraged him to return to his studies, Ender tersely replied: "They aren't studies, they're games. All games, from beginning to end, only they change the rules whenever they feel like it." He holds up a limp hand. "See the strings?"[26] Later, an exasperated Ender states, "I've spent my life as someone's pawn."[27] It seems that the unpredictable nature of the battleroom – and Battle School itself – made Ender feel powerless and manipulated, a resounding echo of Freire's worries about teacher domination.

Does the battleroom actually offer experiences of critical inquiry? Somewhat. While Freire would undoubtedly question whether the challenges Ender faced as a commander were reasonable, both Freire and Socrates would applaud the teachers' integration of social learning into this component of the school's curriculum. The fact that the rules (or lack thereof) in the battleroom tasks are reserved for teachers alone to determine, though, conflicts with Freire's belief that learners should have a say in curriculum construction. He would be concerned about the undemocratic nature of this teacher–student relationship. Card writes:

> And the despair filled him again. Now he knew why. Now he knew what he hated so much. He had no control over his own life. They ran everything. They made all the choices. Only the game was left to him, that was all, everything else was them and their rules and plans and lessons and programs, and all he could do was go this way or that way in battle.[28]

Ultimately, Freire would be unsurprised with the escalating personal struggle that Ender has with his own education.

Educational Skirmishes

Imagine that we invited the philosophers mentioned in this chapter to visit Battle and Command School, perhaps on "Meet-the-Teacher Night." We've somehow transported Socrates, Plato, Mortimer Adler, and Paulo Freire through space and time to examine Ender's situation. What would they think? While Plato would be happy with the vocational foundation of the curriculum, he would be unimpressed with the absence of a liberal education. For him, the I.F.'s training schools would be developing individuals who don't have harmonious souls and are inclined to cruelty. The relative lack of liberal education would, of course, trouble Adler greatly. We'd expect to hear from him some very sharp comments regarding the implications of creating a society that favors specialization over generalization and empowers certain specializations over others.

After engaging Graff in a delightful question-and-answer about the core meaning of war or justice, Socrates would probably express his concern with the lack of dialogic learning. The sort of thinker Graff would produce, for Socrates, would fail to be an active inquirer who lives a reflective, "examined life." While Paulo Freire would be pleased with the amount and variety of problem posing at the two schools, he'd also express his grave concern with the undemocratic relationship between teachers and learners. Such an unbalanced power dynamic forces students learn under a relationship of domination, and quietly encourages them to perpetuate that domination.

Ender's learning experiences illustrate how vocational learning, liberal education, and critical inquiry can coexist, but as conflicting pedagogies. Battle and Command School offered experiences that were predominantly vocational in nature, and their liberal curriculum was virtually non-existent. The degree to which Ender experienced critical inquiry really depends on whose definition we use. As we have seen, *Ender's Game* illustrates just how different views of pedagogy can intermingle and conflict with one another. It also demonstrates how these conflicting pedagogies deeply affect the growth of both individuals and society.[29]

Notes

1. Plato, *Republic*, trans. G.M.A. Grube, revised by C.D.C. Reeve (Cambridge, MA: Hackett, 1992), 88.
2. Mortimer Adler, *The Paideia Proposal: An Educational Manifesto* (New York, NY: Simon and Schuster, 1982), 7.
3. Ibid.
4. Ibid.
5. Orson Scott Card, *Ender's Game* (New York: TOR Books, 1991), 173.
6. Ibid., 109.
7. Ibid., 115.
8. For more insight into *realpolitik* and the politics of Graff and the Enderverse, see the chapter by Ted Henry Brown and Christie L. Maloyed in this book.
9. John Dewey, *Democracy and Education* (New York, NY: The Free Press, 1916), 309.
10. See R.E. Callahan, *Education and the Cult of Efficiency* (Chicago, IL: University of Chicago Press, 1962).
11. Ibid.
12. See H.M. Kliebard, "The Rise of Scientific Curriculum Making and Its Aftermath," *Curriculum Theory*, 5:1 (1975): 27–38.
13. David Snedden, "Fundamental Distinctions between Liberal and Vocational Education," *Curriculum Inquiry*, 7:1 (1977): 51.
14. Card, *Ender's Game*, 20.

15. Ibid., 34.
16. Ibid.
17. Ibid., 32.
18. Ibid., 79.
19. Nicholas C. Burbules and Rupert Berk, "Critical Thinking and Critical Pedagogy: Relations, Differences, and Limits," in Thomas S. Popkewitz and Lynn Fendler, eds., *Critical Theories in Education* (New York, NY: Routledge, 1999), 45–66.
20. Ibid., 46.
21. Paulo Freire, *Pedagogy of the Oppressed*, trans. Myra Bergman Ramos (New York, NY: Continuum, 1970), 80.
22. Ibid., 81.
23. Card, *Ender's Game*, 121.
24. Ibid., 140–141.
25. Ibid., 261.
26. Ibid., 236.
27. Ibid., 312.
28. Ibid., 151.
29. The author would like to thank Kevin Decker and Michael Potter for their astute guidance.

CHAPTER 2

Illusions of Freedom, Tragedies of Fate
The Moral Development of Ender Wiggin

Jeremy Proulx

What is it about Ender Wiggin, his life, his actions, the ruthless pedagogy to which he was subjected, and his eventual destruction of an entire alien species that so many readers of *Ender's Game* find so disturbing? Ender himself is at once a highly sensitive, gifted child and a monster capable of brutal violence. There is also the obvious fact that Ender was manipulated in such a way as to develop and sharpen these violent tendencies, leading him toward a course of action that no child should ever have to take responsibility for.

All of this amounts to a highly discomfiting tale. It's tempting to explain this by pointing out that Orson Scott Card seems to want to create sympathy for undeserving characters, especially Ender. One reviewer of *Ender's Game* suggests that Card models the character of Ender Wiggin on Hitler.[1] Another agrees that there's something morally suspect about Card's attempt to make us sympathize with a child who beats other children to death with his bare hands, but we should just focus on why Card is asking his readers to forget the consequences of Ender's actions and to worry only about his intentions.[2] Ender, after all, never wanted to hurt anyone. Perhaps the details of the story itself aren't as disturbing as are Card's authorial decisions.

But while this all may be true, it doesn't seem to capture very much about the story of Ender Wiggin. Regardless of intentions, the evil acts of violence, manipulation, and neglect in the story strike us *as evil*

Ender's Game and Philosophy: The Logic Gate Is Down, First Edition. Edited by Kevin S. Decker.
© 2013 John Wiley & Sons, Inc. Published 2013 by John Wiley & Sons, Inc.

precisely because of their horrific consequences and, what is worse, because the people responsible for them were able to live with themselves afterward. We all want to think that the evil that occasionally surfaces in humanity can be explained, and that it is just another problem to be solved. Could society or his family have fixed Ender? Is society somehow responsible for creating this moral monster? What went wrong? How can we prevent the anti-humanitarian horrors of the Battle School from ever happening again?

The German philosopher Friedrich Schelling (1775–1854) would say that our desire to explain or justify evil through moralizing about it pushes "philanthropism to the brink of denying evil" in the modern world.[3] In this chapter we'll draw on Schelling's insights about evil to show that the reason we find *Ender's Game* so disturbing is that it points to unnerving facts about our own lives. Evil remains an enduring possibility. Instead of admitting that sometimes people just do evil things, we disguise evil by calling it a "problem to be solved." *Ender's Game* is striking because it has no such pretensions. Far from trying to excuse evil by appealing to good intentions, Card comes right out and tells us that intention is *not* everything. Mazer Rackham, Ender's teacher, makes just this point when he lectures Ender on the morality of war: "Don't start apologizing for them, Ender. Just because they didn't know they were killing human beings doesn't mean they weren't killing human beings."[4] Ender's fate reveals the monstrosity that resides in all of us. Despite his fierce intelligence and obvious intellectual superiority, Ender never understands what compels him to commit brutal acts of violence: "I'm doing it again, thought Ender. I'm hurting people again just to save myself."[5] *Ender's Game* is most disturbing because it reveals to us that despite all our efforts, evil remains a genuine, even necessary, part of what it means to be human.

Putting a Name to Evil

Philosophers have traditionally framed the problem of evil in the form of the question "How can we explain the existence of evil in a world created by an all-good, all-knowing, and all-powerful God?" Why would a good God who knows that evil exists and has the power to eradicate it allow evil to exist, and in such abundance?

The response of St. Augustine (354–430 AD), and perhaps the most intuitive one, is that evil is not a positive force in its own right; evil is a *lack* of good.[6] God creates only good in the universe. Human sin introduces evil into the creation by neglecting God's plan, by straying from the righteous path of creation. Human beings bring about evil by depriving the creation of the goodness that is natural to it. Evil can thus be overcome either by reason or the grace of God. *Ender's Game*, however, forces its reader to confront the simple fact that sometimes evil cannot be overcome. This is where Schelling's philosophy can help us. Schelling was studying at university during the years that followed the French Revolution. The excitement about the revolution was palpable among German students of Schelling's generation, but no one could deny the atrocities that followed from noble intentions during the Reign of Terror in 1793–1794.

Evil, Schelling tells us, is a real and necessary part of reality. He demands we give up the idea that our moral order is immune to the evil that threatens it, and he challenges the idea that evil is always something alien. Instead of treating evil as originating from the animal part of our nature or from an irrational source outside us that opposes our pure, created goodness, Schelling wants us to understand evil as a natural phenomenon deeply entrenched in the human condition and the very existence of the world itself. As Schelling sees things, if evil is defined merely as a lack of good, then evil is ultimately in the service of the good. But part of the very definition of evil is that it completely flies in the face of our attempts to be good citizens in the moral world order, to be in the moral community of human agents. Evil upsets the moral order: it threatens to place the world in the service of its own ambitions. Schelling says that

> ... everything in the world is, as we see it now, rule, order and form; but anarchy still lies in the ground, as if it could break through once again, and nowhere does it appear as if order and form were what is original but rather as if initial anarchy had been brought to order.[7]

Life, for Schelling, is a balance of opposing forces; it's a system whose parts can work harmoniously together, but that could always collapse back into chaos. This collapse is like a cancer. When an organism is functioning well, its parts are working harmoniously together. But when a cancer takes hold, certain cells replicate in non-harmonious ways and, if left unchecked, will subordinate the entire organism to this principle. Cancer is not just an *absence* of proper function; it's a positive force in its own right, subordinating an entire organism to its own principle. Schelling views life as carrying with it the constant possibility of a state in which individuals compete for dominance and upset systematic harmony. At the level of human activity, this means that while we might try to be conscientious members of a moral community, we are always haunted by a selfishness that threatens to take over and subordinate all of existence to our idiosyncratic demands. Evil, for Schelling, is a "contraction into the self," treating my selfish desires as the ruling principle of my life. The evil individual is a kind of systematic cancer that destroys the system from within.

But despite this, evil, like good, is absolutely essential to life. Schelling understands their balance in terms of an organic model: "An individual body part, like the eye, is only possible within the whole of an organism; nonetheless, it has its own life for itself, indeed, its own kind of freedom."[8] As independent individuals, we answer only to ourselves. But we're also dependent on the social order and we can only become individuals in the context of this. On the one hand, we *expand* into our roles as agents in a moral community, becoming more than mere individuals. On the other hand, we *contract* back into ourselves in an effort to define ourselves as individuals. Life is in this way a precarious balancing act that walks a tight rope between *contraction* into complete selfishness and *expansion* into being immersed in a moral community.

The circulation between the self and the moral community is captured in *Ender's Game* in at least two ways. First, Ender Wiggin shows us what "contracting into the self" means. From the very beginning, Ender is aware—and afraid—of the crimes he is capable of committing in the name of self-interest. In the end, his dark tendency is brought to the surface and elevated into the ruling principle of Ender's life. Second, contrary to our natural inclination to treat Hyrum Graff as a diabolical character, the Colonel is the very embodiment of this expansion and contraction that defines life. Graff actually sacrifices his own interests in the service of humanity. And when Graff is forced to defend himself and justify his terrible acts, he contracts back into his selfish core. At the end of the story, we see Ender finally coming to terms with evil as a real possibility and danger for *all* life.

Evil and Its Refrain

"I didn't want to hurt him!" This refrain echoes throughout *Ender's Game*.[9] We hear it from Graff every time he attempts to justify his cruel treatment of the students in the Battle School. But most of all we hear it from Ender. Before whisking him off to Battle School, Graff asks Ender about a fight with a boy from school: "Tell me why you kept on kicking him. You had already won." Fighting back tears, Ender replies, "Knocking him down won the first fight. I wanted to win all the next ones, too. So they'd leave me alone." In admitting this, Ender breaks into tears and tries to justify his actions: "You took away the monitor. I had to take care of myself, didn't I?"[10] But his tears betray his fear of this unknown part of himself. In his actions, Ender recognizes in himself an evil that he can neither understand nor control. When he brutally beats Stilson, when he throws his classmate across the shuttle, breaking his arm, Ender is giving in to violent tendencies he knows are a part of him, but that he doesn't understand. This is equally true when he beats Bonzo to death, when he does whatever he can to win at the games in Battle School, and indeed when he unwittingly enacts the genocide of an entire alien species.

Deep down, Ender knows that in these moments he is just like his brother Peter. He tries to tell himself that he never meant to hurt anyone, but he knows this isn't true.

> Ender felt sick. He had only meant to catch the boy's arm. No. No, he had meant to hurt him, and had pulled with all his strength. He hadn't meant it to be so public, but the boy was feeling exactly the pain Ender had meant him to feel ... I am Peter. I'm just like him.[11]

In these moments, Ender is completely selfish, acting purely out of instinct, with regard only for himself.[12] From Schelling's perspective, this is the very definition of evil. Ender might be acting unconsciously, but this only makes Schelling's framework of ideas more compelling. This part of us that acts out of pure, selfish instinct is for Schelling the dark ground of our individual character. He writes, "This principle to the extent that it comes from the ground and is dark, is the self-will of creatures, which, however ... is pure craving or desire, that is, blind will."[13] This selfish, evil part of Ender—common to us all—constantly upsets the part of him that desperately wants to have a true friend, to be a member of a moral community. Even in the virtual game Ender plays, he discovers that his monstrosity runs very deep. "He hadn't meant to kill the Giant. This was supposed to be a game … I'm a murderer, even when I play. Peter would be proud of me."[14]

In nearly everything he does, Ender flees this part of himself. He quickly develops close and meaningful relationships with classmates like Petra, Bean, and Dink Meeker. He longs for his sister Valentine, who, after all, reminds Ender that he and Peter are different people. "I've spent my whole life in the company of the brother that I hated," Valentine confesses to Ender. "Now I want a chance to know the brother that I love."[15] Ender does everything he can to be a part of the moral community, the world in which relationships matter and people care for more than just themselves. This explains why he is so dismayed at the virtual game's "End of the World" when Peter's face appears in a mirror with a snake "protruding from a corner of his mouth."[16] Symbolic of the temptation to become just like Peter, Ender's vision is too much for him to bear: "This game tells filthy lies. I am not Peter. I don't have murder in my heart."[17] But his heart does have murder in it, and he knows this. Naturally, Ender seeks an end to this existential torment. But much to Ender's frustration, Graff is always there to keep the games going.

Graff's Sacrifice

We might think that Graff is so successful in cultivating Ender's destructive potential because he realizes what Ender is going through. After all, we could easily condemn Graff for what he does to the children at the Battle School, but in Ender's case, Graff does what's necessary to help Ender realize who he really is. Graff puts Ender face-to-face with the purely selfish monster that usually remains hidden. If Schelling's insights are correct, Graff may be the character with the most intimate acquaintance with the human condition. By changing the rules of the game, Graff purposely makes it difficult not only for Ender to win, but much more importantly, he puts Ender in a position to confront his darker side, to wrestle with that monstrous part of him that he shares with Peter.

From the very beginning, Graff deliberately puts Ender in situations designed to bring out his violent instincts. On the journey to the Battle

School, for instance, Graff isolates Ender by making it clear that Ender is intellectually superior, thus compelling his classmates to taunt Ender mercilessly. These episodes escalate progressively until Ender's life is truly in danger in his fight with Bonzo. But Graff always ignores things until Ender has a chance to respond. On the shuttle, Ender thinks, "Again a blow to the head. Laughter from the boys. Didn't Graff see this? Wasn't he going to stop it? Another blow. Harder. It really hurt. Where was Graff?"[18] Of course Graff sees this. But Graff's strategy is to isolate Ender: "I told you," Graff exclaims to his second in command, Major Anderson, "His isolation can't be broken. He can never come to believe that anybody will ever help him out, *ever*. If he once thinks there's an easy way out, he's wrecked."[19] From Graff's perspective, and indeed from the perspective of the entire International Fleet, Ender is humanity's last great chance to make a military stand against the overwhelming force of the buggers. The human race *has* nothing else. If Ender is not subjected to cruel training methods, Graff continually reminds his colleagues, "We'll all be bugger meat."[20]

Graff seems to know that it is only by being isolated that Ender will be forced to contract back into himself and foster his own evil. While Ender is the one who is locked up in Battle School, forced to play war games and fight for his life, Graff is the one who really understands the sacrifices necessary to protect the human race. It may go contrary to our intuitions to say it, but Graff's actions are sacrifices made in the interest of humanity. At times Graff seems to take enjoyment in his cruel tasks, but it's is always in what he accomplishes, rather than the cruel methods themselves, that he rejoices: "There *is* an art to it, and I'm very, very good at it. But enjoy? Well, maybe. When they put back the pieces afterward, and it makes them better."[21] Schelling would note that in preparing the children for war, Graff *expands* into his role, putting his own interests aside in order to save the human race. As the story progresses, Graff puts on more and more weight until, "his belly spilled over both armrests" of his chair.[22] At the end of the story, when Graff has to protect himself from prosecution, we see Graff *contract* back into his selfish core, refusing to take responsibility for his crimes, losing all the weight he originally put on. "One kind of stress puts it on," Graff says, "another takes it off. I am a creature of chemicals."[23]

By putting Ender into situations where his physical safety is threatened and his very life is at stake, Graff forces Ender to contract into his own self. The point is that humankind can't afford to worry about the moral ambiguity of destroying an entire alien species. Earth needs a vicious killer, which is precisely what Graff's training regimen is designed to create. Becoming this monster is of course a highly traumatic experience for Ender. And it's disturbing for the reader not just because we abhor what was done to Ender, but because we all go through a similar process as we reconcile ourselves to the depths to which we are able to sink. One thing that Schelling can help us to notice is that by becoming a selfish monster, Ender passes through an essential phase in his moral development.

The Moral Development of Ender Wiggin

Graff's actions are what make Ender's moral development possible, but Ender ultimately torments only himself. Graff pushes Ender to an early recognition of what so few of us fully recognize: who we are as individuals is a product not of our own choosing. It's a *necessity with which we're born*, one we have to struggle with throughout our lives. This is something that Schelling is uniquely capable of fleshing out.

We all want to think that we are in control of our lives, that our decisions are ours and ours alone; we all want to think that we're free to determine our own lives. But when we take a good hard look at our lives, we realize that our basic motivations are ultimately a mystery to us. According to Schelling, who we are as individuals is something that we spend our lives trying to discover. We always move back and forth from darkness to light, from the mystery of our identity to understanding small parts of ourselves. We might make some important discoveries, yet we never become fully transparent to ourselves. Ender's struggles with his brother Peter, with his peers in Battle School, and with his own demons are examples of this natural human tendency to try to get a better grip on ourselves. The story of Ender Wiggin is disturbing because it reveals the many ways in which all of us are pre-determined to act, ways that are out of our control but that also *define our character as individuals*. We all have a Peter inside of us, a part of us that is completely self-interested and willing to destroy others to protect these interests.

Ender really wants to be a good person, but in striving for this, he becomes something he always suspected, but never thought possible.

He really does mean to viciously defeat his opponents: in a conversation with Valentine, Ender comes clean, saying, "I *destroy* them. I make it impossible for them to ever hurt me again. I grind them and grind them until they don't *exist*."[24] This defines his encounters with Stilson and Bonzo, but it's not until the end that Ender finally realizes that these monstrous forces are not something that can be controlled, but rather must be accepted.

Ender finally begins to grasp the inevitability of evil in human life. Valentine finally breaks it to her little brother: "Welcome to the human race. Nobody controls his own life, Ender."[25] It takes the perspective of someone who's been manipulated and done a good deal of manipulating herself to realize this fundamental truth. Valentine, after all, was manipulated by Peter to become Demosthenes. More than this, Valentine even finds her own identity being manipulated by her virtual role as Demosthenes. She sees the consequences of her ideas fundamentally change the world around her, and she is especially troubled when she hears her own father rehearse political views she penned under her pseudonym.

By this point in the story, Ender too, of course, is intimately familiar with manipulation. The freedom he thought he'd gained through realizing how the I.F. pulled his strings turned out to be an illusion. While it's a terrible realization that you've been manipulated, it's worse to see that you're still the author of your actions in any case. This is driven home when Ender discovers the pupa of a queen bugger on Eros. As it turns out, the buggers are just like Ender—and all people:

> We are like you; the thought pressed into his mind. We did not mean to murder, and when we understood, we never came again. We thought we were the only thinking beings in the universe, until we met you, but never did we dream that thought could arise from the lonely animals who cannot dream each other's dreams.[26]

This revelation does not, however, truly excuse either the buggers' nor Ender's truly evil acts. Rather, the revelation tells us is that while evil can never be justified, it can be understood and perhaps even forgiven. The buggers, just like Ender, never knew what they were doing. But this does not excuse them from moral responsibility. Ender's moral development consists in the recognition that even though he was not aware of what he was doing, he is still responsible. Indeed, in becoming

"Speaker for the Dead," Ender attempts to make up for all the evil that can never be forgiven. No matter how insidious the manipulation, Ender was only acting in accordance with his nature. As Schelling teaches us, when we encounter evil in the world, we like to think that something went wrong, that inexplicable evil is ultimately part of a larger order of the good. But this tempting presumption is mistaken. And indeed by the end of *Ender's Game* we know better. We know that the facts of Ender's crimes can never be justified, least of all by Ender to himself. Ender becomes a "name and a story," much more convenient than a "flesh-and-blood person."[27] Our moral sensibilities won't tolerate a real person capable of real evil—they can't be allowed in our moral community. But Ender's legacy can be re-crafted as the actions of someone who does terrible things for a noble purpose. Ender becomes a hero not as the real boy who beat other children to death, but rather as the boy who saved the human race.

Card's *Ender's Game* is disturbing not only because of what its protagonist does and the manipulation that led him to it. It's discomfiting because it points to something we all suspect about ourselves: that our freedom is really a product of forces that we cannot detect or even imagine. In this way, *Ender's Game* can help us to understand one of the profound truths about freedom, one that Schelling has taught us to recognize. As real as it seems to us, our freedom is still tainted by a necessity over which we have neither conscious awareness nor control. *Ender's Game* is thus revealed as a meditation on the interplay of freedom and fate that defines all of our lives.

Notes

1. Elaine Radford, "Ender and Hitler: Sympathy for the Superman," *Fantasy Review* 102 (1987): 7–11.
2. John Kessel, "Creating the Innocent Killer: *Ender's Game*, Intention, and Morality," http://www4.ncsu.edu/~tenshi/Killer_000.htm, accessed June 8, 2012.
3. F.W.J. Schelling, *Philosophical Investigations into the Essence of Human Freedom*. Trans. Jeff Love and Johannes Schmidt (Albany: SUNY Press, 2006), 39.
4. Orson Scott Card, *Ender's Game* (New York: TOR Books, 1991), 270.
5. Ibid., 115.

6. The classical formulation here is from St. Augustine. A good modern edition of the relevant text is *The Augustine Catechism: The Enchiridion on Faith, Hope, and Clarity*. Trans. Bruce Harbert. Ed. Boniface Ramsey (Hyde Park: New City Press, 1999), 57–84.
7. Schelling, 29.
8. Schelling, 18.
9. Card, *Ender's Game*, 213.
10. Ibid., 19.
11. Ibid., 33.
12. For a very different interpretation of Ender's motivations, see Danielle Wylie's chapter in this book.
13. Schelling, 32.
14. Card, *Ender's Game*, 65.
15. Ibid., 313.
16. Ibid., 117.
17. Ibid., 118.
18. Ibid., 33.
19. Ibid., 38.
20. Ibid., 99.
21. Ibid., 28.
22. Ibid., 190.
23. Ibid., 305.
24. Ibid., 238.
25. Ibid., 313.
26. Ibid., 321.
27. Ibid., 308.

CHAPTER 3

Xenocide's Paradox
The Virtue of Being Ender

Jeff Ewing

Ender's Game, at face value, is a story about a young yet mature and extraordinarily gifted boy manipulated into saving the world. At another level, though, Ender's story raises ethical questions about war, leadership, and character. Perhaps the most important thing about the story is what it says about the virtues that make for good leadership. Ender has particular qualities that distinguish him from Peter, his power-hungry brother, and from the adults manipulating his life. These qualities of character are what make Ender precisely the person humanity needs to survive the buggers. What virtues make Ender the commander that humanity needs? In this chapter, we'll look at Ender's story through the eyes of Plato and Aristotle, two philosophers deeply concerned with the virtues of leadership.

Ender's Game is set in a future in which humanity has fought repeated wars against the Formics, an insectoid alien species referred to by the characters as "buggers." Earth expects a third invasion, and its defense lies in the hands of the International Fleet, whose commanders are carefully bred and trained from a young age in Battle School. The world's most intelligent and promising children are sent to the school, trained in war, and engaged in increasingly difficult games. Andrew "Ender" Wiggin is one of these children, the youngest in a family of child geniuses. His older siblings, Peter and Valentine, had also been tested for Battle School. In a future when families are ordinarily kept to two children, and "Thirds" are normally neither

Ender's Game and Philosophy: The Logic Gate Is Down, First Edition. Edited by Kevin S. Decker.
© 2013 John Wiley & Sons, Inc. Published 2013 by John Wiley & Sons, Inc.

allowed nor respected, Andrew was allowed to be born because Peter was a vicious, heartless genius, while Valentine had exercised too much empathy.

Ender excels in Battle School, stirring increasing hope in his commanders while frustrating some of his peers. International Fleet Commander Graff intentionally isolates Ender from his peers in the hope of developing him into a strong leader. As Ender continues to excel, triumphing over rivals, he soon makes friends, and is put in charge of increasing numbers of fleets in various exercises. What's the secret of Ender's success? Why were Peter and Valentine not suitable for the I.F.? In other words, what does the story of Ender's family tell us about the virtues? Before we examine that, we first need to understand the virtues themselves.

"A Little Private Moral Dilemma"

Virtue ethics is an ancient approach to moral philosophy. Instead of asking, "What is the right thing to do?" a person concerned with virtue poses the question, "What kind of person should I be?" In other words, virtue ethics centers on *character* and, more importantly, the character traits that make a person *good*. Virtue ethics was the dominant ethical approach throughout most of the history of Western philosophy: it was the basic approach in the ancient Greece of Plato (429–347 BC) and Aristotle (384–322 BC)[1] and in the Middle Ages of St. Thomas Aquinas (1225–1274).[2] After going into eclipse for some time, it's regained a foothold in Western moral thinking, starting with G.E.M. Anscombe's 1958 essay "Modern Moral Philosophy," and has been bolstered by influential contemporary philosophers like Alasdair MacIntyre, Michael Slote, Rosalind Hursthouse, and Christine Swanton.[3]

Advocates of virtue ethics agree that the virtues are traits that together make for a "good person." As Alasdair MacIntyre explains, the "immediate outcome of the exercise of a virtue is a choice which issues in right action."[4] That is, virtues give the good person the tendencies to act "rightly." And virtues "are dispositions not only to act in particular ways, but also to feel in particular ways," to *want* to be good, to do right.[5] Most virtue ethicists think of the different virtues as being mutually compatible with each other, so they can exist simultaneously and not compete. Contemporary virtue ethicists often take their inspiration from Aristotle (such as MacIntyre or Hursthouse), or, closer to the present, the eighteenth-century Scotsman David Hume (Slote) or the nineteenth-century German Friedrich Nietzsche (Swanton).

If we're going to examine Ender's moral philosophy, heading straight to the question, "What kind of virtue does Ender show?" seems to jump the gun a little. We first need to determine whether the story of morality in *Ender's Game* can be told through virtue ethics at all. What kind of ethical theory seems to best describe the moral world and lessons of *Ender's Game*? Well, there are three basic *kinds* of moral philosophy: deontology, consequentialism, and virtue ethics. Deontologists emphasize duty. They believe that an individual's duties and intentions determine what actions are moral; actions are right or wrong regardless of their consequences. Consequentialists believe that actions are right or wrong based on their consequences. Of course, judgments on the rightness and wrongness of a given action will vary greatly depending on *which kind of ends* are held to be good. Ethical egoists, for example, will answer every ethical question by asking how consequences benefit the individual, while utilitarians will wonder how they benefit all the people concerned.

Deontology is largely absent in the moral universe of *Ender's Game*, where moral decisions seem to be based on two different ethical stances: utilitarian consequentialism and virtue ethics.[6] Utilitarian reasoning is what finally convinces Ender to go to Battle School. Graff tells Ender that "there's a chance that because you're with the fleet, mankind might survive and the buggers might leave us alone forever."[7] Graff "sells" Battle School and the I.F. in terms of the potentially good consequences for humanity *despite* the fact that signing up might have potentially bad consequences for Ender personally. This is clearly utilitarian logic. But it's worth noting that thinking about consequences is not as alien to virtue ethics as the buggers are to humankind. To understand why, consider what kind of outcomes the traits of benevolence, love, care, and empathy would produce. Most of these would be the kind of consequences that utilitarians are searching for, too.

Ender's Game also teaches that *character* (habitually acting from virtue) is important even when we mull over utilitarian considerations. The sole reason for allowing the Wiggin family to have a third child is that the I.F. wants a certain type of character in its soldiers. Peter "was the best we'd seen in a long time," Graff tells Ender, but "wasn't accepted ... for the very reasons you hate him."[8] Valentine, whom the I.F. wanted to "be Peter, but milder" was "too mild."[9] Ender's thought process is also important. To be virtuous, it's crucial that we act only after deliberating on choices and alternatives, and in the book there's a good deal of emphasis placed on Ender's *reasoning* for actions, rather than solely on the actions themselves. After Ender's "take-no-prisoners" handling of the bully Stilson, Graff tells Ender's mother, "Until we knew what Ender's motivation was, we couldn't be sure he wasn't another—we had to know what the action meant. Or at least what Ender believed that it meant."[10] Here, Graff is less concerned about what Ender did against the bullies than what that action said about the person Ender *was*, that is, about his character. The dominant ethical perspective in *Ender's Game*, it seems, is virtue ethics. But *which* type of virtue ethics perspective governs moral blame and praise in *Ender's Game*? To proceed, we'll have to look to a much more ancient battle between a teacher and his student: that between Plato and Aristotle.

"The Name of Ender is One to Conjure With"

Plato's concept of virtue rests on two ideas: his analogy between the three-part human soul and the state (in his conception, modeled after the Greek city-state, the *polis*), and his four cardinal virtues: wisdom, courage, temperance, and justice. Let's begin with the cardinal virtues. *Wisdom* is the ability to judge which action is right at a given time. To Plato, this is the virtue appropriate to *reason* and needed by rulers of the *polis*. *Courage* is endurance and the ability to withstand fear and anxiety. Again, this virtue has its place: namely, in the warriors in the *polis*. *Temperance* represents self-restraint, needed by the producing classes. *Justice*, on the other hand, represents the balance of all three parts of the human soul: reason controlled by wisdom, the impulse to action organized by courage, and desires restrained by temperance. Does Ender, in his role as a top commander within Battle School, fit into this Platonist model of virtue?

Plato's account of virtues needs to be understood in light of his theory of the *Forms*, a view about the nature of reality. Plato says that each thing in the day-to-day world is an imperfect reflection of an ideal "Form" of that thing. A "Form" is a perfect, non-physical version of the thing existing beyond the physical world, and is something like a paradigm or gauge for imperfect things in the day-to-day world. Horses and humans, for example, are better and more valuable the closer they approximate the Forms "Horse" and "Human." All the Forms are superseded by the Form of the Good, which also gives them their existence. For Plato, the reason why wisdom is a cardinal virtue is that a wise person will understand the lesser degree of reality of the empirical world, and they will value the Good and the world of the Forms more as a result.

Plato believed that though not all *good citizens* are necessarily *virtuous people*, a *virtuous person* must be a *good citizen*. Plato's *just state*, described in the *Republic*, involves a permanent division of the city-state into three classes, the guardians, soldiers, and workers/merchants. Membership in a class is permanent, though children born into one class can be moved into another early in their life, and every individual is expected to accept their class position and obey the wisdom of the guardians. Essentially, for Plato, a *good citizen* respects authority. Though the society of Earth in the Enderverse is not Plato's ideal city-state, its decisions do share the top-down hierarchy structure. The demands of the I.F. for the preservation of humanity take precedence over individual preference. A good citizen is supposed to prioritize what the I.F. needs from them. In the Fleet and Battle School, disobedience to superior officers is heavily sanctioned for the same reason. But, of course, Ender's not known for following rules and respecting orders and the chain of command. Some features of Ender's world and his character traits seem to limit his ability to attain Plato's virtues, in this case the key virtues of wisdom and justice. So what about Aristotle, then?

Aristotle's virtues fall into two broad categories: intellectual and moral. Intellectual virtues sharpen our capacity to reason, whereas moral virtues order the "passive" part of the soul that only acts rationally by following the lead of others. By dividing the virtues, then, Aristotle is in effect arguing that intellectual virtues specifically hone the capacity of the mind to reason, the trait that marks off humanity from the rest of the living world.

To understand how to be morally virtuous, we have to use Aristotle's *doctrine of the mean*, which says that achieving a virtuous character trait is acting according to a mean between two related extremes. For example, acting with courage requires avoiding cowardice and rashness. Among the moral virtues, Aristotle lists courage, temperance, liberality, magnanimity, proper ambition, patience, truthfulness to oneself, wittiness, friendliness, modesty, and righteous indignation. According to Aristotle, moral virtues cannot be *taught*. Rather, they have to be formed as habits by constantly exercising them. Just as there is no way to become stronger except to engage in exercises that strengthen the muscles, so too there is no formula for becoming virtuous except through practice.

Aristotle was also keen on the importance of cultivating intellectual virtues, which fall into five categories: practical reason, scientific knowledge, intuition, wisdom, and artistic or technical skill. He put great stress on the importance of the virtues that would improve relations between people, primarily friendship and justice. Aristotle believed there was a unity of the virtues—they will not conflict, and more importantly, a person is not virtuous until they have attained all the virtues. This is a pretty high bar! This life of virtue is known in Greek as *eudaimonia* or human flourishing. The virtues are excellences of *humanity* in general, traits that collectively make for an excellent human-as-such.

Having very briefly outlined some parts of Platonic and Aristotelian virtue ethics, let's point to some of the virtuous traits that make Ender uniquely capable of beating the buggers. One trait that defines Ender's approach to "problem solving" is the ability to swiftly and resolutely strike with the minimum force necessary to stop the "enemy" for good.[11] While the *goal* of Ender's actions in a conflict is to respond with as much overwhelming, sudden fury as necessary to stop the assault and prevent future assaults, Ender attempts to use the minimum means to do so. He doesn't *mean* to kill Stilson, for example. Rather, he acts out of self-defense, not from malice. This disposition to use moderate force for a particular purpose is also seen in Ender's response to bullying on the flight to Battle School, with Bonzo in the showers, and several other times throughout the story. Ender's virtuous response is at the mean between two vices; he uses neither too much nor too little force. More importantly, Ender doesn't revel in the violence. In fact, after each encounter, he regrets his actions and fears he has become like his malevolent brother, Peter. Ender committed the "simulated" genocidal destruction of the Formics because he judged this to be the minimum means necessary to survive their attack. A genuine xenocide—just like genocide—is never going to be a virtuous act, though. Since Ender didn't know the stakes were so high, on realizing the real consequences of his actions, he fell into depression. Ender fell into the vice of action outside the mean by committing xenocide because at the time he didn't have the benefit of all the relevant information. This is also reflected in Ender's killing of Stilson and Bonzo—in both cases he intends only to make them stop bullying him and to preserve his own life and welfare. But Ender doesn't realize that he's gone too far, and they end up dying.

Ender also has a tendency to solve problems "in the moment," that is, to be fully present in the problem and quickly modify himself and his actions and reactions. In doing so, Ender frequently violates the rules of the games he plays (this is how he's the only person to get past the virtual Giant's Drink game) and disobeys his superiors. He also violates the rules of his peer commanders (for example, Bonzo in Salamander Army) if it benefits the whole, even though insubordination like this is absolutely against the rules. This shows that Ender likes authoritative hierarchies and bureaucracies as little as he likes violence. Indeed, "Ender didn't like fighting. He didn't like Peter's kind, the strong against the weak, and he didn't like his own kind either, the smart against the stupid."[12] Witness the effectiveness of his Dragon Army, which was freed from bureaucracy and allowed a relative independence among the units. His groups were thus more flexible and adaptable than the others.

To sum up, three traits give Ender an edge over the other children in Battle School: (1) the disposition to respond with the minimum force necessary to prevent future attacks, neither too much nor too little; (2) adaptability to new situations; and (3) disregard of rules and hierarchies. These three traits also prove him superior to the buggers.

Plato or Aristotle?

While both Plato and Aristotle believed that a person's exercise of the virtues depend on his or her social role, Aristotle left far more room for stepping outside our roles if virtue dictated this need. Aristotle, then, makes it possible for us to see Ender's second and third key traits as virtues. In turn, the exercise of these virtues made him the formidable opponent and capable leader that humanity needed, a morally praiseworthy person who won the war against the Formics. In this sense, then, Ender seems more Aristotelian in how his character develops than Platonic (though Ender is more clearly anti-authoritarian than Aristotle himself was). Ender's clearest Aristotelian trait is that his moral reasoning treats a *virtuous* act as the *mean* between two extremes.

What about Ender's apparently vicious acts—those that violate the doctrine of the mean? Ender's failure to respond in a virtuous manner to the attacks of Stilson, Bonzo, and the buggers with the *right amount* of force, neither too little to prevent further attacks nor *too much* such that it destroys them, can be explained in terms of Ender's inadequate realization of the *intellectual* virtues. Ender had a level of understanding beyond his years in knowing how to respond forcefully and quickly, as well as to determine who is and who is not a threat, but he erred in deciding *how far to go*, and often lacked crucial knowledge of his own circumstances and the background conditions. So Aristotle's treatment of the virtues provides a better explanation, not only of Ender's dispositions, but also the traits that Ender would need to exercise his skills and traits appropriately. Aristotle's virtues are far more practical than Plato's, and are a better fit for Ender and for the world he lives in. The world of *Ender's Game* is lined with a moral fabric that is virtue-based, and the kind of virtue ethics that make Ender the champion of humanity against the Formic invasion may not be perfectly Aristotelian, but it *is* far more Aristotelian than Platonic.

So, in the end, what's at stake in our discussion? Why is it so important to ask questions about virtue and leadership? A key concern throughout *Ender's Game* is the issue of character—does Ender have the "right stuff" to save humanity? Nothing is more important in a leader than character, because character tells us about strengths and weaknesses, tendencies that will direct how they lead and what they lead toward. Ender's spontaneity and his in-the-moment alertness give him the ability to make quick and accurate decisions. His decisions are always intended to solve the problem once and for all with minimum force necessary. So, is Ender the ideal model of a leader? No, for as we've seen, he often miscalculates the "minimum force necessary." But *Ender's Game* itself teaches the important lesson that we need to look at the *virtues* of a leader and whether or not they have what it takes to solve the challenges of their day.

Notes

1. Interested readers might want to read Plato's *Republic* in Edith Hamilton and Huntington Cairns, eds., *The Collected Dialogues of Plato Including the Letters* (Princeton, NJ: Princeton University Press, 1989), and Aristotle's *Nicomachean Ethics*, in Richard McKeon, ed., *The Basic Works of Aristotle* (New York: Random House, 1941).
2. See St. Thomas Aquinas, *Basic Writings*, Anton C. Pegis, ed. (New York: Random House, 1945).
3. See G.E.M. Anscombe, "Modern Moral Philosophy," *Philosophy* 33 (1958); Alasdair MacIntyre, *After Virtue* (London: Duckworth, 1985); Michael Slote, *Morals from Motives* (Oxford: Oxford University Press, 2001); Rosalind Hursthouse, *On Virtue Ethics* (Oxford: Oxford University Press, 1999); and Christine Swanton, *Virtue Ethics* (Oxford: Oxford University Press, 2003).
4. MacIntyre, *After Virtue*, 149.
5. Ibid.
6. For more on utilitarianism in *Ender's Game*, see Greg Littman's chapter in this book.
7. Orson Scott Card, *Ender's Game* (New York: TOR Books, 1991), 25.
8. Ibid.
9. Ibid., 24.
10. Ibid., 20.
11. For a closer look at the ethics of this tactic, see Lance Belluomini's chapter in this book.
12. Card, *Ender's Game*, 21.

CHAPTER 4

Teaching to the Test
Constructing the Identity of a Space Commander

Chad William Timm

It's ... status, identity, purpose, name; all that makes these children who they are comes out of this game.
—Major Anderson to Colonel Graff

As the only hope of preventing global devastation from the impending bugger attack, Ender Wiggin needed to be transformed from a bright six-year-old child into the most effective military strategist and space commander the world had ever known. To successfully complete this transformation, teachers at the Battle School needed to do more than merely instruct Ender in the nuts and bolts of strategy and leadership. He had to be taught to discipline himself to think and behave like a soldier.

In *Ender's Game* the International Fleet's Battle School subjected children to a rigorous and grueling educational program. This put the Battle School's administrators and teachers in an incredibly powerful position: they had the unilateral power to determine what knowledge and skills were necessary to be a successful soldier. How did this power form Ender's identity? How did the teachers define what it meant to be a soldier and a leader? What role did constant video surveillance play in disciplining Ender's thoughts and actions and in shaping the person he eventually became? As we'll see, the work of French philosopher Michel Foucault (1926–1984) is invaluable in showing how power and knowledge are interdependent in governing the I.F.'s soldiers and in teaching them to be self-governing at the I.F.'s Battle School.

Ender's Game and Philosophy: The Logic Gate Is Down, First Edition. Edited by Kevin S. Decker.
© 2013 John Wiley & Sons, Inc. Published 2013 by John Wiley & Sons, Inc.

"They're Gonna Make You Do Time Out in the Belt ..."

For most people, "genealogy" is about tracing your family history to learn where you came from, like when Ender learned the truth about why he was a "Third." But "genealogy" means something quite different for Michel Foucault. Instead of searching for universal truths as most philosophers do, Foucault looked at history to analyze the conditions that would make something considered to be true. Foucault borrowed the method of genealogy from the philosopher Friedrich Nietzsche (1844–1900), who, like Foucault, was interested in how genealogy could be used as a tool to change the way we view the present. Foucault's genealogies of truth and knowledge uncovered the techniques that powerful institutions like prisons, hospitals, and schools used to determine how and why someone could be called a prisoner, patient, or student. After all, how do we know what it means to be a good student, or what qualifies us as a criminal, if some expert like a teacher or judge doesn't tell us? Foucault argued that people in positions of power and authority use their status as experts to *create* these categories as a means of control through "disciplinary power." The method genealogy allowed Foucault to figuratively trace the family tree of the ideas like "prisoner" and "student" in order to uncover the ways in which these roles are actually created by the institutions that deal with them.

Foucault's special interest was in changes in the methods of governing people in eighteenth-century Europe. Powerful leaders realized they could no longer always use outwardly violent forms of punishment, or "sovereign power," to get people to obey them. Outright violence, Foucault thought, "was ... dangerous in that it provided a support for confrontation between the violence of the king and the violence of the people."[1] When kings pushed subjects to their limit with brutal oppression, the people pushed back with retaliation of their own. As a result, governments developed disciplinary power as a technique to convince people to do what the king wanted, but also to do it without being told. By looking critically at the historical development of the prison, hospital, and school Foucault showed how disciplinary power worked to create certain *kinds* of people. In other words, instead of being completely in control of our own identities, Foucault argues, "the individual is an effect of power."[2] As a matter of fact, Foucault even claimed his notion of power explained what he called "the death of man." Whereas René Descartes (1596–1650) thought we could doubt everything except the fact that we know ourselves (expressed in his famous *cogito ergo sum*, "I think therefore I am"), Foucault argued, "Man is only a recent invention, a figure not two centuries old."[3] There is no "human nature," but only disciplinary power working to create our identities and subsequently to create mankind.

"Leader's Aren't Born, They Are Made"

Modern governments still exercise disciplinary power in two ways. First, government representatives use their positions of power to sort people into specific categories in order to know them and to control them. Second, they use disciplinary power to get people to behave in certain ways so that people will control themselves.

As the director of primary training at the Battle School, Colonel Graff has similar power to define the qualities and characteristics needed to be a potential recruit. This gives a new meaning to Vince Lombardi's saying, "Leaders aren't born, they are made." Graff identifies traits in monitored children, traits like resilience and problem solving, and sends candidates to Battle School on that basis. As conversations between Graff, Anderson, and Imbu show, the characteristics emphasized in the choice depend on the person making the decisions. After all, not every child would have what it takes to be a soldier. Peter was too vicious, for example, while Valentine wasn't vicious enough. The power of *knowing* as it's exercised in disciplinary power in this case allows the teachers to sort children into groups. In turn, this sorting enables school officials to train students in particular ways, like deciding which students will go to which armies, when the armies will battle, and who will lead them. Graff even goes so far as to re-define the rules of the battleroom to challenge Ender because "this is something to be decided by people who know what they are doing."[4] Graff's position of power allows him to determine the very nature of the battle simulations themselves.

It would be impossible for the Battle School's teachers to effectively turn children into soldiers if recruits were allowed to choose their associations freely. As Graff tells Ender, "All the boys are organized into armies ... Everybody starts as a common soldier, taking orders."[5] Once Ender arrived at the school in orbit, this sorting became immediately apparent and "he noticed that the older boys were divided into groups, according to the uniforms they wore. Some with different uniforms were talking together, but generally the groups each had their own area."[6] Foucault explains that the license to sort and categorize people results from having power, and likewise, having power allows leaders to know how to continue sorting and categorizing. Thus power and knowledge operate in a circle, because, as Foucault writes, "It is not possible for power to be exercised without knowledge, it is impossible for knowledge not to engender power."[7] In other words, knowledge can be used in powerful ways, whether benignly teaching your children math facts or Colonel Graff deviously using his knowledge of Ender's whereabouts and health to convince Valentine to help him.

Graff's purpose in sorting recruits was to get the children to act in certain ways. Sorting students into armies, like Centipedes, Scorpions, and Spiders, allowed the teachers to track each student's progress by manipulating the learning environment for maximum impact on the *kind* of student in each group. Once placed into a group, Ender's day was extremely repetitive: "This was school. Every day, hours of classes. Reading. Numbers. History. Videos of the bloody battles in space, the Marines spraying their guts all over the walls of the bugger ships."[8] By controlling his day down to the minute and isolating him so that his only outlet was either the Giant's Drink video game or the battleroom, Ender's teachers gave him just a single choice: to begin seeing himself as the soldier they wanted him to be. His identity as a person became one with his daily learning activities.

This use of disciplinary power parallels the operations of European governments in the eighteenth century. According to Foucault, "By the late eighteenth century, the soldier has become something that can be made; out of a formless clay, an inapt body, the machine required can be constructed."[9] Similarly, Graff saw Ender as formless clay, with Major Anderson even going so far as to say, "He's too malleable. Too willing to submerge himself in someone else's will."[10] But it would take more than identification and sorting to get Ender to embody the identity of a military commander. Teachers would have to observe him, test, him, and train him *to control himself.*

Battle School Panopticon

Perhaps the most important tool of disciplinary power is *surveillance*. The impact of directed scrutiny on human identity was explored in the work of Jeremy Bentham (1748–1832), who devised plans for a unique prison, called the Panopticon. Here, inmates would be led to believe guards they couldn't see were constantly watching them. The architectural plans called for a central guard tower surrounded by rings of cells stacked one on top of another, each cell facing inward toward the central guard tower. With only a small window high in the rear corner of each cell, prisoners were forced to look at the tower and assume they were under surveillance. They never knew if they were actually being watched, because a bright light emanating from opaque windows in the tower allowed prisoners to see only vaguely human shapes behind the glass. According to Foucault, Bentham's intent was that "the inmate must never know whether he is being looked at at any one moment; but he must be sure that he may always be so."[11]

The threat of constant surveillance and the paranoia of never knowing if they were being watched encouraged prisoners to behave in more docile ways. In a sense, the inmate became so used to being watched that he began watching himself, behaving like the guards wanted him to behave. Foucault says, "Hence the major effect of the Panopticon: to induce in the inmate a state of conscious and permanent visibility that assures the automatic functioning of power."[12] The disciplinary power of surveillance served to restrain the inmate beyond bars and shackles.

At Battle School, partitioning, ranking, and ordering the use of time down to the minute provided knowledge and control of recruits, but the teachers also needed to observe and test Ender in order to chart his progress toward their goals. It's obvious that the Battle School mirrors the Panopticon; as a matter of fact, Bentham actually got the idea for the Panopticon from an eighteenth-century military school in Paris where "each pupil ... was assigned a glassed-cell where he could be observed throughout the night."[13] Like Bentham's prison guards, Graff used constant observation through monitors to keep tabs on the potential recruits back on Earth. In the first few lines of the book, Graff clues us into this when he says, "I've watched through his [Ender's] eyes, I've listened through his ears, and I tell you he's the one,"[14] and later when he remarks "We monitored your brother and sister, Ender. You'd be amazed at how sensitive the instruments are."[15]

The Battle School's physical structure also allowed teachers to keep Ender and the other recruits under constant surveillance. Instead of a guard tower, the battleroom served as the central hub on the wheel of the school. Ender assumed his teachers watched him constantly, never knowing for sure if they were. Periodically, his assumptions were confirmed, like when "he noticed how Graff and the other officers were watching them. Analyzing. Everything we do means something, Ender realized."[16] On another occasion, while working alone on his computer desk, the screen goes dark: "Words flashed around the rim of the desk. REPORT TO COMMANDER IMMEDIATELY. YOU ARE LATE. GREEN GREEN BROWN."[17] It seems that even in the "safety" of Ender's cell (I mean *room*!), Graff and the other teachers watched him constantly.

Testing 1, 2, 3 …

In disciplinary power, observation works hand in hand with *testing*. Constant surveillance encourages students to act in particular ways for fear they'll be seen doing something they shouldn't. But examinations are a way for school officials to compare students to their own arbitrary standards of success. For example, Graff and the other teachers determined what qualities and characteristics successful students possessed, and they used testing to encourage the students' striving to identify with, to *be* the standard.

Testing initially helped instructors identify potential soldiers from children on Earth. Valentine remarked to Peter, "Ender and I aren't stupid. We scored as well as you did on everything. Better on some things. We're all such wonderfully bright children."[18] Once at the Battle School, Graff and the other instructors repeatedly tested Ender and the other recruits by engineering battles against other students. This repetitive testing and examining continued all the way to Command School, where Ender realizes "that as the battleroom was to Battle School, so the simulator was to Command School. The early classes were valuable, but the real education was the game."[19] While observing these assessments, teachers "never spoke—hardly anyone ever did, unless they had something specific to teach him. The watchers would stay, silently watching him run through a difficult simulation, and then leave just as he finished."[20]

Observation and testing served to separate students who met standards from those who needed remediation or punishment. Students who didn't test well, like Peter, either fail or are identified as at-risk, while those who are judged to have exceeded expectations, like Ender, are put on an advanced track. Again, Foucault comments, "[Judgment] is a normalizing gaze, a surveillance that makes it possible to qualify, to classify and to punish. It establishes over individuals a visibility through which one differentiates them and judges them."[21] This process of normalization was absolutely necessary if Graff and the other instructors were to be successful at doing their job, namely, "… to produce the best soldiers in the world. In the whole history of the world."[22]

Whereas eighteenth-century sovereign power used outward displays of physical violence and punishment to force subjects to behave in certain ways, disciplinary power has "no need for arms, physical violence, material constraints. Just a gaze. An inspecting gaze, a gaze which each individual under its weight will end by interiorizing to the point that he is his own overseer, each individual thus exercising this surveillance over, and against, himself."[23] The constant observation and testing conducted by Graff and the teachers encouraged Ender and the other students to be their own policemen, to control themselves and become *disciplined*. Beyond this, the fact that Ender's society didn't question the placement of monitors in the heads of small children demonstrates the pervasiveness of disciplinary power. Constant surveillance had simply become the order of things.

"I'm Sure You Can Get Your Training at Someone Else's Expense"

All of this sorting, observing, and testing actually taught students to construct brand new identities for themselves, because as Foucault says, "Discipline 'makes' individuals; it is the specific technique of a power that regards individuals both as objects and as instruments of its exercise."[24] Ender may have come to Battle School with the identity of a child, but he left with that of a warrior.

Forming an identity in Battle School relies on rejecting weakness, as when Ender "… wanted to stop at Petra's bunk and tell her … about what his birthdays were usually like … But nobody told birthdays. It was childish. It was what landsiders did."[25] More importantly, it is guided by affirmations of strengths. Ender approaches Graff to demand his own army, saying, "You want to make me the best soldier possible … Look at the all-time standings. So far you're doing an excellent job with me. Congratulations."[26] Eventually Ender's identity reflected a complete transformation. Aspects of his new identity emerge in an encounter with Bean, a new member of Ender's Dragon Army. The scene is at the end of a rigorous practice session. While chastising his team for performing poorly, Ender quizzed Bean, complimenting his answers with, "Excellent. At least I have one soldier who can figure things out."[27] Ender proceeded to praise Bean while criticizing the rest of the team, all the while thinking, "Why am I doing this? What does this have to do with being a good commander, making one boy the target of all the others? Just because they did it to me, why should I do it to him?"[28] This episode is nearly identical to Ender's experience on the flight to Battle School when Graff singled him out and used him as an example. "When I tell you Ender Wiggin is the best in this launch, take the hint, my little dorklings," Graff warned. "Don't mess with him."[29] When Ender questioned Graff's treatment, Graff responded with "So? What will you do about it? Crawl into a corner? Start kissing their little backsides so they'll love you again? There's only one thing that will make them stop hating you. And that's being so good at what you do that they can't ignore you."[30] Ender's treatment of Bean reflects his complete metamorphosis into a commander when Bean asked him for his own toon. Ender replies, "Why would any soldier want to follow a little pinprick like you?".[31]

Although Ender questioned his own actions, thinking "Is it some law of human nature that you inevitably become whatever your first commander was?" he nonetheless continued with Bean's brutal training, rationalizing it with the thought, "I'm hurting you to make you a better soldier in every way … That's why they brought you to me, Bean. So you could be just like me. So you could grow up to be just like the old man."[32] Just like the giant in the virtual Giant's Drink game, who was transformed into a woodland playground upon his death, the six-year-old child who entered Battle School as Ender Wiggin had died and been resurrected as a ruthless battle commander.

Every Action Has an Equal and Opposite Reaction

It may be surprising to hear that the strategies used by instructors at the Battle School are the same kind of strategies used by teachers in public schools every day. Sure, we don't take six-year-olds away from their parents and send them into space to learn military tactics and strategy. We *do* sort, observe, and test children over and over for the purposes of making them into certain kinds of human beings. Instead of Battle Commanders, our schools strive to create what they term "twenty-first-century learners."

President Barack Obama's education program, "Race to the Top," "encourages states to award bonuses to teachers whose students get higher test scores ... and to fire teachers if their students get lower test scores."[33] This isn't Ender-level pressure of saving the earth, but today's teachers are under a great deal of pressure to produce results. So they use "fill-in-the-bubble" standardized tests to sort students into the categories of "proficient" or "not-proficient." In theory, this makes teachers more effective because they can then address the specific learning needs of each student. By sorting children into categories or groups with certain identified qualities like "struggles to solve multi-step problems" or "doesn't read with fluency," the teacher can then work with those students in specific ways similar to how sorted battle groups are trained in Battle School.

Yet this is precisely where the danger lies. Education officials who design standardized tests decide what knowledge to assess, and it's generally rote knowledge through memorization. This knowledge gives officials tremendous power, since schools that don't show improvement on test scores can lose funding. The power/knowledge relationship is then passed on to classroom teachers who sort, examine, observe, and discipline students until they develop identities as twenty-first-century learners. Thus teachers are affected by power and in turn use power on their students. The students themselves exert some degree of power over each other when they label, exclude, and create cliques that include and exclude their peers. This is because *all relationships* are power relationships—another of Foucault's controversial views.

Foucault calls attention to "... the significance of methods like school discipline, which succeeded in making children's bodies the object of highly complex systems of manipulation and conditioning."[34] This manipulation and conditioning arbitrarily creates students instead of letting them grow and develop in their own way. Being subject to this power and knowledge is hard on children: When Graff announced, "Pay attention, please, Ender. Today is your final examination in Command School," Ender reflected, "Final examination. After today, perhaps he could rest."[35]

Hold on a minute, you might be thinking. Disciplinary power has to be better than sovereign power, right? After all, isn't it a good thing that governments and their representatives no longer use public punishment and torture to get people to do what they want? Well, while the modern government claims its methods are more humane, the hidden manner in which disciplinary power operates might be even more unethical than giving someone a beating. Instead of schools allowing children to fulfill their innate potential, teachers *create* identities for students, like when Imbu says to Graff "The mind game is designed to help shape them, help them find worlds they can be comfortable in."[36] Like the prison that teaches the inmate to be disciplined or the mental institution that teaches the patient to be mentally healthy, schools teach children to be certain kinds of learners. Foucault asks "Is it surprising that prisons resemble factories, schools, barracks, hospitals, which all resemble prisons?"[37]

What makes understanding this power so complicated is that teachers and educational administrators aren't evil tyrants seeking to harm students. Instead, their identities as teachers are *also* wrapped up in Foucault's power/knowledge relationships, because these relationships are inevitable in modern societies. In every case, knowing anything involves the power to determine which kind of knowledge matters and, conversely, having power always involves knowing what matters. Its invisibility is what makes disciplinary power so dangerous and, at the same time, so effective. We take the "knowledge" being assessed on the tests for granted and don't ask, "Who gets to decide what's on the tests?"

Foucault argues that disciplinary power *is* everywhere, but "to say that one can never be 'outside' power does not mean that one is trapped and condemned to defeat no matter what."[38] Resistance is possible, and it begins with recognizing the power/knowledge relationships in the first place. Making disciplinary power visible begins the process of resistance because, as Foucault professed, "There are no relations of power without resistances."[39] Whether we see it or not, our children may already be resisting. They are tired of all the testing.

Ever the model student, even Ender resisted when he thought, "It was funny. The adults taking all this so seriously, and the children playing along, playing along, believing it too until suddenly the adults went too far, tried too hard, and the children could see through their game."[40] Unfortunately this resistance wasn't enough, and Ender completed the task that he had been created to achieve: the annihilation of the bugger civilization.

Notes

1. Michel Foucault, *Discipline and Punish: The Birth of the Prison*, trans. Alan Sheridan (New York: Vintage Press, 1995), 73.
2. Michel Foucault, *Power/Knowledge: Selected Interviews & Other Writings 1972–1977*, ed. Colin Gordon (New York: Vintage Books, 1980), 98.
3. Foucault, *The Order of Things: An Archaeology of the Human Sciences* (New York: Vintage Books), xxiii.
4. Orson Scott Card, *Ender's Game* (New York: TOR Books, 1991), 98.
5. Ibid., 24.
6. Ibid., 41.
7. Foucault, *Power/Knowledge*, 52.
8. Ibid., 45.
9. Foucault, *Discipline and Punish*, 135.
10. Card, *Ender's Game*, 1.
11. Foucault, *Discipline and Punish*, 201.
12. Ibid.
13. Ibid., 47.
14. Card, *Ender's Game*, 1.
15. Ibid., 47.
16. Ibid., 28.
17. Ibid., 74.
18. Ibid., 13.
19. Ibid., 259.
20. Ibid.
21. Foucault, *Discipline and Punish*, 184.
22. Card, *Ender's Game*, 34.
23. Foucault, *Power/Knowledge*, 155.
24. Foucault, *Discipline and Punish*, 170.
25. Card, *Ender's Game*, 92–93.
26. Ibid., 191.

27. Ibid., 161.
28. Ibid.
29. Ibid., 34.
30. Ibid., 35.
31. Ibid., 165–166.
32. Ibid., 166, 168.
33. Diane Ravitch, "How, and How Not, to Improve the Schools," *The New York Review of Books*, March 22, 2012, http://www.nybooks.com/articles/archives/2012/mar/22/how-and-how-not-improve-schools/?pagination=false, accessed May 24, 2012.
34. Foucault, *Power/Knowledge*, 125.
35. Card, *Ender's Game*, 290.
36. Ibid., 120–121.
37. Foucault, *Discipline and Punish*, 227.
38. Foucault, *Power/Knowledge*, 141–142.
39. Ibid., 142.
40. Card, *Ender's Game*, 293.

Part Two

GAME

COOPERATION
OR CONFRONTATION?

CHAPTER 5

The Enemy's Gate Is Down
Perspective, Empathy, and Game Theory

Andrew Zimmerman Jones

One of my most cherished books is a hardcover copy of *Ender's Game*, containing the following inscription from Orson Scott Card: "A survival guide for geniuses."[1] What key lesson should geniuses (or any of the rest of us) take from the pages of *Ender's Game*? While there are many candidates, the one most important one, I think, is this: *Winning a conflict is best achieved by truly understanding an opponent.* This key lesson is not only closely linked to *empathy*, but also to *game theory*, or the art of "understanding how other people think. And consequently being able to figure out what they will choose to do."[2] The author of this quote, Tom Siegried, even briefly mentions *Ender's Game* as really being *about* game theory:

> [*Ender's Game*]'s all about choosing strategies to achieve goals—about adults plotting methods for manipulating young Ender Wiggin, Ender choosing among maneuvers to win on a simulated battlefield, and Ender's siblings' devising tactics for influencing public opinion.[3]

Developed in the mid-twentieth century, game theory is a mathematical discipline that now drives fields as diverse as warfare, economics, evolutionary theory, and foreign policy. It's a field in which the rules of games are defined, outcomes are calculated, and (if you're lucky) analysis reveals an optimal strategy, just like what came naturally to Ender Wiggin.

Ender's Game and Philosophy: The Logic Gate Is Down, First Edition. Edited by Kevin S. Decker.
© 2013 John Wiley & Sons, Inc. Published 2013 by John Wiley & Sons, Inc.

In this chapter, we'll explore the importance of understanding others to Ender's military brilliance. For Ender, this understanding was not merely intellectual, but also emotional. We'll also see how Ender's instinctive ability to understand his enemies places him in a prime position, according to game theory, to redefine the game to create a path to victory. This is the lesson that *Ender's Game* teaches about how to find a path to victory even when one doesn't seem to exist.

But before you can win the game, you have to set the rules ...

Understanding Your "Enemy"

Ender faces four basic types of conflict in the book:

1. *Military*. Battles against other Battle School armies and the "simulations" against the buggers.
2. *Leadership*. Forming alliances, both with peers and subordinates.
3. *Vendettas*. Intense personal clashes against tormentors who hate him (Stilson, Peter, Bernard, and Bonzo).
4. *Rebellion*. Conflict against the teachers at Battle School and Command School.

The brilliance of Card's storytelling comes out in how these various forms of conflict play off each other. For example, it's specifically Ender's military success that escalates Bonzo's hostility. When Ender finally "resolves" the conflict with Bonzo, his enemy becomes the school itself, which drives his insane (but militarily successful) strategy in his final battleroom game.

Each conflict places Ender in opposition to some other participants. In game theory, each participant is called a "player" and the parameters of the conflict are a "game." The game-like nature of Ender's military conflicts is pretty obvious, but some of the other conflicts don't seem like games. Despite this, they can all be approached using the tools of game theory. For example, Ender's leadership skills are best exemplified in three cases: first, when he unites his Launch unit under Alai; second, when he mentally critiques the errors in Bonzo's leadership; and third, when he must organize Dragon Army in short order.

In all of these cases, he's able to analyze the motivations and objectives of different players involved, and he acts in a way that fulfills everyone's ends. The result is a method of leadership that focuses on the needs and abilities of those being led, not on the leader's ego. In many ways, it is similar to what's called "servant leadership." Whereas Bonzo worries about what the unit can do for him, Ender genuinely cares about what he can do for the unit. Ender's method is so compelling that it was even used by a Marine captain to teach leadership at the Marine University at Quantico.[4]

Though Ender enjoys varying levels of success in "winning" his conflicts, ultimately, he loses the game that matters most to him, the one that he didn't even know he was playing. By misunderstanding the scope of Graff's manipulations, his final sacrificial gambit, intended to end his involvement in the battle simulations on his own terms, goes horribly awry. Across all of his conflicts, Ender's degree of success or failure is dictated by how well he understands his enemy and how well he recognizes the game the enemy is playing. Let's call this type of understanding of others "empathy." One of the main lessons of *Ender's Game* is that we have to strive for empathy with our opponents if we want to resolve any conflict.

The need to understand opponents has an ancient pedigree in philosophy. Socrates considered it in Plato's dialogue *Laches* when he implied that being courageous partly depends on our ability to accurately size up our position relative to the enemy:

> ... [T]ake the case of one who endures in war, and is willing to fight, and wisely calculates and knows that others will help him, and that there will be fewer and inferior men against him than there are with him; and suppose that he has also advantages of position; would you say of such a one who endures with all this wisdom and preparation, that he, or some man in the opposing army who is in the opposite circumstances to these and yet endures and remains at his post, is the braver?[5]

This scenario almost perfectly matches Ender's final Battle School combat, when his Dragon Army is forced to face off against the combined might of Griffin and Tiger armies. Undoubtedly, the troops in Dragon Army required more "courage" than anyone in Griffin or Tiger, given the heavily skewed odds of the combat. But if cultivating courage is too specific, the more practical purpose of understanding the enemy, from a game theory perspective, is to figure out what their options are.

Understanding, Empathy, and Love

Empathy might seem to be too "touchy-feely," but, on the other hand, getting lost in emotion doesn't win wars. Bean describes it this way when he later discusses Ender with his three children:

> Ender knew how to love. I'm not talking about warm gooey emotions ... I'm talking about putting yourself inside someone else and embracing their needs, understanding what they hunger for, and also what will actually be good for them. Understanding them better than they understand themselves. Like a mother who can tell when her child is sleepy even as the child absolutely denies that he's sleepy at all.[6]

Presumably the mother described by Bean loves her child, but it's not clear that she *empathizes* with him. "Empathy" implies that we feel what others feel, and the mother doesn't need to *feel* tired to know this is true of her child. In this case, what she experienced was not empathy, but more like sympathy. The distinction between empathy and sympathy is a slippery one, however. Sympathy also can imply a general understanding of another person without necessarily sharing their emotional state. Ender makes it clear that, at the very least, sympathy is at work in his own life:

> Every time, I've won because I could understand the way my enemy thought. From what they did. I could tell what they thought I was doing, how they wanted the battle to take shape. And I played off of that. I'm very good at that. Understanding how other people think.[7]

The contemporary philosopher Michael Slote provides some clarity by pointing out that the word *empathy* "didn't exist in English till the early twentieth century."[8] So the eighteenth-century thinker David Hume was really talking about empathy when he made the following observation, even if the word wasn't yet available to him:

> No quality of human nature is more remarkable, both in itself and in its consequences, than that propensity we have to sympathize with others, and to receive by communication their inclinations and sentiments, however different from, or even contrary to our own,[9]

"Empathy" is a word that's certainly available to Card, but he chooses not to use it. Nor does he use "sympathy"; instead, he uses the word "love." Ender uses the same word to describe his understanding of his enemy:

> In the moment when I truly understand my enemy, understand him well enough to defeat him, then in that very moment I also love him. I think it's impossible to really understand somebody, what they want, what they believe, and not love them the way they love themselves.[10]

Unfortunately, this quote confuses more than clarifies what's precisely at work in Ender's head. Is he empathizing with his enemies as in "feeling their emotions and motivations," or sympathizing with them by merely understanding their emotions and motivations? Or does Ender truly love them? Or is some combination of the three at work?

Loving Your Enemy

It's hard to specify Ender's use of the word "love" in this context without thinking of the broad Christian religious tradition from which Card's Mormonism springs. This form of love is related to the Greek word *agape*, which includes not only the religious love of God but also the love extended toward one's fellow man ... or even fellow buggers, in Ender's case.

In this regard, we might note Jesus's notable and paradoxical instruction, "Love your enemies and pray for those who persecute you."[11] If this quote is rarely seen as a strategy for conflict resolution, this is in part because Jesus advocates it on spiritual, rather than practical, grounds. But it's not necessarily an abstract aspiration, and I have always viewed it as sound practical advice, even if I don't particularly embrace the theology behind it.

The advice to love your enemy, though difficult to act on, is useful to reframe a conflict. If you love an opponent, your mental perspective changes. The person ceases to be an *enemy* and becomes a person who simply has goals opposing yours. The conflicting goals are still a problem, of course, but it's a far better environment in which to work out a solution.

While this reframing could take place without love, its introduction creates a powerful motivator to create understanding. Most people don't want to fight with someone they love, so from a practical standpoint the religious command to "love your enemy," if taken seriously, forces a person to think of ways to avoid conflict. In fact, if you truly love someone, you want to do things for them. This matches very closely with the way Bean compares his own strategic perspective to Ender's:

> I hated the enemy, I let my fear of the enemy drive me. What will he do, where will he move, what can he do, I must be ready to counter it. And I was very, very good. Very quick. Very creative. But Ender didn't think like that at all. He was thinking: What does the enemy want and need? How can I give them what they need, in such a way as to leave them vulnerable? How can I take away the enemy's will or capacity to fight? It's a different mindset ...[12]

Bean's method does involve a *sympathetic* understanding of the enemy, but he's stuck reasoning from within the conflict framework. He is trying to *win* the conflict, but not necessarily to *end* the conflict, and perhaps he can't think in terms different from those that constitute a traditional victory.

Consider Ender's conflict with Peter, the megalomaniacal child who hated his younger brother with a passion and threatened to kill him on a number of occasions. In every reasonable sense of the word, Peter was Ender's enemy. Yet Ender loved Peter. "I don't want to beat Peter," he told Valentine. "I want him to love me."[13] Because of Ender's love for Peter, there is at least a door open for conflict resolution. If Peter sincerely wanted to resolve things, Ender would have immediately been receptive. Years after the events of *Ender's Game*, when Peter does approach Ender via ansible, there is a resolution of sorts between the two estranged brothers.

But consider a situation where Ender takes the easy and understandable road of hating Peter. Upon beating the buggers, Ender could have taken Valentine's advice. "Beat the buggers. Then come home and see who notices Peter Wiggin anymore. Look him in the eye when all the world loves and reveres you. That'll be defeat in his eyes, Ender. That's how you win."[14] However, Valentine would have been naïve to think that Peter would have conceded defeat at that point. For Ender to have accomplished a traditional victory over Peter, he would have had to crush him in the same way he crushed Stilson and Bonzo, but these were both lightweights compared to Peter. All-out war between the Wiggin brothers would leave a lot of collateral damage. Instead,

Ender chose another route: he refused to even engage with Peter and hopped on a spaceship to avoid the whole conflict. But that option was *only* available to Ender because he loved Peter (or at least because didn't hate him). An Ender Wiggin who hated Peter would not have been able to allow him the victory of interpreting Ender's refusal to engage as a retreat.

To conclude this line of thinking and get back to the game, we now can clearly recognize two things. If you begin loving someone, this provides a motivation for understanding them. But according to Ender, if you truly understand someone, then you will begin to love them. For Ender, at least, it seems that sympathy, empathy, and love are not fundamentally different. Instead, they lie on a continuum. Love and sympathy, experienced simultaneously, allow empathy. Ender and Bean both believe that this stance of empathy is the best way to win a war ... or, at least, a game.

Back to the Game

Love helps resolve conflicts if it can help us avoid them entirely; if we are committed to the game, though, it's good only to the point that it provides insight into the other player's strategy. One thing that's key to this insight is learning the opposing player's goals. To return to the idea of game theory, the typical goal for a player is called a "payout," if the value is a positive benefit, whereas the opposite is a "loss," or a negative outcome. Some games are very elaborate (like Peter's geopolitical games as Hegemon), so putting a number to the payouts or losses is hard, but fortunately for us, the battleroom isn't a game of that kind. In the battleroom, the army gets credit for each opponent who's frozen or disabled in an exact one-to-one ratio. This makes it a "zero-sum" game. So one primary goal of the battleroom game is to minimize your losses. Interestingly, the mathematician John von Neumann proved in 1928 that it was always possible to do just that—to win through attrition—with his "minimax theorem." This was the birth of game theory.

Chess is also a zero-sum game, but very different from the battle-room. In chess, you can always see all of your pieces as well as your opponent's pieces. Nothing is hidden from the players, so it is a game of "perfect information." Backgammon, checkers, go, and tic-tac-toe are also perfect information games, yet many other common games are not. Poker, where the opponent's hand is kept hidden, is a game of "imperfect" information. What von Neumann mathematically proved in 1928 is that, for any zero-sum game with perfect information, it's possible for both players to determine a strategy that minimizes their loss. He calls this an "optimal strategy." To use this strategy to win games, I have to figure out each possible outcome from a potential move and choose the move that will minimize the overall negative outcome for my own side. Of course, the commander in the battleroom doesn't have quite this level of omniscience about the layout of forces, so the game doesn't qualify as a perfect information game. Still, the strategy can work. Sixteen years after his groundbreaking minimax theorem, von Neumann showed that the theorem also applied to zero-sum games of imperfect information!

Applying the theorem is certainly not a *simple* thing to do, though, even for a relatively straightforward game like chess. As in many games, in chess the number of possible moves is fairly large. With the incomplete information that battleroom commanders have and the degree of freedom they have to move their soldiers, they obviously aren't in a position to work through each and every sequence of possible events. It would take a supercomputer (like IBM's chess grandmaster Deep Blue or the computer running the Giant's Drink scenario) to literally compute all possible strategies and outcomes. Battle School does have the best and brightest minds, though, and those who rise to the rank of commander typically do have intuition that comes into play. Even Bonzo and Rose de Nose can figure out strategies and tactics that have a fairly decent chance of minimizing the number of soldiers lost.

They can certainly be blindsided, though. When Salamander Army is given a major head start in the battleroom, they position themselves around Ender's gate, thinking that they'll easily be able to pick off Dragon Army as they enter. Bonzo completely failed to recognize that there was a strategy in which his own Salamander losses could be massive. He positioned himself for a big payout without any thought about his own potential "fatalities." He never once asked himself, "What will Ender do when he realizes where I am?" If Bonzo had been the sort of person who asked that question, a person who could empathize (or even sympathize) with an opponent to that degree, he would have not only been a better commander, he probably would have lived longer.

The Enemy's Gate

Ender's adaptability raises some questions for game theory. Ender demonstrates his ability to view a situation from a new perspective on the shuttle to Battle School, where he's the first to orient himself to the new gravity standard. In the video game room, he quickly proves himself superior to much more seasoned players, developing elaborate game strategies they can't defend against. When he finally makes it into the battleroom, this skill is represented by the classic phrase that can be recognized by any Ender fan immediately: *The enemy's gate is down*. The success of his flexible perspective revolutionized the way his soldiers (and, ultimately, all of Battle School) approached the game.

We might predict, then, that Ender could exploit certain problems with game theory to his advantage. Game theory is dependent upon the rules of the game being "well-defined." Ender's adaptability actually *threatens* the well-defined nature of the battleroom game. We find him constantly exploiting loopholes no one had ever thought of, forcing the teachers to modify the game to throw fresh challenges in his way. When he became concerned that he wouldn't be able to stay ahead of them, he enlisted Bean to form a special forces toon with the specific goal of thinking up things that even their commander wouldn't dream of.

After his brutal confrontation with Bonzo, Ender has had enough. He gives up on the game but wants to "go out in style."[15] He completely casts aside all the rules he's ever learned about the game, except for one: the victory condition. He sacrifices the majority of his army to get a handful of troops straight to the enemy's gate ... and wins his final Battle School game by throwing out the rulebook. Ender no longer cares about winning the battleroom game. He expects that this will be his swan song and he'll be drummed out of Battle School, but instead he gets promoted to Command School. In fact, the battleroom game never really mattered. There was a far larger game going on all along, with Graff and the school as the enemy.

In his first training with Petra, Ender realizes that "the most important message was this: the adults are the enemy, not the other armies. They do not tell us the truth."[16] This echoes Bonzo, who thought Ender's promotion to an officer was a case of the I.F. "playing tricks" on him and an attempt to thwart Salamander's rise in the standings. Perhaps the most nuanced conflict in the book is between Ender and Graff and the entire I.F. training system. Graff, forced to train a superb commander, gives Ender stark terms when he arrives at Battle School. "There's only one thing that will make them stop hating you. And that's being so good at what you do that they can't ignore you. I told them you were the best. Now you damn well better be."[17] Luckily for the human race, Ender seems to accept the trials and tribulations that Graff puts in his way. He isn't thrilled with them at any point, but he doesn't often lash out directly against that authority. And when he does lash out, this coincides with his greatest military victories.

In fact, everything that Ender encounters from the moment he steps on the shuttle is part of Graff's bigger game. The Giant's Drink virtual scenario, the video games, and even the battleroom game are all just *sub-games*, well-defined games within the larger game. They're well-defined, of course, until the teachers start messing with them. Ender cares about the integrity of the battleroom subgame, but Graff is perfectly willing to implement a strategy that destroys the battleroom subgame if it's needed to achieve his larger objective.

And it's in missing Graff's long game that Ender's ability to empathize crucially fails him. Though he is able to empathize with every opponent, from other commanders to the buggers, from Peter to Bernard, he never really comprehends Graff or Rackham's real objectives. When he defies them in the last battleroom game, he doesn't realize that the outcome they desire is *exactly* his breaking of the rules. They need a commander who'll do anything to end the game once and for all, even if it means throwing out traditional notions of victory and military strategy. Ender's empathy fails to help him discern why Mazer Rackham is so frustrated with him when troops die in the "simulation": they are actual people, and personal friends.[18] He doesn't understand the depth to which the adults are willing to manipulate everything about his world.

The reason why Ender doesn't understand them is that he never considers them the enemy, not truly. He never really tried to get into their heads the way he did with Peter, the other commanders in Battle School, or Bonzo. Adults were more unfathomable to him than the alien buggers, who, ironically, he soon grows to understand at a deep, intuitive level. Ender does win Graff's game, but he also suffers massive, unquantifiable losses. He sacrifices his youth, his innocence, and his future. Out of the ashes of the life he allowed them to destroy, he creates a new future, as an exile, then the Xenocide, then a Speaker for the Dead. In that future, it would be a long time before Ender played another game with stakes so high.

Notes

1. Another one that always makes me grin is his *The Call of Earth*, inscribed with "A tale of husbands, wives, and other mythical beasts."
2. Tom Siegried, *A Beautiful Math: John Nash, Game Theory, and the Modern Quest for a Code of Nature* (Washington, DC; Joseph Henry Press, 2006), 218.
3. Ibid., 217.
4. Orson Scott Card, *Ender's Game* (New York: TOR Books, 1991), xx.
5. Plato, *Laches* (New York: Classic Books International, 2009), 27–28.
6. Orson Scott Card, *Shadows in Flight* (New York: TOR Books, 2012), 80.
7. Card, *Ender's Game*, 167.
8. Michael Slote, *The Ethics of Care and Empathy* (New York: Routledge, 2007), 13.
9. David Hume, *A Treatise of Human Nature, vol. 1* (Oxford: Oxford University Press, 2011), 206.
10. Card, *Ender's Game*, 168.
11. Matthew 5:44, *The Green Bible*, New Revised Standard Version of *The New Testament* (New York: HarperCollins, 2009).
12. Card, *Shadows in Flight*, 79.
13. Card, *Ender's Game*, 170.
14. Ibid.
15. Ibid., 156.
16. Ibid., 59.
17. Ibid., 25.
18. An insight that is not lost on the less empathic Bean, as revealed in *Ender's Shadow*.

CHAPTER 6

War Games as Child's Play

Matthew Brophy

Ender, for the past few months you have been the battle commander of our fleets. This was the Third Invasion. There were no games, the battles were real, and the only enemy you fought was the buggers. You won every battle, and today you finally fought them at their home world, where the queen was, all the queens from all their colonies, they all were there and you destroyed them completely. They'll never attack us again. You did it. You.
—Mazer Rackham[1]

Ender is eleven when he commits xenocide. He pulls the trigger on a molecular disruption weapon that explodes the bugger home planet, obliterating the race in its entirety. Ender believed he was just playing a game. He exclaims in terrifying realization, "I didn't want to kill anybody! I'm not a killer! ... you tricked me into it!"[2] The unwitting architect of annihilation, Ender suffers a nervous breakdown.

Ender was indeed tricked, as were his fellow child compatriots. Only by presenting war as a game was the I.F. able to get brilliant children—Ender in particular—to accomplish its military tasks. Representing war as a game is a common, effective misrepresentation that allows otherwise moral human beings to commit the inhumane violence war requires. Treating hurtful actions as a "game" psychologically distances the person from considering consequences,

Ender's Game and Philosophy: The Logic Gate Is Down, First Edition. Edited by Kevin S. Decker.
© 2013 John Wiley & Sons, Inc. Published 2013 by John Wiley & Sons, Inc.

insulating them from a feeling of moral responsibility, and may protect the individual from a corruption of moral character.

This chapter explores the masquerade of war as a game and how it manipulates human psychology to effectively accomplish destructive goals. We'll look at philosophy, psychology, and sociology to illuminate the I.F. High Command's strategy of using child's play to destroy an alien race, and thereby save humanity.

Paradox of the Heart and the Head

Know your enemy and know yourself; in a hundred battles, you will never be defeated.

—Sunzi[3]

Knowing a man well never leads to hate and nearly always leads to love.

—John Steinbeck[4]

Sunzi instructs us in *The Art of War* that understanding our enemy is crucial to victory. The I.F. High Command recognized his wisdom: before one of their commanders can achieve victory, he first needs to understand the buggers. Yet getting into the head of any enemy leads to a psychological paradox: it requires empathizing with the enemy, but this would likely render a person incapable of callously destroying them. This paradox between the heart and the head demands reconciliation. So how can the I.F. get Ender Wiggin to empathize with the buggers, and also make him capable of obliterating them? The solution is for Graff and the I.F. to psychologically manipulate Ender. Legendary commander Mazer Rackham explains the paradox to Ender, trying to justify their manipulation of him:

> We had to have a commander with so much empathy that he would think like the buggers, understand them and anticipate them ... But somebody with that much compassion could never be the killer we needed. Could never go into battle willing to win at all costs. If you knew, you couldn't do it. If you were the kind of person who would do it even if you knew, you could never have understood the buggers well enough.[5]

Valentine and Peter, initially considered by the I.F. as potential command material, were rejected because they didn't fit these parameters. Only

Ender, the "Third," possesses the heart tempered by the head, and vice versa. Fighting Stilson, Ender demonstrates a willingness to coldly calculate and execute preemptive defense. He lashes out at Stilson, and—while Stilson is limp on the ground—kicks him in the face and groin. Unintentionally, Ender kills him, but he only wanted to injure him badly enough to deter him and others like him from coming after Ender again. After his brutal triumph, Ender cries at the bus stop. His empathy is a double-edged sword, enabling him to be an effective combatant, yet torturing him with reflections of the damage he's done. Ender confides in his beloved sister Valentine the excruciating nature of this paradox:

> In the moment when I truly understand my enemy, understand him well enough to defeat him, then in that very moment I also love him. I think it's impossible to really understand somebody, what they want, what they believe, and not love them the way them love themselves. And then, in that very moment when I *love* them ... I *destroy* them. I make it impossible for them to ever hurt me again. I grind them and grind them until they don't *exist*.[6]

How can the I.F. train Ender to kill, while still protecting him against the psychological trauma that tortures him? To reconcile the paradox, they develop an ingenious solution: train Ender (and other children) to regard war *as a game*.

War Games

"The Battle School was so enclosed, the game so important in the minds of the children, that Ender had forgotten there was a world outside."[7] Training focuses on the battleroom, where brigades of schoolmates combat each other in null-gravity. Scoreboards track their triumphs and defeats. When Ender graduates to Command School, the game takes the form of a "simulation," where he controls fleets of starships to defeat (what he believes to be) a simulated enemy supposedly controlled by his mentor, Mazer Rackham.

Similarly, war games in twenty-first-century America teach children and adults alike to view war as a game. Recently, military-themed video games have outstripped even blockbuster movies in terms of popularity and profit. *Call of Duty: Modern Warfare 3* earned over $400 million dollars in the first day of release compared to the current movie-record holder, *The Dark Knight*, which garnered a comparatively paltry $67 million in its first day.

Capitalizing on the popularity of such war games, the US military put out its own free online game, *America's Army*, to boost recruitment. The video game is billed as an educational tool, teaching army values like teamwork, as well as specific skills. A 2008 study by researchers from the Massachusetts Institute of Technology found that "30 percent of all Americans age 16 to 24 had a more positive impression of the Army because of the game and, even more amazingly, the game had more impact on recruits than all other forms of Army advertising combined."[8] Surprisingly, *America's Army* and its brethren—such as *Call of Duty* and *Medal of Honor*—are a dominant pastime with deployed soldiers. The *New York Times* featured one platoon sergeant who "actively encouraged his soldiers to play these games during their off time."[9]

For better or worse, the army is aware of Orson Scott Card's seminal science-fiction book. "*Ender's Game* has had a lot of influence on our thinking," states Michael Macedonia, director of the army's simulation technology center in Orlando, Florida. This center plans to build a "virtual Afghanistan," a scenario that could host hundreds of thousands of computer players over its network.[10] Yet some military officers have expressed misgivings about presenting war as a game. "The video game generation is worse at distorting the reality of it [war] from the virtual nature," claimed an air force colonel. "They don't have that sense of what is really going on." His opinion was that games made it harder for individuals to weigh the consequences of their acts. "It teaches you how to compartmentalize it."[11] Similarly, Donald J. Mathes, a captain in the Marines, worries about young people becoming desensitized to violence. "Here you have to learn by dying," he told a class of marines in his lecture after their fourth simulated combat mission in a city eerily similar to Baghdad. "But you have to remember, you can't get desensitized."[12]

But the I.F. High Command holds desensitization and compartmentalization as key virtues. A combatant who's not desensitized, after all, might hesitate to kill, and a soldier who cannot psychologically distance herself from violence might be tortured by her deeds later. It does take a steely kind of character to be able to kill an enemy, face-to-face. Mazer Rackham realizes this, and misrepresents the final battle as a "simulation" so that Ender can save humanity from possible extinction. Only then can Ender, once a gentle child, accomplish a brutally decisive victory.

The Problem of Dirty Hands

For Ender to remain an effective weapon, Graff and the I.F. have to protect his innocence. Yet how can anyone, much less a child, plunge his hands in the "filth and blood" of war, without dirtying them?[13] Contemporary philosopher Michael Walzer has written about this question as the "problem of dirty hands."[14] If a person commits a "lesser of evils," isn't she still perpetrating evil? And if someone else seeks refuge in moral absolutism—refusing even the "lesser" evil—isn't he morally responsible for stepping aside and allowing the greater evil to prevail? Morally speaking, it seems when you're confronted by evil, "you're damned if you do, and damned if you don't."[15]

In *Ender's Game*, the I.F. High Command finds itself in the "dirty hands" dilemma. It has to decide whether to obliterate the buggers or to leave humanity vulnerable to attack by passively hoping the Formics won't attack. The I.F. chooses war, and commences the Third Invasion, what they see as a preemptive strike upon the bugger's home planet. In real life, political and military leaders often have to confront just such a moral dilemma, where they must choose between expediency and an absolute moral prohibition against violence. In war, the question becomes, should they opt for a cost–benefit-driven decision to kill some (including innocents as collateral damage) to save more? Or should they choose the morally pure path of pacifism and imperil the lives of the people they've sworn to protect?

Ender would ultimately have to face the dirty hands dilemma himself, putting him in a position to choose between the brutality of war and the precarious withdrawal of pacifism. Ender chooses war, largely out of love for Valentine. Graff manipulates a disillusioned Ender by reuniting Ender with his loving sister at a reclusive lake house retreat. "I may have used Valentine," said Graff, "and you may hate me for it, Ender, but keep this in mind—it only works because what's between you, that's real, that's what matters. Billions of those connections between human beings. That's what you're fighting to keep alive."[16] Because he values these precious human relationships, Ender accompanies Graff to Command School to see the war through to the end.

For its own reasons, the I.F. shields Ender and the other children from the truth that they are, in fact, soldiers. The I.F. ensures that the children's hands remain clean; their innocence is untainted by war and the tragic moral compromises it demands. While Ender later suffers stabs of guilt for the destruction he's unwittingly wrought, he could always wash his hands clean with the rationalization that he believed it only to be a game. The dirty hands are the hands of the politicians, not those of children like him.

Death Games and Moral Decision-Making

A widely accepted assumption in ethics is that an individual can only be held morally responsible for their actions if she is a "moral agent." That is, she has to be free, rational, and informed about what she's doing.[17] Ender may have satisfied the first two conditions, since he's a rational individual who's freely engaging in the battle "simulations" at Command School. Yet Ender doesn't meet the third condition: he doesn't have the correct information that his alleged strategy "games" are real. He's unaware that the "points of light" in the holographic space in front of him are actual starships, and that his war-game "play" determines who lives and who dies.

But placing individuals in what they see as a game *neutralizes* their sense of moral agency. People begin to view themselves and others as mere players of a game in which rules of objective morality don't apply. This, is turn, can make someone far more capable of torturing and killing without feeling morally responsible. *The Game of Death*, a 2009 French documentary, is a macabre illustration of this.[18] It follows a fake game show named "The Extreme Zone," in which a "candidate" contestant tries to answer trivia questions. When the candidate gets the answer wrong, the "player" contestant apparently inflicts an electric shock on him. With each wrong answer, the voltage of these shocks increases from 80 to 460 volts—and so do the candidate's protests. At first, they yelp in pain, then plead for the game to stop, and finally fall eerily silent, as if passed out or dead. Out of 80 contestants, 64 obligingly did things they had reason to believe tortured the "candidate" to the very end. Player contestants weren't rewarded for inflicting the shocks, but they did have both the host and audience (all actors) egging them on to continue shocking the candidate. Unknown to the player contestant, the candidate was a paid actor, and was not actually being shocked.

This fake game show was based on the classic 1961–1962 psychology experiments of Stanley Milgram at Yale University in which Milgram tested how far subjects would go in administering shocks to another person. The show validates the experiment's results.[19] Milgram's experiments exposed the dark nature of humanity by demonstrating that otherwise decent people are capable of committing atrocities. Participants later defended themselves by explaining that they were merely following the rules of the game, or "following orders." In essence, they gave away their moral agency to something bigger than themselves: they viewed themselves as mere cogs in a machine.

Likewise, Ender's "final exam" is set up like a game show that he's playing for the audience of the I.F. officials and his fellow trainees over his headset. Ender sees himself as playing the I.F.'s game and ignores any potential consequences. Of course, that is exactly Graff's intent: "You had to be a weapon, Ender. Like a gun …"[20] When Ender views the actual invasion as a mere simulation, he can avoid the moral crisis of soberly having to decide to kill a sentient race. After the fact, he can think of himself as a victim, duped by the military complex. In that way, he can live with the xenocide, maybe absolving himself of moral, though not causal, responsibility. In fact, it's possible to say that the I.F. does Ender a favor by giving him the dark gift of deception and allowing Ender to rationalize that he is morally innocent.

Moral Distance Makes the Heart Grow Fainter

The increasingly computerized warfare of the twenty-first century parallels Ender's "simulated" battles. The US armed forces frequently employ drones to kill overseas enemies. To carry out a drone strike, a human being sits at a console, remotely controlling the small aircraft to seek out and "neutralize targets." This makes warfare seem eerily similar to a game. This new face of remote military action has been called "Nintendo warfare" because it relies upon the use of remote computers and consoles to achieve destruction and replaces much of the "face-to-face" warfare of twentieth-century wars.

Bill Maher, host of the TV talk show *Politically Incorrect*, was fired in 2001 partly for criticizing Nintendo Warfare as cowardly: "We have been the cowards, lobbing cruise missiles from 2,000 miles away. That's cowardly."[21] Most controversial of Maher's comments was his rejection of President George W. Bush's description of the 9/11 terrorists as "cowardly." Maher stated, "Staying in the airplane when it hits the building, say what you want about it, it's not cowardly." Maher's view is that bravery is required for a combatant to kill face-to-face, even when this is done for evil ends. Maher's more important point, however, is that it is psychologically easier to kill when there is a "moral distance" between the attacker and the human targets. Nintendo warfare maximizes the "moral distance" between the killer and the human casualties. Moral distance is a key psychological phenomenon about human beings: it shows that emotional distance and separation in time and space significantly affect our moral judgments. For human beings, moral distance makes it easier to kill.

In the Milgram experiment, individuals were twice as likely to shock another person from a remote desk where they couldn't see or hear the person than they were if they were in the same room and had to place the person's hand on the shock plate themselves. In his book, *Causing Death and Saving Lives*, Jonathan Glover notes that moral distance "is especially evident in war ... There is the feeling that because killing at a distance is easier, one would not have to be such a monster to do it."[22]

The psychological power of moral distance is vividly illustrated through a scenario called "the trolley problem," which was first proposed by Philippa Foot.[23] Imagine that a runaway train is hurtling toward five innocent people, who'll certainly die if you, a bystander, do nothing. Luckily, there is a switch nearby that you can easily flip, and so divert the train onto a secondary track. This will kill only one innocent person. What should you do? Stand and watch while the five die? Or flip the switch, saving five, but causing the death of one? Empirical research reports that most people, given the choice, will choose to flip the switch and divert the trolley.[24] A second trolley scenario places you, as the bystander, directly behind an innocent man whom you can easily push in front of a train that is going to hit the original five people. The man is of ample enough proportions to bring the runaway train to a halt and preventi the death of those ahead on the track. According to the same research, subjects are morally uncomfortable with the option that involves physically pushing the person, and more often opt to allow the five people to die.

Yet what's the *moral* difference between these two scenarios? Both situations seem to present the same option: killing one to save five, or allowing the five to die. Isn't the difference between flipping a switch from far away or pushing a person from up close pretty arbitrary, morally speaking? Maybe, but it doesn't *feel* as morally wrong to kill a human being from a remote distance as it does to kill a human being up close and personal. Our differing moral intuitions about the two scenarios point out an inconsistency in our moral psychology. Our conscience is less disturbed when we cause another's death from a great distance than when do it face-to-face, but no *morally relevant* difference can justify treating one case differently from another. By psychologically distancing the combatant in war from the moral impact of the violence (she is merely "flipping a switch" as in the trolley case), it becomes much easier to motivate the combatant to do harm. The distance insulates the agent from any personal connection with the loss of life, the collateral damage, the suffering.

Mazer Rackham conveys this sentiment to Ender after the final battle, "Any decent person who knows what warfare is can never go into battle with a whole heart. But you didn't know. We made sure you didn't know."[25]

Ender's a Willing Pawn

Ender blanches when it's revealed that his "final exam" wasn't a game at all. "They weren't just points of light in the air, they were real ships that he had fought with and real ships he had destroyed. And a real world that he had blasted into oblivion."[26] As Ender reckons with the truth, he protests, "I didn't want to kill anybody! I'm not a killer! ... you tricked me into it!"[27]

A commonsense interpretation of *Ender's Game,* one painted in black and white, has Ender as an innocent child, manipulated by the big, bad military into doing its dirty work. Certainly it's easy to vilify the I.F. High Command as puppet-masters, and it's easy to see a child as an innocent pawn.

Yet Ender may not be as innocent as we might think. An alternative interpretation begs consideration: that Ender *allows* himself to be deceived—that he lets himself be used as a weapon to save humanity. As Ender decides to leave with Graff to go to Command School, he acknowledges that "Graff was only acting like a friend ... [yet] everything he did was a lie or a cheat calculated to turn Ender into an efficient fighting machine. I'll become exactly the tool you want me to be, said Ender silently, but at last I won't be *fooled* into it. I'll do it because I choose to, not because you tricked me ..."[28] Ender's internal dialogue shows the wisdom behind his perception that his teachers and the I.F. are his adversaries, not his friends. And Ender's greatest talent is to know his enemy.

Even Ender's dreams betray awareness that the war "games" he plays at Command School are real. One night he dreams of drowning his sister, after which, "he dragged her out of the lake and onto the raft, where she lay with her face in the rictus of death. He screamed and wept over her, crying again and again that it was a game, a game, he was only playing!"[29]

Ender realizes that even "games" have deadly consequences. Ender explicitly endorses the end-game of the Third Invasion: the extinction of the buggers. In his exchange with Colonel Graff on their flight to Command School; Graff tells Ender, "So if we can, we'll kill every last one of the buggers, and if they can, they'll kill every last one of us." "As for me," said Ender, "I'm in favor of surviving." "I know," said Graff. That's why you're here."[30]

But while Ender recognizes the necessity of wiping out the buggers, he's also far too sensitive to engage in the recurring brutality it requires. Ender's bloody history of triumphing over his enemies always leads him to self-deception about the murderous consequences of his actions. Yet these incidents still haunt him. Realizing Ender's sensitivity, the I.F. conceals Stilson's (and then Bonzo's) death from him. To shield Ender from the psychological trauma of war, which would otherwise debilitate him, the I.F. trains him to regard war as a game, where he is a mere player, not an executioner.

This tactic of gaining consent from the executioner, but shielding him from the violence he inflicts, mirrors a common method of firing squads. In order to ensure that such squads are reliable and to lessen the guilt suffered by the executioners, one or more of the shooters in the squad are equipped with guns that contain only blank cartridges, instead of live rounds. All of the firing squad shooters know that some of the guns contain blank cartridges, but it's kept secret which particular guns shoot blanks instead of live ammunition. This tactic provokes the phenomenon known in sociology as the "diffusion of responsibility," which makes it easier for each shooter to pull his trigger without having to admit that he is the one killing the prisoner. This tactic also allows for self-deception: by allowing each shooter to rationalize that his gun shot blanks, the shooter can evade the guilt he might otherwise feel for killing another human being.

Yet is it reasonable for the firing squad executioner to believe that his gun will always contain blanks? And does it matter if the shooter happens to be shooting blank rounds, if he endorses the execution by participating in it? Likewise for Ender, is it reasonable for him to think that *none* of the battles would be real? And would it matter if the battles were merely simulations, given that Ender endorses the war's xenocidal goal?

In the end, methinks Ender doth protest too much. Ender's confusion after the final battle smells suspicious: "Men in uniform were hugging each other, laughing, shouting; others were weeping; some knelt or lay prostrate, and Ender knew they were caught up in prayer. Ender didn't understand. It seemed all wrong."[31] How could a savvy military genius like Ender have ended up so thoroughly deceived at the end of the story? The single plausible explanation is that he allowed himself to be conned. He participated in a conspiracy predicated upon his willful ignorance, where he allowed himself to be used as a weapon to save humanity.

The meaning of the title *Ender's Game* invites many interpretations. Ultimately, it may just refer to the game Ender plays with himself. To save the human race, Ender deceives himself into believing war games are but child's play, that starships are mere points of light, and that an entire alien planet is mere pixels. And while the dying breath from the bugger race forgives Ender his sins, a question will still haunt him until the end of his days: should he forgive himself?

Notes

1. Orson Scott Card, *Ender's Game* (New York: TOR Books, 1991), 296–297.
2. Ibid., 297–298.
3. Sun Tzu, *The Art of War* (New York: Oxford University Press, 1971), Chapter III, para 31.
4. From Steinbeck's 1938 journal entry, in Tracy Barr and Greg Tubach, eds., *Cliff Notes: On Steinbeck's Of Mice and Men* (New York: Wiley Publishing, 2001).
5. Ibid., 298.
6. Ibid., 238.
7. Ibid., 111.
8. Peter W. Singer, "Video Game Veterans and the New American Politics," *The Washington Examiner*, Nov. 17, 2009.

9. Tim Hsia, "Virtual Reality War," *New York Times*, Mar. 11, 2010.
10. Peter W. Singer, "Video Game Veterans and the New American Politics," *The Washington Examiner*, Nov. 17, 2009.
11. Ibid.
12. Ibid.
13. Jean-Paul Sartre, "Dirty Hands," in *No Exit and Three Other Plays* (New York: Vintage Interational, 1989), 218.
14. Michael Walzer, "Political Action: The Problem of Dirty Hands," *Philosophy and Public Affairs*, 2:2 (1973): 160–180.
15. Read more about the evil that Ender does in Jeremy Proulx's chapter in this book.
16. Card, *Ender's Game*, 244.
17. Toddlers and mentally impaired adults, in contrast, are not moral agents in that they lack sufficient rationality and awareness of relevant facts when acting. This is why children are not tried as adults, and a significant reason as to why the death penalty in the United States is rarely applied to adults with mental retardation.
18. Time Magazine, "*The Game of Death*: France's Shocking TV Experiment," Mar. 17, 2010; *Le jeu de la mort*, directors Thomas Bornot and Gilles Amaod (2010).
19. Stanley Milgram, *Obedience to Authority* (New York: Harper and Row, 1974).
20. Card, *Ender's Game*, 298.
21. *Politically Incorrect*, ABC, Sept. 17, 2001.
22. Jonathan Glover, *Causing Death and Saving Lives* (New York: Penguin, 1977).
23. Philippa Foot, *The Problem of Abortion and the Doctrine of the Double Effect* in *Virtues and Vices* (Oxford: Basil Blackwell, 1978).
24. Joshua D. Greene, "The Secret Joke of Kant's Soul," in *Moral Psychology*, vol. 3, ed. Walter Sinott-Armstrong (Cambridge, MA: MIT Press, 2008).
25. Card, *Ender's Game*, 298.
26. Ibid.
27. Ibid., 297–298.
28. Ibid., 252.
29. Ibid., 282.
30. Ibid., 254.
31. Ibid., 296.

CHAPTER 7

Forming the Formless
Sunzi and the Military Logic of Ender Wiggin

Morgan Deane

Early in *Ender's Game*, Colonel Hyrum Graff asks Ender Wiggin why he attacked the leader of a gang of kids with such apparently sadistic force. Ender replies that he had to win not only that fight, but win so convincingly that the leader's gang wouldn't think twice about attacking him. "Knocking him down won the first fight. I wanted to win all the next ones, too. So they would leave me alone." Ender's parents were shocked, recoiling from their son's violence. But Graff both understood and ultimately admired the military logic behind his decision. In response to his mother's disgust he said, "It isn't *what* he did ... it's why."[1]

According to the Chinese military philosopher Sunzi (or Sun-Tzu), a commander's actions must be "formless."[2] Ender displays this formlessness in the fact that when we try to analyze his actions we're left with a sense of confusion about his reasoning. Yet Ender's strategies follow a hidden logic that closely resembles the military philosophy of Sunzi, incorporating wisdom on how to become a successful leader. Sunzi is traditionally held to be the author of *The Art of War*, but its authorship is still debated. He may be a leading figure from the late spring and autumn period (722–481 BC) of China. Other historians argue, based on anachronisms and other evidence in the text and recent archeological finds of ancient bamboo strips, that he's a figure from much later, the Warring States Period (481–221 BC).[3] Sunzi's thought crucially affected Chinese military decision-making for

Ender's Game and Philosophy: The Logic Gate Is Down, First Edition. Edited by Kevin S. Decker.
© 2013 John Wiley & Sons, Inc. Published 2013 by John Wiley & Sons, Inc.

thousands of years. Military commanders, from ancient times through Napoleon to today continue to read and apply his teachings. Sunzi'a thought influenced other ancient writers whose works are included in *The Seven Military Classics of Ancient China*. This text consolidated the writings of major Chinese theorists and it became standard educational literature for Chinese generals.

Sunzi advocates tactics including strengthening the martial spirit of your own soldiers through rewards and punishments, targeting the enemy's martial spirit through tricks, exploiting their fear and anger to inspire or sap their abilities, and outwitting the opponent through a mix of orthodox and unorthodox maneuvers. He also recommends the skillful use of intelligence to mask your own "form," or plans and intentions, while knowing the form of your opponent.

Sunzi stressed the importance of psychological self-control, unfeeling and cold analysis driven by practical considerations, and adroit maneuvering of soldiers and formations on the battlefield. As we'll see, Ender's own military decisions can be illuminated by the writings of Sunzi and other seminal Asian philosophers like Confucius and Laozi. By these standards, Ender qualifies as a military genius.

"Of Course We Tricked You Into It"

Ender already knew how to manipulate others by the age of six. Perhaps inspired by fear of his psychotic brother, he knew winning one battle would not necessarily prevent future conflicts. He knew he had to inspire fear and with it an aversion to attack again, with a decisive win. In Battle School, Ender continued to capitalize on others' emotional flaws. As a new member of Salamander Army, he often clashed with the commander, Bonzo Madrid. Ender recognized that his own anger was "cold" while his commander's was "hot"—and exploitable. Ender understood that Bonzo's type of anger lessened his self-control, while his own "cold" anger instead aided Ender. Later, in the showers, Ender faced off with Bonzo, now the leader of a murderous cabal of other students. Ender exploited Madrid's anger and sense of honor, maneuvering him into a one-on-one fight. As with the six-year-old bullies back on Earth, Ender not only won, but did so decisively to put fear into other potential challengers.

As a leader, Ender used manipulation in a positive way to build *esprit de corps*. He instituted a series of rewards and punishments. For example, on his first day in command he set a strict timeline for leaving for the battleroom, forcing those who couldn't dress fast enough to fight in whatever clothing they had on. As a new commander, he challenged and stimulated Bean, modeling his own motivational strategy on Graff's. After a particularly astounding victory Ender remained stoic, but allowed his toon leaders to share the reward.

The government manipulated Ender—through Valentine—even as he manipulated his enemies. Graff structured Ender's training in terms of isolation and anxiety to elicit the greatest effort from him. Once Ender began to adapt and thrive at school, Graff stacked the battleroom game against him. Finally, in a poignant moment, we learn that Graff tricked Ender into committing xenocide, circumventing his empathy by making him think he was just playing a game.

The writings of Sunzi and other classical Chinese philosophers rely on harnessing manipulation. The ancient Mongols put this into practice by stacking the bodies of enemy dead to inspire terror and a subsequent surrender by the next city on their path. Even fictional armies do it: the deformed orcs from Tolkien's *Return of the King* (2003) launched the severed heads of fallen soldiers into the besieged city of Minas Tirith.

Chinese thought prescribes specific routines and interactions to harness the martial spirit and increase discipline among the home forces, but it also recommends draining the martial spirit of enemies. The impetus to influence soldiers' martial spirit comes from Daoist thought, which derives from the *Dao De Ching* written by Laozi (c. 6th century BC). *Dao* simply means "Way." Many Westerners translate *Dao* as "*the* Way" but that often distorts its nature. Way is the creator of the universe, sustainer of the universe, and the process, flux; it is simply the *way* of the universe. Much like the Force from *Star Wars*, the Way is the power that flows throughout the universe, a portion of which can reside within and strengthen people. Our duty is to stay in harmony with that process or Way, often sloganized as "going with the flow." Hence, strong leaders sought to channel the Way for their benefit, while seeking to upset the Way of their enemies.

Ender's actions closely resemble Daoist methods for overpowering opponents. Chinese history tells of many examples of ruses like feigned flights, ambushes, tricks, and traps. Strategists sought to mislead their enemies not only toward the goal of victory, but also to destroy their enthusiasm in the current battle and for future conflicts.[4] Toward this goal, Sunzi dictated that "the ... [power] of the [enemy] can be snatched away; the commanding general's mind can be seized ... Thus one who excels at employing the army avoids their ardent [spirit] and strikes when it is [made] indolent or exhausted. This is the way to manipulate [their martial spirit]."[5] In a similar way, Ender pressed the attack against already-defeated enemies to drain their future fighting spirit.

Chinese governance has always relied on Confucian values as well as Daoist ones. Confucius (551–479 BC) is known through the *Analects*, a book that preserves a collection of his sayings. The picture of Confucius in the *Analects* is of a man who sought moderation, optimism, good sense, propriety, and wisdom. Confucianism stresses the duty a person has to his station: a ruler must rule correctly, a father must be a good father, and a son a good son. Chinese military philosophers used these stable roles to build stronger armies. During the Warring States Period, beginning in 481 BC, the size of armies increased from roughly 30,000 men to almost 300,000. The commander controlled his army by positioning himself as a father with his troops as his sons. As Sunzi writes, "When the general regards his troops as young children, they will advance into the deepest valleys with him. When he regards the troops as his beloved children, they will be willing to die with him."[6] Graff and the I.F. also harnessed such manipulation to win the war by using a general-as-father's ability to cast his soldier-as-sons into hopeless situations in order to harness the utmost effort.

Sunzi called these kinds of decisions the use of "fatal terrain." Of the soldiers, he said "Throw them into a place from which there is nowhere to go, and they will die rather than flee. When they are facing death, how could one not obtain the utmost strength from the officers and men?"[7] At the beginning of Ender's training, Graff was asked if he "enjoyed breaking" students. He replied that he did, but only when they "put the pieces back afterward, and are better for it."[8] The modern slogan "sink or swim" nicely captures this concept. In a military context, a commander would deliberately place his troops in hopeless situations, with their backs to the river or in a position with no chance of escape. The fatal terrain tactic was intended to quickly stimulate the discipline and effort needed to survive the battle. Graff used fatal terrain when he stacked the game against Ender. Faced with daily battleroom contests and twice the normal number of opponents, and students seeking to kill him on top of that, Ender had to quickly learn how to "swim." The final product supported the thinking of both Graff and Sunzi when Ender showed himself a victorious commander. Commanding the fleet in attacking the bugger home world, Ender was thrown in the deep end, hopelessly outnumbered and outgunned. But he called upon his resolve from his earlier "hopeless situations" and achieved total victory.

Like the I.F., Ender uses a system of rewards and punishments for those under his command. This is idea is found in Legalism in early China. Its representatives Han Feizi (d. 233 BC) and Li Si (d. 208 BC) argued that human nature is inherently selfish. Humans like comfort and rewards and dislike punishments and pain, so true peace required a united country and strong state. A state guided by Legalism would institute severe punishments for breaking laws, while also offering incentives for bravery in battle, loyalty, diligence, and frugal living. Another military theorist who wrote in the *Seven Military Classics*, Wuzi, said:

> The people do not take pleasure in dying, nor do they hate life, [but] if the commands and orders are clear, and the laws and regulations carefully detailed, you can make them advance. When, before [combat], rewards are made clear, and afterward punishments are made decisive, then when [the troops] issue forth they will be able to realize an advantage, and when they move they will be successful.[9]

Ender used the same techniques to elicit greater effort from his soldiers, giving them rewards after victory and fairly harsh discipline for failures. As a result of their policies, the early Legalists quickly faced revolt from the people. Likewise, Ender's martinet-like command made him enemies and inspired brutality between groups of students.

"The Enemy Outnumbered Him a Thousand to One"

One way to protect yourself against manipulation is to analyze the facts of the situation as it really stands. Victory for Ender often came because of such mental exercises. For example, battleroom contestants had always fought with the enemy gate facing their chest, but Ender changed this, pointing their feet at the gate instead. This tactic made his team smaller targets and improved his chances, even if Ender's comrades at first complained that they couldn't fight on their backs. This position only made sense if "the enemy's gate is down" and not "across" from the individual. Ender not only manipulated the anger of bullies, but more importantly he coldly analyzed and exploited their actions. This routinely led bullies into unwise choices. When one recruit taunted Ender on board the shuttle to Battle School, Ender's quick analysis of the pattern of the boy's behavior in zero gravity dictated that he grab the bully's arm to fling him across the room.

Outside of battle, Ender understood that an army's "down time" mattered. He analyzed the barracks environment of the different armies. Salamander's quarters were a model of order and Rat's of chaos. Ender used this difference to formulate a strategy accordingly. When an old man (Mazer Rackham) suddenly appeared in his room and attacked Wiggin, Ender admitted that he'd failed to analyze the situation. He should have treated the old man as a potential enemy after his first attack. This was a critical mistake he wouldn't repeat.

Sunzi also calls for self-knowledge: "Thus it is said that one who knows the enemy and knows himself will not be endangered in a hundred engagements ... In antiquity those that excelled in warfare first made themselves unconquerable in order to await [the moment when] the enemy could be conquered."[10] Throughout the story Ender constantly wonders who he really is. His fear was that he was too much like Peter, while Graff was banking on the fact he wasn't like Valentine. Despite these pressures, Ender consistently strived to live his own life as much as possible. Eventually, his reflections produced an unconquerable inner self, a victory that the government could never take away.

While a formal, indifferent analysis is required to determine the best conditions for battle, once battle is joined, the movement of troops is all-important. It's true that Chinese history displays a preference for civil over martial values and an avoidance of battle. But conflicts did sometimes require a military solution, and the Chinese had innovative ideas on the forms combat maneuvers should take. Sunzi's description of *fluid movement* is particularly insightful. Inspired by Daoist beliefs that a person must adapt to the flow or Way that surrounds them, Sunzi described the flexible movement toward battle as being like water:

> Water's configuration avoids heights and races downward. The army's disposition of force avoids the substantial and strikes the vacuous.

Water configures its flow in accord with the terrain; the army controls its victory in accord with the enemy. Thus the army does not maintain any constant strategic configuration of power; water has no constant shape. One who is able to change and transform in accord with the enemy and wrest victory is termed spiritual.[11]

Likewise, Ender noticed that the practice army groups often had fixed formations, but such formations were often unresponsive to the flow of the battle. In his first combat as a member of Salamander Army, Ender faced a highly mobile and aggressive enemy that seized the initiative as well as the spirit of the Salamanders. As an army commander himself, Ender organized his toons in innovative ways, giving them the ability to operate independently. This helped Ender adapt to quickly changing situations as well as to use and reward the initiative of commanders like Bean. Against a deadly ambush, he organized his troops into mutually supporting positions allowing a win. In battle with the buggers he noticed the same kind of organized, yet organic movement. The constant and flexible movement of Ender's toons, and later his army, proved how deadly flexible formations can be.

Sunzi also stressed the value of speed to seize objectives. Just as a commander must first realize the conditions for victory, then fight for those conditions, a leader must seize the terrain he wants and fight to keep it. Sunzi said that "analyzing the enemy, taking control of victory, estimating ravines and defiles, the distant and near, is the Dao of the superior general."[12] As we've seen, Ender exploited this tactic through moving his soldiers according to the dictates of cold analysis.

One case deserves special attention. In command of Dragon Army, Ender was facing his second battle of the day. To make things worse, Bonzo's soldiers had been given enough time to prepare elaborate ambush positions at the battleroom entry point. Ender took advantage of a unique formation to solve a unique problem: his strategy was to partially freeze some of his men, who then were used as a protected firing platform against Bonzo's army. This is similar to the response to a situation faced by the Chinese in the sixteenth century. In response to attacks by pirates, the military theorist Qi Jiquang (1528–1588) established the "Mandarin Duck" formation. This consisted of an 11-person unit led by a squad leader with two teams of five. Each team included one soldier armed with a multiple-tipped spear (think of a long pole tipped with a giant and deadly sharpened can opener) whose job it was to entangle the enemy's weapons. Four infantrymen form the rest of the team: a shield person to protect the spear-carrier, two other spear-wielding infantry who would thrust at the entangled enemy, and one sword bearer for additional combat power.

Qi Jiquang ordered squads to repeatedly drill in this formation to coordinate the functions of individuals with their cooperative aims. While the function of individual members always remained the same, the specific configuration could be changed in three different ways, similar to a modern-day rifle platoon. Both Ender's army, and the bugger's army, employed a series of individually trained units that acted organically with each other in this mutually supportive fashion, much like in the strategies of Sunzi and Qi Jiquang.

Mazes and Formlessness

As we've seen, ancient Chinese military theory dictates that political and military leaders should marshal the spirit of soldiers. It also stresses how analysis of information and the movement of an army can guide a leader's actions to sure victories. When generals used these strategies against each other, they often found themselves having to navigate a metaphorical "maze of mirrors" of deceptions and counter deceptions. A commander must hide his "form," his strategic plans and feelings at the same time that he attempts to know the form of his enemy. A leader must also hide the tactical goals that might be guessed from his army's movement and formations. The successful execution of these factors makes the leader unknown or "formless" to his enemy.

A conflict between Peter and Ender early in the book illustrates this: when Peter chokes Ender, Ender at first doubts that Peter will kill him, but then changes his mind. "Ender could not speak; the breath was being forced from his lungs. Peter might mean it. Probably didn't mean it, but then he might." "I do mean it," Peter said.[13] Peter claims that he would do it if killing Ender fit his plans. In other cases, though, Ender hid his feelings because he didn't want to add to the enemy's strength. He thought that "any form of weakness would tell the Stilsons and Peters that his body could be broken."[14]

This ability to make his feelings "formless" benefits Ender during the bugger war. From Mazer Rackham, Ender learned that while he can certainly learn from the enemy, he has to avoid teaching them in turn. The buggers constantly innovated, only for Ender to do the same.

Chinese tradition, influenced by Sunzi, advocated this as well:

> In battle one engages with the orthodox and gains victory through the unorthodox. Thus one who excels at sending forth the unorthodox is as inexhaustible as heaven, as unlimited as the Yangtze and Yellow rivers ... In warfare ... the unorthodox and orthodox can never be completely exhausted. The unorthodox and orthodox mutually produce each other, just like an endless cycle.[15]

The *orthodox* pins down, or "spikes"[16] an enemy to prepare for the army's *unorthodox* or "tilting" maneuver. But the difference between the two can become blurred. If an enemy is actually expecting a surprise flank attack, the surprising unorthodox attack instead becomes the expected orthodox attack. So the definitions of these terms can often change in the course of one battle, depending on the intent of the attacker and the perceptions of those being attacked.

In plain language, a soldier should always "expect the unexpected." And sometimes the most surprising move can be the expected one. A conversation from the film *The Princess Bride* (1987) serves as a memorable illustration. Westley, the hero, enters into a battle of wits with Vizzini the Sicilian. In the course of trying to outwit each other, Vizzini describes how he knows that his opponent knows his mind well enough to predict Vizzini's next action. Vizzini goes on to say (with dazzlingly circular logic) that, sometimes, his opponent knows that he knows, so he must do something completely different. But his opponent must know that he knows that he knows ... so he must do what was originally predicted. The repetition of "he knows that I know" represents the inexhaustible permutations between opting for the orthodox and unorthodox, and describes the difficulty in trying to know your enemy while trying to keep your own strategy a secret.

Since the unsuspected nature of an attack is vital to its success, and armies constantly try to carry off devastating psychological attacks against the enemy, intelligence is critical. Sunzi advised, "Warfare is the way [Dao] of deception."[17] On the importance of not letting the enemy know your plans, he said:

> When someone excels in attacking, the enemy does not know where to mount his defense; when someone excels at defense, the enemy does not know where to attack. Subtle! Subtle! It approaches the formless ... Thus he can be the enemy's Master of Fate ... Thus if I determine the enemy's [form] while I have no perceptible form, I can concentrate [my forces] while the enemy is fragmented ... Thus we are many and the enemy is few.[18]

Ender confused and mystified his enemies by being unpredictable and "formless." Nobody expected he would gouge the giant's eyes out in the Giant's Drink scenario, or go directly for the "goal" in the battle near the buggers' home world.

This formlessness came at a steep personal price, reminding us that genius and victory demand sacrifices. Ender's knowledge of his opponents led to his developing sympathy and compassion for them.[19] While these are normally admirable traits, they initially made him avoid the final solution needed to beat the buggers. So Graff had to trick Ender into committing xenocide. Yet, it seems that Graff's paternal feelings toward Ender kept him from relishing the deadly games he forced Wiggin to play. In fact, both Graff and Ender loathed the role they played in winning the war: at the end of the book, they were broken soldiers who despised themselves as they lived in forced retirement, with Graff barely surviving a court martial. This is why Sunzi advocated a "cold" approach to waging war, a controversial suggestion that was often seen by Confucian historians as amoral or even wicked. In displaying the heart-wrenching moral cost of Ender's victory, Card mirrored his own society's recoil from the violent calculus of war.

Ender Wiggin qualifies as a military genius, if only a fictional one. His own "art of war" mirrors that of Sunzi. Ender was a master of the manipulation of the spirits of his soldiers and his opponents. He earned his victories through his ability to navigate his enemy's deceptive "maze of mirrors" and psychological ploys. Through his unfeeling analysis and the "fluid" movement of soldiers, he executed plans that mirror those of historical Chinese military maneuvers. Sunzi started his text by saying that, "Warfare is the greatest affair of state, the basis of life and death, the Dao [Way] to survival or extinction. It must be thoroughly pondered and analyzed."[20] We can learn much about the way of warfare not only from Sunzi's words, but also through Card's book and the strategies and tactics it embodies.

Notes

1. Orson Scott Card, *Ender's Game* (New York: TOR Books, 1991), 19.
2. Ralph Sawyer trans., *The Seven Military Classics of Ancient China* (New York: Westview Press, 1993), 324.
3. Ibid., 149–151.
4. David Graff, *Medieval Chinese Warfare: 300–900* (New York: Routledge Press, 2003), 168.
5. Sawyer, *Seven Classics*, 170.
6. Ibid., 177.
7. Ibid., 179.
8. Card, *Ender's Game*, 20.
9. Sawyer, *Seven Military Classics*, 245.
10. Ibid., 162–163.
11. Ibid., 168.
12. Ibid., 177.
13. Card, *Ender's Game*, 12.
14. Ibid., 43.
15. Sawyer, *Seven Military Classics*, 165.
16. Benjamin Wallacker, "Two Concepts in Early Chinese Thought," in Peter Lorge, ed., *Chinese Warfare to 1600* (New York: Ashgate Publishing, 2005), 235–240.
17. Sawyer, *Seven Military Classics*, 158.
18. Ibid., 166–167.
19. Read more about how Ender puts himself in the place of his opponents in Andrew Zimmerman Jones' chapter in this volume.
20. Sawyer, *Seven Military Classics*, 157.

CHAPTER 8

Do Good Games Make Good People?

Brendan P. Shea

Ender Wiggin spends much of *Ender's Game* playing games of one sort or another. These range from simple role-playing games with his siblings ("buggers and astronauts"), to battleroom contests, to the strange free play Giant's Drink video game in which he must kill a giant and confront his deepest fears.

These different games teach Ender skills that prove critical to his development. For example, the battleroom contests teach Ender how to think in three dimensions, how to command soldiers, and how to think strategically. Playing buggers and astronauts with Peter, by contrast, forces Ender to consider what it would be like to *be* a bugger. This empathy—the ability to "get inside the buggers' heads"—proves crucial to Ender's eventual success as a military commander, since it allows him to predict how they'll respond in combat situations. It also gives Ender a reason to eventually dedicate himself to finding a new home for the bugger species (as he does in the sequels, starting with *Speaker for the Dead*).

While the games that Ender plays are different than the games most of us are familiar with, it would be a mistake to conclude from this that Ender's experience has nothing to teach us. After all, games—whether they are computer games, sports, cards, or games of make-believe—occupy a crucial role in almost every society, and many children and adults devote lots of time to playing them. In this chapter, we'll examine the role that games play in Ender's development as both

Ender's Game and Philosophy: The Logic Gate Is Down, First Edition. Edited by Kevin S. Decker.
© 2013 John Wiley & Sons, Inc. Published 2013 by John Wiley & Sons, Inc.

a military commander and as a human being. We'll consider a number of interrelated questions: What is a game? Is it really appropriate to call Battle School activities "games," given how serious they are? What is the relationship between a good game and the development of a good person?

So What Is a Game, Anyway?

In order to determine the effects that playing games has on Ender's development, we need to define what we mean when we call a certain activity a "game." This is more difficult than it might sound. After all, Ender plays a wide variety of games throughout the novel. Some are games that require physical skill, others can be "won," while others have no winner or loser, and so on. Given the differences between these various activities, it might seem impossible to offer a completely satisfactory definition of a "game." This puzzle has led one famous philosopher—Ludwig Wittgenstein—to declare that it's impossible to precisely state the criteria that distinguish games from non-games.[1] According to Wittgenstein (1889–1951), any definition of "game," no matter how satisfying it appears, will mistakenly classify some games as non-games. On the other hand, some definitions will register some non-games as games, or could end up making both mistakes. So, for example, it might seem that a game such as Giant's drink (a single-player computer game that cannot be "won" or "lost") has nothing in common with the team-based, competitive battleroom games.

Not all philosophers agree with Wittgenstein that it's impossible to define a game, though. Bernard Suits offers one influential definition by succinctly describing a game as a "voluntary attempt to overcome unnecessary obstacles."[2] Suits further says that games are activities with the following four components:

1. A *prelusory goal*, the purpose independent of the game that the players aim to accomplish. "Prelusory" comes from the Latin *ludus* (for "game" or "sport") and names an objective that exists prior to the beginning of the game. So, for example, the prelusory goal of the battleroom contests is to open the opposing team's gate by having four of your players touch their helmets to the side while a fifth player passes through it. You *could*, in theory at

least, achieve the prelusory goal without playing the game; for example, a sufficiently clever student could perhaps sneak into the battleroom at night and pry open the door.

2. One or more *constitutive rules* that forbid players from using the most efficient methods for achieving the prelusory goal. Here, *constitutive* refers to the fact that the game's very nature is made up of just this set of rules. In the battleroom, one direct way to get the enemy's gate down would be to knock out the opposing team with sleeping gas and then open their gate while they were unconscious. But the constitutive rules of the game (which in other cases might be unwritten) forbid this. Constitutive rules are what make striving for the prelusory goal challenging and worthwhile; without such rules, there would simply be no game to play.

   Constitutive rules are different from other sorts of rules that are relevant to game playing. For example, most games have a variety of "rules of thumb" that dictate how successful players ought to play. So, for example, one good rule of thumb for battleroom games might be "the members of each team must communicate effectively." This rule is not a constitutive rule, since it's perfectly possible to play the game without following it. It's simply that teams that don't follow this rule are likely to do poorly.

   Likewise, constitutive rules are different from *moral* rules, which pertain to the way that players ought to treat one another in general (and not just while playing a game). While some constitutive rules will line up nicely with moral rules, this isn't always the case. For example, you *could* alter the constitutive rules of the battleroom contests so that the children were given live ammunition, and players who were hit would be wounded or killed. Students who willingly participated in this sort of game would clearly be breaking the moral rule "don't kill innocent people"; however, they would still be following the constitutive rules of the game.

3. A set of *lusory means*, or methods to achieve the goal permitted by the constitutive rules. One way of achieving the prelusory goal in the battleroom that Ender devised is to freeze your own legs and use them as a shield. Doing this doesn't violate the constitutive rules of the game. Good game players must learn how to master the lusory means of their chosen game. By contrast, the strategy of knocking out the opposing players using poisonous gas would not be among the lusory means.

4. One or more players who possess the *lusory attitude*, which means that they obey the constitutive rules *because they want to play the game*. In Battle School in general the students have very good reasons to want to obey the constitutive rules of the game for, if they don't obey the rules, they will lose games and might be thrown out of school.

Looking at games as activities with these four components allows us to tell games apart from the rest of ordinary life (cooking, driving to work) by the fact that they involve the *voluntary acceptance of inefficient methods* for pursuing a particular goal, and these means are *accepted for the reason that they make the game possible*. So, while the battleroom contests clearly count as games, many of the students' other goal-directed activities don't. For example, the students clearly have a goal for eating—to nourish themselves and to enjoy their food—but they pursue it using relatively efficient means. They use silverware to bring the food to their mouths. The students might make eating into a game if they wanted to—they need merely introduce some constitutive rules. For instance, they could require that all food must be thrown a distance of at least ten feet before being caught in a student's mouth.

Many other goal-directed activities, such as doing homework, are similar. Here, the case is a bit more complex. In theory, the most efficient means of getting the right answer might involve cheating. But does the possible choice of an efficient method mean that students choosing the inefficient method of actually studying and writing are treating homework as a game? Clearly not. The key difference between honest students and game players is that students adopt less efficient means in the service of some larger goal, in this case, the goal of learning the material well. In games, the inefficient methods are chosen *only* because we want to play the game.

Games Without Goals?

Suits' view of games clearly applies to the I.F.'s battleroom contests. In this case, it's relatively easy to identify prelusory goals ("open the opponent's gate") and constitutive rules ("no gassing of opponents"). Some of the games that Ender plays, however, have more complex structures. Consider, for example, the make-believe game of buggers and astronauts or the Giant's Drink computer game. These clearly seem to be games, but it's much more difficult to determine what the prelusory goals are, or what constitutive rules curb the players' choices.

In *The Grasshopper: Games, Life, and Utopia*, Suits contrasts *closed games* that have a predetermined end-point (the battleroom or platform video games) and *open games*, in which there is no "winning" that marks the end. Suits' definition can also handle games without a clear conclusion. Just because players can't "win" an open game, players may still be aiming at prelusory goals and follow rules in their pursuit of them.

To see how open games work, consider the free play computer game with the giant. Unlike traditional computer games, Ender couldn't "win" the Giant's Drink by aiming at an easily describable state (such as "beat level 8-4," "rescue the princess," or "get to the screen that says 'You win!'"). However, this doesn't mean that students who enter the Giant's Drink scenario have no prelusory goals in mind when they sit down to play. When we look at the main reason the students play ("because they want to"), the most important prelusory goal is simply to *make the game continue*. The reason that Ender wants to get by the giant is not because this allows him to "win" the game; he wants to find out what happens next. This goal is typical of open games. Engaging in role-playing or make-believe games, we "play along" because this is what allows the game to continue.

Once we see this, we can also see what sort of constitutive rules are needed to rein in players' choice of means toward this goal. Consider how Ender would react if some other brilliant player (perhaps one of his siblings) simply told him through step-by-step directions how to beat the giant. Presumably, Ender wouldn't have found this nearly as rewarding as beating the giant himself (he certainly wouldn't have learned as much). He might have felt the same way if he had hacked the computer system and deleted the giant from the game. This suggests that one constitutive rule of the Giant's Drink is something like, "You must figure out the answer yourself, using only the resources the software makes available to you." This is typical of open games. It would simply ruin the point of make-believe games such as buggers and astronauts if our lines and actions were entirely scripted ahead of time.

This Game Is Deadly Serious

One thing we haven't mentioned yet is how "trivial" the prelusory goals of many games appear. There's nothing inherently valuable, for instance, about getting a little white ball in a hole (in golf), or arranging the chess pieces on a board in such-and-such an arrangement. This same thing is true of the games Ender plays—there's nothing objectively worthwhile about opening an opponent's door in the battleroom contests, or getting to the next area in the "Giant's Drink." But this fact about many games doesn't stop people from playing or enjoying them. That games are not "for" any practical purpose is part of what distinguishes them from work, or from mere habits. In many cases, people work because they *have* to, but play games because they *want* to and because playing games is fun.

This feature has led contemporary philosopher Randolph Feezell to propose that games are a type of *play*, where play is, roughly speaking, any activity engaged in for its own sake.[3] Feezell does think that games are different from other sorts of play because they have constitutive rules and prelusory goals. If Ender and Valentine were anything like normal children, we can imagine that they played a great deal in the years before the book begins. When they played "hide and seek" they were engaged in both play and in a game. When they built model spaceships or splashed in the bathtub, on the other hand, they were engaged in play, but not in a game.

The war games that Ender plays in Battle School are very different from the games played by ordinary children. But for at least some of the students there, the *reasons* for playing the games are not so different from the reasons that most of us play games. Like us, they simply enjoy them. Consider Dink Meeker: when Dink and Ender first meet, Dink is deeply suspicious of both the government and the Battle School teachers, and is doubtful as to whether there's really any bugger threat to be afraid of. When Ender questions him about why he sticks around, he says that he "can't give up the game."[4] Feezell would say that Dink has the right attitude toward the game—he knows that it's not really serious, but he enjoys playing it despite this.

While the idea that "playing games" always involves "playing" is certainly attractive, an immediate problem presents itself: not every game player is (or should be!) motivated by love of the game.

Professional baseball players, for example, don't just play baseball because they enjoy it, and people betting in high-stakes poker matches in Las Vegas don't just like playing cards. Ender is much more similar to these professional game players than most of us. The main reason that Ender plays buggers and astronauts at home is because of Peter's physical threats; his motivation for participating in the battleroom contests is to become a more skilled commander. In very few cases does Ender simply play a game "because he feels like it."

Ender's experience suggests that it is perfectly possible to play a game without "playing" in the ordinary sense of the word. Games often have goals that are fairly trivial, and to play the game at all you do have to try your best to achieve this goal. Yet it simply doesn't follow that game players should always be motivated by a "love of the game." Game players will instead have a wide variety of motives. Some, like Ender, play games to improve themselves or because social circumstances have forced them to. Others, like Peter Wiggin, play games to exert power over others. Still others, such as Dink Meeker, play games because they love them.[5]

Do Good Games Make Good People?

So far, we've talked about what games are, the difference between open games and closed games, and the possibilities of "playing a game" without engaging in "play." We still haven't answered the question we started out with: Do good games make for good people, in Ender's case as well as our own? Or is the relationship more complex than this?

It's a common idea that playing games and sports make people better morally and in other ways. So it's not unusual to hear people say things like, "playing chess teaches children to think strategically" or "playing football helps build toughness and team spirit." Ender's teachers at the Battle School clearly buy into this philosophy because they've designed a curriculum in which game playing dominates. It does seem that playing certain games can help to develop our abilities. After all, some games are extremely challenging, especially when compared to the more mundane activities that characterize daily life. For example, Ender's success in the battleroom contests requires him to develop a wide range of abilities: physical skills such as strength and agility, intellectual skills like strategic and tactical decision making, and psychological skills such as the ability to lead others effectively.

Playing challenging games is crucial to Ender's development as a successful military commander. What's less clear, however, is whether playing these games helps or hinders Ender's developing good *moral* character. A person's moral character is, roughly, the tendency to treat other creatures as they deserve to be treated. So, for example, a person with good moral character is kind, generous, and patient; one with poor moral character is cruel, selfish, and impatient. In our own society, it's clear that games and sports can help—but also hinder—the development of moral character. While playing organized sports can teach children the moral importance of "playing fair" and sticking up for teammates, we need only consider the behavior of some professional athletes to see that these are not the only things that sports teach. A number of skilled professional athletes, though certainly not all, behave in morally abhorrent ways: they're willing to cheat to win, they treat their teammates and opponents badly, and they seem motivated entirely by greed instead of love of the game.

So what sort of games should we play, and how should we play them, if we want to develop good moral character? Again, Ender's experience provides some valuable clues. Ender's success—as both a military commander and as a human being—seems closely tied to his ability to *empathize* with different sorts of beings. Empathy, the ability to adopt another being's perspective, is central to the development of moral character. Since an empathetic person can "feel" the pain that selfish or hurtful actions cause others, he or she is less likely to do these sorts of actions.

As Ender's experience shows, one way of developing this sort of empathy is to play the right sorts of games—that is, to play games in which success requires we adopt another's perspective. In simple games of make-believe, this requirement is directly built into the constitutive rules of the game, which require that players "pretend they are buggers" or "pretend they are astronauts." In other cases, the role that empathy plays is less direct, but no less important. So, for example, much of Ender's success in both the Giant's Drink and the battleroom contests depends upon figuring out what the game designer, or the other players, have taken for granted, and to exploit this knowledge. The designers of the Giant's Drink game had failed to consider that a player could kill the giant; the battleroom strategists (at least before

Ender) didn't expect an opposing team to attack immediately out of the gate. Ender's creative, successful strategies in these games are possible only because he has figured out what his opponents expect of him, and he promptly violates these expectations.

Another important factor in whether games aid or hinder the development of moral character is the attitude that game players have toward winning (achieving the prelusory goal) and fair play (following the constitutive rules). In the battleroom, students are encouraged to view winning as the *only* thing of genuine importance, while fair play is less important. Games like these teach students something like: in life, the most important thing is to be successful, but the means you choose are irrelevant. In some ways, this lesson does prove valuable for Ender's development, as it's his willingness to break the "don't attack the planet" rule that leads to his eventual victory over the buggers. This same experience shows why games of this sort aren't, in general, a good way for students to develop moral character. After all, it's possible that if the I.F. had learned to question the apparently elementary importance of the maxim, "we must defeat the buggers, or face annihilation," it's possible that they would have discovered the buggers weren't hostile in the first place.

In our own world, as well as in Ender's, the idea that "winning isn't everything; it's the *only* thing" is a dominant way of looking at games. And while it's unlikely that anyone adopting this attitude in games will end up committing xenocide, as Ender does, it would be a serious mistake to suppose that a person's attitude toward games is morally irrelevant. Ender's experience clearly shows that the games we play are important, and even more important is the way we choose to play them.

Notes

1. In *Philosophical Investigations* (Cambridge, UK: Blackwell Publishing, 2001), Wittgenstein argues that while games have "family resemblances" to one another, it is not possible to describe explicitly what it is that all games have in common.
2. Suits details his theory of games in *The Grasshopper: Games, Life, and Utopia* (Toronto, CA: University of Toronto Press, 1978). Suits also discusses games in "What Is a Game?" *Philosophy of Science* 34, no. 2

(1967): 148–156 and "Tricky Triad: Games, Play, and Sport," *Journal of Philosophy of Sport* 15, no. 1 (1988): 1–9.

3. Randolph Feezell, *Sport, Play, and Ethical Reflection* (Champaign, IL: University of Illinois Press, 2006).

4. Orson Scott Card, *Ender's Game* (New York: TOR Books, 1991), 108.

5. A similar diversity of motives is evident in Suzanne Collin's hugely popular *Hunger Games* (New York: Scholastic Press, 2009), which describes a game in which children are forced to fight to the death, with the "winner" being the sole survivor. Many of the characters (like Katniss, the main character) play because they "have to," but others seem to find genuine enjoyment in hunting and killing other children.

Part Three

HIVE-QUEEN

ALL TOGETHER NOW

CHAPTER 9

Bugger All!
The Clash of Cultures
in *Ender's Game*

Cole Bowman

It may seem strange to think this, but the moment that the Enderverse's Formics, or buggers, ambushed human soldiers on their interstellar outpost may well have been the "beginning of the end" of the Human/Formic war. While it's always true that the beginning of a thing will lead to its eventual end, the moment in question is much more important than this implies. In fact, what happened in that ambush provides the very means by which the two races gained the ability to understand, and even care for each other. That violent instant, fueled by the adrenalin of the defending humans and the obedience of the Formic drones, propelled the two into a future in which there are only three degrees of separation between them in Demosthenes' "hierarchy of foreignness."[1]

Like the soldiers floating through space in that station, the human race was forced out of its isolation in the universe when it made contact with a seemingly malevolent species of aliens. The great tragedy of the violence that erupted from their meeting was that it occurred as a result of two deep misunderstandings. The Formics not only failed to grasp the capabilities of humanity, but humanity also deeply misunderstood the creatures that they would come to nickname "buggers." These misunderstandings may have resulted from what's sometimes called "cultural incommensurability," a philosopher's term for the lack of commonalities between two cultural standpoints. Cultural incommensurability, if it's true, suggests that because their

Ender's Game and Philosophy: The Logic Gate Is Down, First Edition. Edited by Kevin S. Decker.
© 2013 John Wiley & Sons, Inc. Published 2013 by John Wiley & Sons, Inc.

ways of life were so different, the two species came to inevitable conflict upon their initial encounter. The problem may be deeper, though, than even this suggests. Formics and humans didn't go to war just because they had different lifestyles, but because of a chasm between the ways that they view and interact with their universe.

In philosophy, this is explained by differences in their respective "conceptual schemes." At its heart, a conceptual scheme is the means by which we understand … well, everything! An appropriate way to think of a conceptual scheme is that it serves as a "schematic," if you will, of all the mental tools we use to learn and to know. We often say that two people or two different groups disagree with each other not because they disagree on the facts, but because they actually have two very different conceptual schemes. Because humans claimed to understand concepts like "good" and "evil," "war" and "defense," but these don't make sense to the buggers. Since the reverse is likely true also, they each fail to understand the very nature of the life-forms that believe them.

In the Enderverse, misunderstandings and the wars they lead to point to something deeper than a failure to communicate. They may be explained by the fact that the two species involved were so radically different in their perceptions and conceptions that they literally *cannot* understand one another. And while it's entirely possible that two such species could meet and find no common ground, it's likely that this *isn't* the case with humans and Formics. Donald Davidson (1917–2003), an intellectual powerhouse in the area of philosophy of mind, warns us not to *assume* that our culture is incommensurable with others in his essay, "On the Very Idea of a Conceptual Scheme," even when we seem to have no common ground with them. So, were the humans and buggers really too different to "just get along"?

Two Sides of the Same Coin, but Which Side Is Which?

Your conceptual scheme is the way that you understand the world. It encompasses all that you know, all that you're able to perceive and all the minute details that your culture, species, position amongst the stars, and disposition have embedded you with. This scheme sets the parameters of what you're *able* to know, and this makes Donald Davidson suggest there's no way to understand what lies outside of your scheme. He writes, "Reality itself is relative to a scheme: what counts as real in one system may not in another."[2]

But to assume that there's no way to reconcile the Formic and human conceptual schemes would be to treat their situation as what Davidson refers to as a "complete failure of translatability." Ultimately, if their cultures do truly exist outside of each other's conceptual scheme, this is why the humans and Formics must come to conflict. There would simply be no way that they *could* get along, as they could not understand the others' desires, values, or needs. And without this comprehension, there's no way to for us to know them as *beings* rather than just as *things*.

If we look at some of the key players in the Battle School, we see how this need for familiarity really works. Ender, Dink, and Alai all have different understandings of the school itself, but all of them subscribe to the same conceptual scheme. This is because each of them participates in the culture of the school itself and so they've been conditioned to see the world in a similar manner. Yes, their personal details make them perceive the same things from different angles, but this is simply a matter of perspective, which is a different order of magnitude from their conceptual scheme. Davidson explains, "Different points of view make sense, but only if there is a common coordinate system on which to plot them."[3]

Their differences are many: Ender is appreciably shorter than the other two, while Alai has a particular religious background that informs his opinions in a much different way than does Dink's. Dink's initial position as a toon leader for the Rat Army primes him for assessing people in different ways than the other two boys would. However, they're all human, they all speak English, and they are all students at Battle School. They, therefore, are likely to share a basic standpoint, a set of fundamental concepts.

The role that *language* plays in a conceptual scheme is even more significant than experience. Language is a defining characteristic of culture and, as Davidson and many other philosophers of language point out, it may be the most important one. While understanding itself is not derived from any given language, every language is a means by which a shared concept or idea can be conveyed. It's the *symbolism* behind the language that makes the framework for a particular conceptual scheme. Because Ender, Alai, and Dink share a fluency in English by which they express their understanding of their world, they're able to participate within the same scheme. They can speak to one another—so they can *understand* one another.

If a person were to come into the school who doesn't speak English (or a language that some of the students could understand), they would be an outsider among the soldiers in training because of their lack of ability to express the symbols manipulated within communication. Though they could likely improvise some means of expressing themselves, through drawing or interpretive gestures, there would be few ways for them to communicate a *wide range* of ideas effectively with the others. This new student would remain isolated until they could find a way to convey meaning to the others. And yet the degree of alienation between humans and Formics is even greater than this, as it's likely that Formic bodies can't perform simple human gestures, and the Formics have no recognizable forms of art that can be interpreted.

What's important about symbolism in the conceptual scheme is this: it enables the fluent user of a language to access the concepts underlying the symbolic modes of the language itself. English, for example, utilizes both *connotation* and *denotation* in expressing ideas. Connotation allows abstraction; it's what connects meaning to specific words. Denotation allows us to specify what we're talking about, like pointing at the particular student in Battle School who will be our commander. These two dimensions of the symbolism of language are parallel to the terms "scheme" and "content" in a conceptual scheme, where *scheme* is to the abstract as *content* is to the specific. To understand this, we can turn again to our favorite soldiers. Each of the boys would diverge in the sense they make of the word "mother." While they all know the word, each has different experiences that shape his understanding of the connotation or meaning of that word, just as they would with "father" or "sister." What's important is that each boy is capable of using the *concept* "mother" in a way that shows they know what it does (and doesn't) apply to (the denotative principle). While their individual meaning behind a word may vary, each can act in ways that shows he understands the idea of "mother" or "father." Words and concepts are key elements that allow them to participate in the conceptual scheme they share.

But this wouldn't be the case if the boys' experience was informed by different schemes. Davidson comments, "There may be no translating from one scheme to another, in which case the beliefs, desires, hopes and bits of knowledge that characterize one person have no true counterparts for the subscriber to another scheme."[4] It seems as though buggers *don't* participate in the same conceptual scheme as do the boys at Battle School. Their kin structure doesn't include the concept of "father" as the boys know it. It's not just that Formics don't have biological fathers in their culture, but they don't have the means of understanding the very *notion* of what "father" means. Perhaps the closest approximation within the bugger knowledge base is a mix between their image of a male (which exists only to breed with a queen) and their image of a mother (the queen herself). But what would result would be an impoverished and inaccurate image of what "father" or "fatherhood" means to a human. Generating a concept of "father" for the Formics would simply imply the "slug-like male" of their species that dies shortly after mating with the all-powerful queen. Attempting to shoehorn the concept of "father" into the context of the Formic conceptual scheme results in a basic distortion of the concept. This certainly isn't what Dink or Alai might think of when they use the word "father."

This sort of effort to fit a concept into an alien framework (literally, in this case!) almost always inaccurately represents what we're attempting to convey by the word at hand. This is what Davidson would call a "complete scheme failure," which happens when a concept simply can't be accurately translated into another scheme. Perhaps because the Formics and the humans are so incredibly different, they suffer from complete scheme failures. The buggers were unable to understand that humans were sentient because humans didn't follow the Formics' "rules" for sentience. And because they had no means of communication with the humans after the invasion, they were unable to convince the humans of their desire for forgiveness after they realized we were sentient after all. The differences between their conceptual schemes alienated each species from the other.

To bring this into even clearer focus, Davidson uses an elegant analogy to explain the difference between content and scheme:

> We cannot attach a clear meaning to the notion of organizing a single object (the world, nature etc.) unless that object is understood to contain or consist in other objects. Someone who sets out to organize a closet arranges the things in it. If you are told not to organize the shoes and shirts, but the closet itself, you would be bewildered. How would you organize the Pacific Ocean? Straighten out its shores, perhaps, or relocate its islands, or destroy its fish.[5]

He cautions us, however, not to consider scheme and content as two completely different things. By this he means that, while the two are *defined* as separate things, they cannot be understood one from another. One cannot effectively exist without the other. He refers to this dualism as "a dogma of empiricism"[6] as you can't separate what is being organized from the principles of its organization and continue having meaning, just as you can't fundamentally separate the word used to describe something and the thing itself.

When One Face Is Up, the Other Face Is Down

After their initial conflict had passed into memory, the differences between humans and the Formics were continually reinforced in the cultures of Earth. Because the human conceptual scheme didn't already have a place for the Formics, we put them into the closest possible conceptual category that we had: *bugs*. Formics are "buggers," a derogatory term that establishes the Formics as something bad, something wrong every time that it is said. The words and ideas surrounding the fear and distaste of "bugs" within many human conceptual schemes made the Formics into "others"—that is, everything that humanity is *not*. By calling them names, by playing games like "buggers versus astronauts," and by wearing bugger masks, humans reinforced the "us versus them" mentality that spurred the fighting.

This binary opposition of "us versus them" bolstered the unfolding political climate of Earth during the war. The countries of the world, despite their unresolved political tensions, banded together in the face of a mutual enemy. But this unity was because of an outside threat that they all feared, and the differences between humans and the Formics were much exaggerated because of the demonizing perspective of Earthlings.

While Ender's siblings and his fellow trainees hold steadfast to the concept of "bugger as enemy," Ender's perspective on the Formics is very different from the start. When Ender and Peter play a game of buggers versus astronauts, Ender puts on a Formic mask. In this moment, he assumes the perspective of a bugger, asking himself how they might view their human opponents. By doing this, Ender has taken the first step in a complex process of reconciling the two species' perceptions of each other. Because Ender is able to project himself into the attitudes and perceptions of the Formics—if only in a very limited way—he's shown that there's room for inclusion of the buggers within his own conceptual scheme, and perhaps in all human understanding. This moment, though just a trivial piece of child's play, confirms that Davidson's skepticism about the possibility of complete scheme failure is correct: the *very idea* of genuine cultural incommensurability seems doubtful.

The First Invasion occurred because the Formics had no idea that humans were sentient, and humans had no way to communicate that they were. The Second Invasion came about because the Formics had no way to express that they were reaching out for forgiveness. Finally, the Third Invasion occurred because the humans didn't yet understand the Formics as sentient—as beings, and not just things. The problem, therefore, lies *in translation*. Language plays a key role in sharing of conceptual scheme, since it allows alien cultures to share the symbolic system of another scheme. Davidson suggests that there is always a way to appreciate a different scheme so long as one scheme's means of symbolic expression can be translated into the other. "Studying the criteria of translation is therefore a way of focusing on criteria of identity for conceptual schemes," he writes.[7]

Davidson suggests that to grasp the importance of translatability we must realize that we can't assume to know the minds of others, even people like ourselves. "Since knowledge of beliefs comes only with the ability to interpret words, the only possibility at the start is to assume general agreement on beliefs," Davidson says.[8] That is, the only way to translate the words, gestures, or symbols of an "other" is to begin by assuming that most of our beliefs are like the beliefs of the "other." Davidson writes, "The agreement may take the form of wide spread sharing of sentences held true by speakers of 'the same language,' or agreement in the large mediated by a theory of truth contrived by an interpreter for speakers of another language."[9] With these resources, Davidson rejects the possibility of complete untranslatability.

The philosopher Thomas Kuhn (1922–1996), whose theories about culture Davidson relies heavily on, suggests that scientists working in two different historical periods "live in different worlds." Imagine what an astronomer from the early European Renaissance would have in common with a modern astrophysicist. While he could be a pioneer in his own time, highly regarded as an expert in his field, it would likely take many years for that astronomer to clue into the modern view of cosmic order (if he ever grasped it at all). While this example suggests a sort of "progress" in developing scientific ideas, it's important to keep in mind that we are comparing humans to humans here. It's like comparing an apple to a slightly different apple. When contrasting the Formics and the humans, we're looking for similarities between an apple and a radial control knob. While they are both made of matter, they correspond in very few other ways.

The astrophysicist can *never* look at the world from a Renaissance perspective; the modern advances that have been made constantly color his perception of the universe, helping to establish order in all that he experiences. Likewise, the astronomer is trapped, despite his attempts to learn, in the husk of a pre-modern understanding of things. While he could potentially come to talk about relativity and quantum mechanics, his conceptual scheme is built from mental structures appropriate to Renaissance culture.

What's important for both Davidson and Kuhn is that the possibility of communication itself doesn't rely so much on anything particularly mysterious, but merely on a number of commonly held beliefs between the two parties. That is, to be able to communicate with another being, there must be shared and symbolically meaningful practices or behaviors. Davidson thinks we have to assume these beliefs are present in order to get the work of translation off the ground in the first place; Kuhn thinks that over the history of science, beliefs have changed so drastically that a contemporary astrophysicist would not be able to talk shop with a Renaissance astronomer. The entire problem of translation and understanding in the Human/Formic War is handily summed up in a conversation between Ender and Colonel Graff:

> "So the whole war is because we can't talk to each other."
> "If the other fellow can't tell you his story, you can never be sure he isn't trying to kill you."
> "What if we just left them alone?"
> "Ender, we didn't go to them first, they came to us. If they were going to leave us alone, they could have done it a hundred years ago, before the First Invasion."
> "Maybe they didn't know we were intelligent life. Maybe--"[10]

If you were trying to communicate with beings who couldn't understand the idea of "an individual" (like the Formics), they wouldn't understand why you were using words like "I" or "you" in your sentences.

Two Faces of the Same Coin, and I Am the Metal in Between

While Davidson doesn't eliminate the possibility of a total failure of translation between two schemes that are different enough, in the case of humans and Formics, the parties have at least one shared point at which their conceptual schemes overlap: their initial encounter. Because the humans and the Formics have engaged in war, they each have a space for their opponent within their conceptual scheme. Imagine two circles drawn next to one another on a page with a space between them; they have no area that overlaps. If, however, we redraw the circles with one point shared in common on their circumferences, this would no longer be true. Though neither circle would encompass any part of the other, there would be sharing between the two at the single point where they touch. This single point of intersection represents the first contact between the Formics and the humans. Ironically, it is their first war that is the mutual ground on which they could come together to understand each other's perspective.

So what does all of this really mean? Davidson suggests that *charity* is necessary when we're trying to reconcile different schemes. Being charitable to another in the process of communication assumes that they share beliefs with you, and that many of their beliefs are *true*. Beyond this, charity relies on shared experience to be able to flourish. To be able to truly understand each other, the humans and the Formics would have to grant a certain validity to each other in their perception of the universe, but this didn't happen until Ender (bred for his compassion) and the Formic hive-queen (bred for her own) came into contact. They validated each other in a way that had not happened before. "Charity is forced on us …," Davidson writes, "… whether we like it or not, if we want to understand others, we must count them right in most matters."[11] Being charitable toward the other's perspective was not a choice for both Ender and the queen, but in a sense, they were bred for it. Ender was granted the basics he needed to understand the Formics through his ansible communication with the queen's own mind. Meanwhile, the former hive-queen, who had created her specifically to reconcile the conflict, had also taught her this form of communication. They literally shared in the other's mind, discovering from this connection that the other was sentient and, therefore, valuable.

At the end of the book, when Ender is told that the "game" he's been playing in the simulator has been real, he breaks down. Instead of fighting against accepting the moniker of "killer," as he did in the rest of his training, he acknowledges that he's committed the murder of billions. When he refers to himself as a *murderer* in this moment, rather than as a soldier, victor, or even just a killer, he affirms his sympathy for, and identification with, the Formics. If he were to have killed a mere nest of ants, he wouldn't have been a murderer. Through his acceptance, a recognition of the intrinsic value of the buggers emerges; this is the beginning of a long and fruitful process of translating his scheme to the Formics' and vice versa. He is the single point at which the human conceptual scheme meets the buggers' scheme.

By this point, both humans and Formics have entered a new era. They've created an entirely *new* scheme by acknowledging the existence of their former "others" within it, and this effectively changes their entire perspective on the universe. Once this change was initiated by their first meeting, there would be no way for them to undo what has been done to their points of view. Their conceptual scheme has been stretched to fit the other species' existence within it, and to attempt to shrink that back down would be impossible.

The philosophy of Paul Feyerabend (1924–1994) suggests one interpretation for what has happened to both the humans and the Formics. The older theories of both races about the nature of their "others" become inconsistent with the new concepts that the Queen and Ender have about each other. So, as Feyerabend would say, "... the principles involved in the determinations of the meanings of older theories or points of view are inconsistent with the new ... And it concludes by showing that such a procedure will also lead to the elimination of the old meanings ..."[12] In this way, "we get a new scheme out of an old," according to Davidson.

This shows that what's most important about Ender is not merely his ability to understand his "enemy," but his ability to love them. "I think it's impossible to really understand somebody, what they want, what they believe, and not love them the way they love themselves," he tells us.[13] Through love, he's connected to another species so that he can begin to tie the two schemes together. This connection is more meaningful than one stemming from a simple book- or vid-knowledge of the other beings, and it enables him to challenge human perceptions of the Formics. He's able to harness the sympathies of the humans and change their minds about the buggers. Along with the Formic hive-queen, Ender now occupies the space in between the two conceptual schemes—a space he can never retreat from—and has begun translating their meanings.

Notes

1. Orson Scott Card, *Ender's Shadow* (New York: TOR Books, 1999).
2. Donald Davidson, "On the Very Idea of a Conceptual Scheme," *Proceedings and Addresses of the American Philosophical Association*, Vol. 47 (1974): 5.
3. Ibid., 6.
4. Ibid., 5.
5. Ibid., 14.
6. Ibid., 11.
7. Ibid., 6.
8. Ibid., 18–19.
9. Ibid., 19.
10. Orson Scott Card, *Ender's Game* (New York: TOR Books, 1991), 178.
11. Donald Davidson, "On the Very Idea of a Conceptual Scheme," 19.
12. Paul Feyerabend, "Explanation, Reduction, and Empiricism," in *Scientific Explanation. Space, and Time: Minnesota Studies in the Philosophy of Science*, Vol. II (Minneapolis, 1962): 82.
13. Card, *Ender's Game*, 238.

CHAPTER 10

Why Ender Can't Go Home

Philotic Connections and Moral Responsibility

Brett Chandler Patterson

Toward the end of *Ender's Game*, after the manipulations of the Battle School officials stand exposed, Ender Wiggin must face the terrible consequences of what's really been going on during the last simulation. And those involved in the Third Invasion confront the inevitable question, "What happens to all these child soldiers now that the interstellar war is over?" The two problems these questions imply converge in another: "Can Ender go home?" Several characters, most notably Ender's brother Peter, have been anticipating his return in light of Earth politics. The tentative alliance of nations, including the Hegemony and the Warsaw Pact, has been breaking down, each country clamoring to get their hands on the highly trained military geniuses of Battle School.[1] Ender's alliance with one of these countries, even his home the United States, would have a tremendous impact on the political map.

In the spirit of diplomacy, political leaders decide that Ender will not return home, since his presence on Earth could spark a war. Instead, he will be part of the pioneering groups launched out into space to explore and to establish settlements on the "bugger worlds." Discerning readers who've followed Ender's story know that feels like an excuse, yet Ender doesn't put up a fight. We gradually realize that Ender has another destiny—revealed through the significant connection that the Formic hive-queen has made with him—the new role of Speaker for the Dead. This connection with the Formic leader creates

Ender's Game and Philosophy: The Logic Gate Is Down, First Edition. Edited by Kevin S. Decker.
© 2013 John Wiley & Sons, Inc. Published 2013 by John Wiley & Sons, Inc.

a relationship of responsibility that Ender cannot ignore. Ender learns that he has to be the one who will restore the Formics. The special nature of his connection with the buggers is the real reason Ender can't go home.

Philosophy helps us better to understand the nature of the relationship between Ender and the hive-queen, a relationship made possible by "philotes" that allow communication over vast distances. Card's "philotes" bear an intriguing resemblance to the "monads" of Gottfried Wilhelm Leibniz (1646–1716), which form the basic metaphysical building blocks of reality. Card describes a new form of communication arising from philotic interconnection. Once this relationship is established, the parties involved encounter the Other, the Strange, the Alien. In other words, they confront the basic ethical situation that Emmanuel Levinas (1906–1995) explored so effectively. According to Levinas, when we come face-to-face with the Other, we discover a moral relationship that's prior to our own self-understanding. Ender gives himself up to these moral demands, eventually deciding to use the rest of his life rebuilding the Formic species and civilization. The philotic connection has forever changed Ender. He can't go home, for he now has a mission.

Communicating Across the Galaxy

Where does this connection with the hive-queen originate? Ender has just been a child playing video games and battle simulations in orbit around Earth, so how could there ever be a bond between him and the Formics on the other side of the universe? After the Third Invasion, Ender, Valentine, and other settlers make a home on one of these unexplored bugger worlds. Surveying the planet, Ender discovers a landscape that resembles the virtual territory he had once explored in the Giant's Drink fantasy game in Battle School. Ender emphatically believes that the buggers built this landscape for him. Brushing aside the possibility that the landscape is a trap built to take revenge on him, Ender makes his way to the tower and the central mirror in its upper room. Instead of deadly snakes in the mirror, Ender finds a fertilized egg bearing a new hive-queen.

Standing there with the Formic pupa, Ender experiences visions of its kind, learning about their culture from the inside. Here Ender feels a "philotic connection" in its overwhelming immediacy—alien images and thoughts engulf him. Although Card is introducing complex ideas that he will explain further in later novels in the series (notably *Xenocide*) there's enough context in *Ender's Game* for readers to understand that the virtual "game" Ender played had evolved from a program devised by the Battle School technicians and officials to keep an eye on the children, into a bugger-engineered means for him to establish a philotic connection with the hive-queen.

One of the calling cards of science fiction is providing predictions of phenomena that we have yet to discover, and to do so in a way that fits well with the science and philosophy we already have. So in *Ender's Game*, we have the ansible, a machine allowing lightning-quick messaging across the galaxy.[2] The most telling discussion about the ansible and philotes occurs in a conversation between Ender and Graff while they're headed to Eros. Ender directs a series of questions to Graff: he's been studying the vids of the two Formic wars and wants to understand how the buggers communicate with one another. Graff tells him that Formic communication, "however they do it," is instantaneous. Contact with the buggers led human scientists to look for how communication "faster than light" could take place. Though Ender pushes for more, Graff admits, "I can't explain philotic physics to you. Half of it nobody understands anyway. What matters is we built the ansible."[3] Graff finally confesses to Ender that when the first working ansibles were built decades ago, I.F. Command launched ships into space to reach the buggers' home system. For the Third Invasion, Graff explains, the ships are lining up and a master ansible—the means for communicating with them—has been installed at I.F. Command. They just need a battle commander to tell the fleet what to do.[4]

How can such miraculous interstellar communication take place? Card offers us only a tantalizing glimpse into this special form of communication in Ender's discussion with Graff. We learn that "philotic physics" lies behind the technology of the ansible. Careful readers will have also noted much earlier in the book that Ender's brother Peter had been studying the "philotic collation of DNA"— even before hatching his plan to dominate net politics through the personas of Demosthenes and Locke.[5] The further development of the technology, though, becomes important in the succeeding novels *Speaker for the Dead*, *Xenocide*, and *Children of the Mind*. In *Xenocide*, Card defines philotes as "the fundamental building blocks of all matter and energy," that they "have neither mass nor inertia," only "location, duration, and connection."[6]

Remarkably, Card's cosmology, which lies behind his conceptions of Formic telepathy and ansible technology, resembles Leibniz's own view of the basic nature of the universe in his *Monadology*. They agree particularly closely when they describe the qualities of the most simple and fundamental building blocks of reality and in explaining the essential interconnectedness of these indivisible parts.[7] Today, particle physicists can speak of quarks and Higgs bosons, but Leibniz, in the seventeenth century, found that rationally reflecting on the nature of matter and mind revealed both were composed of "monads." A monad is a "simple substance that enters into composites." Because they're the simplest kind of things, they can't be broken down into more basic parts; they are the "true atoms of nature."[8] And while similar things differ because of a divergence between the arrangements of their parts, simple monads vary from one another *internally*. They have an internal complexity which "enfolds a multiplicity in unity." For Leibniz, "God alone is the primary unity or the original simple substance, of which all the created or derivative monads are products."[9] This divine creator organized the monads that make up everything in the universe into a hierarchy: (1) basic monads, (2) those with consciousness and memory, and (3) rational souls or spirits. Monads come together to form composite things, both inorganic (like rocks) and organic (like human bodies). Surprisingly, they also make up minds and their ideas. The "totally bare," basic monads do not have consciousness, but animals made up of these can develop sentience and memory if they also have the second kind of monad.[10] Human beings are even more distinctive because they have a rational soul or spirit, which includes "knowledge of necessary and eternal truths," the source of our capacity for reasoning about ourselves and God.[11]

Organisms and animals have a dominating monad, what Leibniz calls an "entelechy" or soul. What we call an "organism" is really just a harmonious union between body and entelechy; this union between body and soul is what we mean by an "animal." Part of the internal complexity of the monads we mentioned earlier is that *the order of the entire universe* is represented by *the order reflected in the organism or animal*, so it's correct to say that each living being is a "divine machine." God's hierarchy of order extends, uninterrupted, from the macrocosm all the way down to microcosm. Although bodies and souls conform to different laws, they work together according to the "pre-established harmony" of the universe. God elevates "spirits or rational souls" to the highest order of monads, and these spirits can share communion with God.[12]

After an all-too-brief mentioning of philotes in *Ender's Game*, Card offers a more extensive description in *Xenocide*, explaining how these basic building blocks come together as composites. It is the "twining" of "philotic rays" that allows the ansible to work.[13] Philotes "twine up" to make structures, each philote connecting "along a single ray, a one-dimensional line that connects it to all the other philotes in its smallest immediate structure, a meson."[14] Every more complex structure—neutrons, atoms, molecules, organisms, planets—follows this pattern with threads continuing through each level.[15] Individual rays, always present in the twines, keep "reaching on forever." Philotic connections can be broken, but despite the breaking, the old philotic twining lingers for a time. It is this breaking and lingering that is at the heart of ansible technology: "The principle of the ansible is that if you suspend a meson in a powerful magnetic field ... split it, and carry the two parts as far away as you want, the philotic twining will still connect them" instantaneously.[16]

In describing the fundamental interdependence of these building blocks, Card's theory again unnervingly resembles Leibniz's monadology. Leibniz notes that monads are fundamentally interconnected too: each monad has an internal coding (its "complete concept") that reflects the coding of all others, making it a mirror of the universe. The perfection of God's creation can be found in this picture, which consists of the greatest possible variety within the greatest possible order, a "universal harmony, which makes every substance express exactly all the others through the relations it has to them."[17] Although each created monad is limited, having only internal relations to those things nearest to them, all monads "reach confusedly to the infinite, to the whole."[18] Because all matter is interconnected, there is an "intercommunication" that "extends to any distance, however great" so that "all bodies feel the effects of everything that happens in the universe."[19]

In the Enderverse the breaking and lingering of philotic connections within the ansible mirrors the "intercommunication" in Leibniz's model. Card, though, doesn't stop at the level of cosmology: he also suggests that human beings unconsciously make philotic connections with family and dear friends. Valentine and Ender were twined, despite their separation while he's in Battle School. One of the characters in *Xenocide* speculates, "When a human being chooses to bond with another person, when he makes a commitment to a community, it is not just a social phenomenon. It's a physical event as well. The philote, the smallest conceivable physical particle—if we can call something with no mass or inertia physical at all—responds to an act of the human will."[20] Such a bonding has moral implications. When we interact with someone else, there is always the possibility of *bonding* with that person.

That Blasted Fantasy Game

This complicated cosmology sets the stage for crucial scenes in *Ender's Game*. Someone reading the story for the first time is unlikely to pick up on these connections, though. As a result, readers of the evolving story in the Ender novels may feel that Card "retconned" what was going on in the fantasy game that Ender played in Battle School and in his later dreams on Eros.[21] *Xenocide* explains that the hive-queen was reaching out philotically to bond with Ender, possibly to subjugate him to her will.[22] The ending of *Ender's Game* and its chilling description of the landscape tells us that a connection was made. Readers eagerly anticipate how Ender will respond to this contact.

The buggers do not need a machine, that is, an ansible, to communicate across the philotic web. In the crucial conversation between Ender and Graff on the way to Eros, Ender asks why Graff thinks the Earth is at war with the buggers. After listing a series of possible explanations, Graff finally admits what he personally thinks: "They must talk to each other directly, Ender, mind to mind. What one thinks, another can also think; what one remembers, another can also remember. Why would they ever develop a language?"[23] Graff says that if the buggers do not have a language, then human beings can't translate back and forth. Ender summarizes, "So the whole war is because we can't talk to each other."[24] Graff says that if you can't speak to each other, then you're never certain whether the other is plotting to kill you or not. Ender asks if there was some way to avoid war, but Graff says that war was inevitable once the buggers killed human beings in their first contact.[25]

As we saw earlier, Ender becomes capable of this kind of communication when he discovers the pupa of the hive-queen on the colony world. Images and thoughts arise in his mind, and he wonders where they've originated. Yet the landscape around him is a testimony that this isn't the first time they've reached out to Ender. When he sees the "Giant's corpse," Ender confirms what he has already suspected, that the Formics did make a connection with him through the fantasy game and its world of images.

The Giant's Drink game started as part of the manipulations of the Battle School administrators, including Graff. It offered one more way to spy on the children, while also testing them with apparently no-win scenarios. During his time at Battle School, Ender becomes obsessed with two such scenarios: the guessing game of the Giant and the mysterious upper room in a castle tower. In both, after repeatedly experiencing the death of his own character, he realizes that he has to kill, first the Giant, then the snake, to advance. The Giant's decayed body becomes the part of the landscape, opening the door to further vicious adventures. The killing of the snake leads Ender to a mirror in which he sees the image of his brother Peter, blood on his chin, snake tail in his mouth. Ender is horrified at this vision, and Graff can't understand how this computer game could have such a picture of Peter. Major Imbu suggests that the computer has a large database from which to draw, but Graff says that the picture must have originated from Earthside computers. Something unexpected and strange has happened, and first-time readers may be surprised to find out that this is a sign that the Formics are reaching out to Ender.

After what seems an eternity later, Ender finds the physical embodiment of this fantasy land: "Now Ender knew why it had looked familiar. The Giant's corpse. He had played here too many times as a child not to know this place. But it was not possible. The computer in the Battle School could not possibly have seen this place."[26] Ender tells Abra that the Formics built it for him, and he travels over the land and climbs the tower. At the top he discovers the room with a rug with a snake's head carved into the corner; the buggers had pulled these images from his mind to leave him some sort of message. He then turns to the mirror, and it is there that he discovers the pupa for the hive-queen.[27] Ender experiences direct philotic communication, and it's then that he realizes he's been encountering the alien for a long time (since his days in Battle School) without fully being aware of it.

Although the landscape Ender discovers is not built in terms of a "language" in the traditional sense, it does become the means of communication between two radically different forms of life, forms that had previously known only violence and warfare. Emmanuel Levinas helps us to understand what is ethically at stake in these kind of encounters in his books *Totality and Infinity* and *Otherwise Than Being*. The moment of face-to-face communication between two persons fascinated Levinas. His concerns arose as a counter to the self-centered quality of the philosophy of his teachers Edmund Husserl and Martin Heidegger. Being, existence, and thought were central concepts for Husserl and Heidegger. As a result, the focus in their existentialist philosophy was on the inward-looking self. Levinas, however, pulled this focus outward, analyzing the claims that *other persons* place on us.

To illustrate Levinas's point, imagine that you are home one evening by yourself. Suddenly, there's a loud knock at the front door. You try to guess who would be visiting at this time of the day. You decide to go to the door, pausing for a second to wonder if you should refrain from opening the door, but then decide to open it anyway. As soon as it opens, you're startled that your visitor is standing so close and that you do not recognize him. In the "immediacy" of this meeting and your unconscious reaction, you realize that you're vulnerable. You start to draw back until you make eye contact with this stranger. There's a moment of silence, as you each try to size up each other.

Levinas would have us go back to this kind of simple situation to pay attention to the "immediacy" of encounters with other people. There's always something startling about meeting someone "different." Levinas focuses on how difference or "alterity" challenges our perceptions of ourselves and the worlds in which we live. An *ethical* relationship already exists between us and others before we are able to reflect upon it, Levinas says.[28] "Responsibility is to bring to light a bond in which one is already held."[29] Our own sense of individuality as a "subject" arises in this kind of relationship with another. There's always a moment of vulnerability when we meet someone else, as we receive the advances from the one who pulls us out of ourselves.[30] Our sense of identity always depends upon our relationships, but we're rarely aware of this connection. Encounters with those radically different from us help us to see (by exaggerating difference and reactions to it) a fact that's always with us.

Card himself makes a similar point in his afterword to the *Ender's Game* sequel *Children of the Mind.* In a section defending the literary "seriousness" of his writings, Card asks, "Is the world of the Stranger and the Other not as vital to me in understanding what it means to be human as the world I actually live in?" Card is arguing that science fiction is able to illuminate exactly what Levinas describes: how we come to understand ourselves more clearly in our relationships with what's outside of us. Science fiction, through exaggerated difference, exposes what happens in *all* encounters with other life forms, human or not.[31]

Levinas claims that we disclose ourselves to those who provoke us, and that knowledge is only possible because of a basic relationship of *receptivity*—that is, being open to what's outside us.[32] We see this in the process of communication. When someone's speaking to us, we passively listen. We surrender ourselves to a moment when the other person dominates. As the other person speaks, we experience some vulnerability as we receive what is presented to us, as we participate in what Levinas calls the "saying."[33] Afterward, we remember what was "said"; we have a souvenir that connects us back to the immediacy of the moment of communication.[34]

Art and written language record what's "said"; they are fossils that give testimony to living moments of communication.[35] The landscape that the buggers have shaped for Ender is just such a testament, and Ender has to work to discover the meaning of it. This quest for understanding motivates Ender to push past any sense that he might get going into a trap; he takes risks, exposing himself to potential harm, to discover what the buggers intended. When Ender finally discovers the pupa of the hive-queen and experiences the direct nature of the philotic bond, he *experiences* the receptivity that comes in the moment of communication, receiving what Levinas would call the "free initiatives" of the other.[36] The "saying uncovers the one that speaks" and places a relationship of responsibility on the one who listens.[37] Once the hive-queen makes a philotic bond with Ender, a new world opens to him.

Ender's Quest for a New Home

Few people recognize the correct order of the relationships that Levinas illuminates: first, a responsibility for the other, then self-knowledge. In fact, we often reject such responsibility and turn to violence. Readers find out in *Xenocide* that the hive-queen's motivations might have led potentially to violence. When she reached out to Ender, she had hoped to exert her will over his, to make him a "drone" who would do her bidding. She discovered that he had a strong will of his own. The hive-queen couldn't tame Ender, but instead "twined" with him.[38] This bond gave Ender an insight that he didn't have previously: "They found me through the ansible, followed it and dwelt in my mind. In the agony of my tortured dreams they came to know me, even as I spent my days destroying them; they found my fear of them, and found also that I had no knowledge that I was killing them."[39] They then built a new language, the fantasy landscape, so that they could communicate with him and pass on a crucial message: "We are like you; the thought pressed into his mind. We did not mean to murder, and when we understood, we never came again. We thought that we were the only thinking beings in the universe, until we met you."[40] When Ender understands this tragic fact, he envisions a new purpose for his life, a destiny that he'll be able to choose and embrace on his own terms.

We know that Graff selected Ender because of his potential to be a commander with empathy. That empathy, supported by his bond with Valentine, is what guides Ender to recognize the importance of this philotic twining. The empathy and the bonding give him the insight necessary to write *The Hive Queen* and to pave the way for forgiveness between humanity and the buggers. The bonding pushes him to assume the true calling of his life, to *become* the Speaker for the Dead, a title and role that he creates for himself to acknowledge these changes. In searching for a way to bring back the Formics, Ender has to establish a new community. This mission is the real reason he cannot return to Earth; his new home lies before him.

Notes

1. Card details this story in his *Shadow* series: *Ender's Shadow*, *Shadow of the Hegemon*, *Shadow Puppets*, and *Shadow of the Giant*.
2. Card borrows the term from sci-fi and fantasy author Ursula K. Le Guin.

3. Orson Scott Card, *Ender's Game* (New York: TOR Books, 1991), 249.
4. Ibid., 251.
5. Ibid., 124.
6. Orson Scott Card, *Xenocide* (New York: TOR Books, 1991), 38.
7. As a result of Card's Mormon upbringing and commitments, the theology of Orson Pratt may also be an influence here. Pratt's cosmology also resembles Leibniz's monadology. See http://www.libertypages.com/clark/10660.html, accessed February 4, 2013.
8. Nicholas Rescher, *G.W. Leibniz's* Monadology: *An Edition for Students* (Pittsburgh: University of Pittsburgh Press, 1991), 17.
9. Ibid., 21.
10. Ibid., 18–19.
11. Ibid., 20.
12. Ibid., 28.
13. Card, *Xenocide*, 38.
14. Ibid., 40.
15. Ibid., 39.
16. Ibid., 41.
17. Rescher, *G.W. Leibniz's* Monadology, 24.
18. Ibid.
19. Ibid., 25.
20. Card, *Xenocide*, 43.
21. Card just about admits to such in his "Introduction" to the revised version of *Ender's Game.*
22. Ibid., 124–126.
23. Ibid, 253.
24. Ibid.
25. For more ponderings on whether the buggers and humans were born to misunderstand each other or not, see Cole Bowman's chapter in this volume.
26. Card, *Ender's Game*, 317.
27. Ibid., 319.
28. Emmanuel Levinas, *Otherwise Than Being* (Pittsburgh: Duquesne University Press, 2002), 90.
29. Alphonso Lingis, "Translator's Introduction," in Levinas, *Otherwise Than Being*, xix.
30. Ibid., 14, 25.
31. Card, *Children of the Mind* (New York: TOR Books, 1997), 348.
32. Levinas, *Otherwise Than Being*, 28, 32.
33. Ibid., 75.
34. Ibid., 34–35.

35. Ibid., 40, 45.
36. Ibid., 47.
37. Ibid., 49, 56.
38. Card, *Xenocide*, 126.
39. Card, *Ender's Game*, 224.
40. Ibid., 321.

CHAPTER 11

Of Gods and Buggers
Friendship in *Ender's Game*

Jeffery L. Nicholas

Andrew "Ender" Wiggin is a genius—a boy wonder who shouldn't exist except that his older siblings showed such promise that the government allowed his parents to have a "Third." Ender is so smart that he never loses a military strategy game at a school for geniuses. He's such a genius that when fighting the alien buggers, he loses a few battles but wins the war. Orson Scott Card writes the story of Ender to make us believe that Ender's genius rests on his ability to empathize with his enemy so that he can anticipate their strategy and use it to defeat them. Yet, he writes Ender as though he has no friends, and we have to wonder, "Can someone with such empathetic sensibilities lack friends?" Despite Card's best attempts—and they are really good—to paint Ender as Friedrich Nietzsche's "superman," he instead gives us a meditation on the truth of Aristotle's claim that human beings are political animals.

Ender seems to be more a superhuman or a god than a normal human being. Nietzsche (1844–1900) believed that an authentic person is one who exercises mastery of himself and creates new values rather than settling for the values of others. Nietzsche's superman, though, is alone in his world. It's an interesting parallel that Colonel Graff structures Ender's life to support Ender's maturation into a superman, too. Graff's strategy keeps Ender isolated; Ender feels he can't depend on anyone, including close friends, for support. We're sympathetic with Ender's isolation because we see his constant

Ender's Game and Philosophy: The Logic Gate Is Down, First Edition. Edited by Kevin S. Decker.
© 2013 John Wiley & Sons, Inc. Published 2013 by John Wiley & Sons, Inc.

longing for companionship—for his sister, Valentine, for friends, like Alai or Petra. In fact, Card nicely distinguishes Ender from his brother Peter by emphasizing Peter's sociopathy and lack of need for friends. Ender occupies a middle position between Peter and the buggers, who share a hive mind. His development fleshes out insights that Aristotle (384–322 BC) had about friendship and humanity over two thousand years ago. For Aristotle, a person outside a community was either a god or a beast. Peter is the beast in the novel—more beastly even than the buggers. If Peter is a beast, though, Card sets Ender up to become a god. Yet Ender never transforms into that god. Through all his ups and downs, Ender strives simply to be a friend and to have friends—that is, to simply be human after all.

Ender, the Superman

Ender's Game opens with two anonymous people (we find out later they're Graff and Anderson) whose conversation sets up the rest of the book:

"Too willing to submerge himself in someone else's will."
"Not if the person is his enemy."
"So what do we do? Surround him with enemies all the time?"
"If we have to."[1]

The conversation contrasts those who submerge themselves to the will of another and those who dominate others as if they were enemies. A focus on the power of the human will—over oneself or over another—frames the story of Ender. In order to prevent Ender from submitting to others, Colonel Graff and Major Anderson are determined to surround him with enemies all the time, even though they recognize this will be torture for Ender. "I thought you said you liked this kid," Anderson says.[2]

This focus on the power of the will is not accidental. Card's interest in military history led him to study the generals of the civil war. In them, he discovered something that inspired the writing of *Ender's Game*: "I understood at levels deeper than speech, how a great military leader imposes his will on his enemy, and makes his own army a willing extension of himself."[3] For Card, a military genius imposes his will: first on his own army, making it an extension of himself, then, on the enemy. Someone who had completely surrendered to the will of others couldn't be such a military genius, according to Card.

So, Graff sets to conditioning Ender. Ender is only six, a child in preschool when the story begins. He's afraid of Peter, but loves Valentine, and we know through word and deed that Valentine loves Ender as well. Graff, however, must separate Ender from Valentine and every other potential ally. "I'll have him completely separated from the rest of the boys," he declares.[4] At the beginning of the novel, Ender thinks that he and Graff will be friends, but Graff soon dispenses with that notion: "My job isn't to be friends. My job is to produce the best soldiers in the world."[5] In Ender's case, Graff desires to produce nothing less than a genius. "We need a Napoleon or Alexander," he tells Ender. Humanity wants to survive and "the way we do it is by striving and straining and, at last, every few generations giving birth to genius."[6]

We might think that Graff is setting himself up for failure. After all, Graff is imposing his will on Ender. Graff's own genius lies, though, not in imposing his own will on his enemy, but rather in creating someone who could do this in his stead. Graff also denies all freedom to this military genius: "Human beings are free except when humanity needs them. Maybe humanity needs you. To do something. Maybe humanity needs me—to find out what you're good for. We might both do despicable things, Ender, but if humankind survives, then we were good tools."[7] Graff knows he's doing despicable things to Ender in hopes that Ender will do something despicable: xenocide. Yet, he believes they'll be vindicated if humankind survives.

In many ways, Graff endorses Nietzsche's philosophy of the superman. Nietzsche believed that human beings survive as a species through struggle—the struggle, particularly, of "overmen" or "supermen" in history. For Nietzsche, the vital powers of the human species are dwindling, and individuals are required to rise above the riff-raff to bring new life to the species. The overman, in a sense, acts as a B-12 injection for a sick species.

Nietzsche never explicitly labeled any historical person a superman, but he did have high praise for certain superior individuals, including Jesus Christ. Nietzsche was an atheist, so his praise of Jesus had nothing to do with belief in him as the son of God. Rather, Nietzsche saw in Jesus someone so dedicated to his own values that he wasn't willing to betray those values, even through his crucifixion. In that way, Jesus transformed the values of the world. By his own suffering, Jesus imposed his will on the world, showing everyone the value of humility and pacifism. The reason Christianity thrived, according to Nietzsche, is not because God intended it to, but because one man was willing to bear the ultimate sacrifice and, through that sacrifice, change the world. This position doesn't contradict Nietzsche's anti-Christian stance. He respected Jesus Christ and St. Paul the apostle for their abilities while rejecting the herd-mentality of the religion they left behind. For Nietzsche, Jesus was a bird of prey because he changed the world, but those who followed him are sheep because they wallow in their self-pity and deny their will to power.

For Nietzsche, the Greek myths embrace a very different morality than that of Jews and Christians. This morality of nobility, Nietzsche's "master morality," valued strength and pride. A master imposes his will upon the world, which doesn't necessarily mean that the master enslaves others or makes them suffer. Rather, the key to the master's psychology is that he bears his own suffering, and through it gets stronger: "What does not destroy me, makes me stronger" is a saying from Nietzsche that has found its way into the popular consciousness.[8]

Peter and Ender should be judged differently according to Nietzsche's maxim. Peter takes joy in making others suffer; the first time we meet him, he's angry at Ender. He forces Ender to play buggers and astronauts and beats his brother, who is masked and four years his junior. Peter threatens to kill Ender, and seems to relish crushing Ender's chest. Later, we discover that Peter enjoys capturing squirrels, crucifying them, and, while they're still alive, cutting them open to study their muscles. Ender, on the other hand, tries to avoid causing pain and suffering to others. Reluctantly and without intent, he kills the bully Stilson. After the shuttle launch, he sits patiently in his chair as another bully hammers at his head, and then, intending minimal suffering, breaks the boy's arm. At Battle School, Ender is attacked by six larger boys. Again, without intending to do so, he kills Bonzo. While it's Ender who kills, it's Peter who relishes the suffering of others. When Ender learns about the deception that led him to xenocide, he collapses in bed and refuses to move for weeks. "Of course we tricked you into it. That's the whole point," said Graff. "It had to be a trick or you couldn't have done it ..."[9] Throughout we have to wonder, can those who have power ever truly be happy?

Happiness or Power?

No one in *Ender's Game* appears particularly happy. We see Graff being threatened several times with prosecution, being questioned by his I.F. superiors, and, in the end, being tried. Peter doesn't appear happy, although maybe psychopaths are limited in their ability to feel happiness. Even Valentine is sad throughout the book, working with the brother she hates and tricking the brother she loves.

Why aren't they happy? Ender wins every time and saves humanity! He's fed, clothed, taught—Ender has such genius and talent that it's hard to imagine why he wouldn't be happy. Yet, he most certainly isn't. Valentine, too, has many gifts: just 14 years old, she's able to influence the world through her writing as Demosthenes.[10] Graff sits at the top of his world. It's his plan, after all, that saves the world through Ender. Even the legendary war hero, Mazer Rackham, isn't happy: "I am not a happy man, Ender. Humanity does not ask us to be happy. It merely asks us to be brilliant on its behalf."[11]

Nietzsche offers an answer to why they aren't satisfied with their lives. Anything that "is a living and not a dying body," he writes,

> will have to be an incarnate will to power, it will strive to grow, spread, seize, become predominant—not from any morality or immorality but because it is *living* and because life simply *is* will to power ... "Exploitation" ... belongs to the *essence* of what lives, as a basic organic function; it is a consequence of the will to power, which is after all the will to life.[12]

All life is simply exploitation, and happiness has no place or meaning in the totality of exploitation. Graff exploits Ender; Peter exploits Valentine; Valentine exploits Ender; Ender exploits Stilson, Bonzo, even Bean. They are living beings, so they take advantage of each other, according to Nietzsche. After defeating Bonzo, Ender reaches an epiphany about the harsh truth that Nietzsche offers: "Peter might be scum, but Peter was right, always right; the power to cause pain is the only power that matters, the power to kill and destroy, because if you can't kill then you are always subject to those who can, and nothing and no one will ever save you."[13]

Can Nietzsche truly believe that human life—the will to power— has no room for happiness? In fact, Nietzsche says something quite different: "What is happiness?—The feeling that power *increases*—that resistance is being overcome."[14] We might think that for Nietzsche, it's precisely when Ender kills Stilson and Bonzo and when he destroys all the buggers that he should be happy, because that is when he's overcome the resistance of other wills. His power has increased as theirs wanes. But it is the process of struggling and overcoming that brings happiness according to Nietzsche. Once a foe has been vanquished, the will to power cannot simply rest content but rather seeks a new obstacle to overcome.

In Nietzsche's eyes, it's no use pitying Ender, even if his struggles seem unjust. After his last battleroom skirmish, Ender, frustrated with the unequal odds and unfair rules, asks Anderson: "'What is it next time? My army in a cage without guns, with the rest of the Battle School against them? How about a little equality?' There was a loud murmur of agreement from the other boys, and not all of it came from [Ender's] Army."[15] Later, Ender is talking to Bean in his room when Anderson and Graff arrive to give Ender his transfer orders to Command School. Ender's frustration is subdued, but "Bean was still feeling insubordinate, and he didn't think Ender deserved the rebuke. 'I think it was about time somebody told a teacher how we felt about what you've been doing.'"[16] Bean and the other students at the school would agree with Anderson that it's unfair what they've done to Ender. Even Graff thinks it's despicable.

Nietzsche, having no time for such pity, writes,

> The most intelligent men, like the *strongest*, find their happiness where others would find only disaster: in the labyrinth, in being hard with themselves and with others, in effort; their delight is in self-mastery; in them asceticism becomes second nature, a necessity, an instinct. They regard a difficult task as a privilege; it is to them a *recreation* to play with burdens that would crush all others.[17]

According to Nietzsche, the Battle School staff should thrill in the challenge of developing the abilities of the brightest student the school has ever seen. If we think of Nietzsche's "labyrinth" as Ender's Battle School, the application is obvious. Ender should treat his working on the most difficult tasks as a privilege. Early on in the story, as a matter of fact, we see him do just this. On first arriving at Battle School, he makes his way to the games the older boys play. He watches them for some time, and when he thinks he has the game down, he challenges one of them. He wins two out of three of the games, and "felt good. He had won something, and against older boys."[18] Ender does sometimes take happiness in the will to power, but not when the odds are stacked too high against him. We must ask, "Why? Why does he reject this god-like superiority?"

Ender, the Political Animal

Card, great storyteller that he is, reminds us what it's like to be alone and away from loved ones. When we first meet Ender, he's a six-year-old afraid of his older brother, in love with his older sister whom he relies on for protection, and an outcast in both his family and society as a Third. Colonel Graff whisks him away from all of this, explaining to Ender that he won't see his family members again until he is 18. This separation is hard on Ender. On his first night at Battle School, Ender lies in bed listening to other boys cry. "Then he could not help himself. His lips formed Valentine's name. He could hear her voice laughing in the distance, just down the hall. He could see Mother passing his door, looking in to be sure he was all right. He could hear Father laughing at the video. It was all so clear, and it would *never* be that way again."[19]

Ender constantly searches for friends in the persons of Graff and Alai—"I the sweetest friend you got"; Petra and Bean—"I'll be watching you more compassionately than you know." Yet when he reaches Command School, even though all his friends are there, things change: "As their trust in Ender as a commander grew, their friendship remembered from the Battle School days, gradually disappeared."[20]

Graff maintains, "His isolation can't be broken," but Ender is allowed to come out of isolation twice. In both cases, Valentine intercedes to save him from depression. Graff's motivation is that he needs Ender to move on to the next stage of training. Ender has fallen into depression from his isolation and the constant stress of training. Since he also enjoys the games, we might ask why the great genius would fall to this sort of depression? In the book's introduction, Card tells us, "[W]e're hungry for another kind of truth: the mythic truth about human nature in general, the particular truth about those life communities that define our identity, and the most specific truth of all: our own self-story."[21] Our self-story is tied up with community—a community that defines our identity. And so the problem with stories like Ender's is that it's too easy to see our heroes as examples of Nietzsche's superman, people with no ties or connections to anyone else.

Our heroes—Superman and Batman, John Wayne, Clint Eastwood, and Ellen Ripley—stand alone against the forces of evil. You and I, however, *come from somewhere.* No matter how unique, our identity is still defined by our community. Aristotle recognized this more than twenty-three hundred years ago. In his *Politics*, he declared, "Man is by nature a political animal. And he who by nature and not by mere accident is without a state, is either a bad man or above humanity."[22] By "political," Aristotle means something broader than the modern meaning of this word. While the state helped the individual become both a good citizen and a good person, the state is not just the government.

Peter is what Aristotle calls "a tribeless, lawless, hearthless one." Valentine "couldn't think of anything so terrible that she didn't believe Peter might do it," and Ender hates himself because he thinks he might be a more heinous killer than Peter.[23] Graff and the I.F. couldn't use Peter because he had no empathy for anyone. Peter clearly seems to be either a "bad man" or "above society."

When Aristotle further explains what he means by "political animal," what he says also seems, surprisingly, to apply to the buggers in *Ender's Game*:

> Now, that man is more of a political animal than bees or any other gregarious animals is evident. Nature, as we often say, makes nothing in vain, and man is the only animal whom she has endowed with the gift of speech .... the power of speech is intended to set forth the expedient and inexpedient, and therefore likewise the just and the unjust. And it is a characteristic of man that he alone has any sense of good and evil, of just and unjust, and the like, and the association of living beings who have this sense makes a family and a state.[24]

Aristotle makes the ability to communicate central to the definition of the political animal. But it's communicating about the just and unjust, good and evil, "and the association of living beings who have this sense [that] makes a family and a state."

Aristotle carefully points out that human community is not like insect community. Today's evolutionary biologists, like Richard

Dawkins and E.O. Wilson, have tried to understand human social life through the lens of insect species. Yet, Aristotle contends that this approach tells us nothing about human beings because human beings have the power of speech and insects do not. Readers of *Ender's Game* can see Aristotle's point clearly. Fundamentally, humans and buggers don't recognize each other as sentient. The buggers couldn't see that individuals of the same species could have distinctive identities requiring them to coordinate their activities through thought and speech. Humanity—except for perhaps Mazer Rackham—couldn't understand the collective thinking and action of the Formics. The buggers—or more correctly, the hive-queen—finally learn to communicate with Ender by reading his playing of the Giant's Drink game. They develop an ansible connection with his mind alone.[25]

The fact that the queen is able to communicate with Ender establishes a form of "political" community between them in Aristotle's sense. At the end of the novel, Ender discovers a larval queen put there just for him to discover. The queen shared—through a type of speech, for pictures are "a thousand words"—a common good with Ender. Now Ender's goal is to establish a new hive so that the buggers can be resurrected from oblivion.

The buggers prove, in two different ways, Aristotle's thinking about political animals. Because they have no power of speech, they lack a common good: the only good for the buggers is the good of the queen herself. Without her, the buggers die because they have nothing to aim for. In contrast, when the queen establishes communication with Ender, she develops a common good with him. She rises above mere animal life to human life.

"I the Sweetest Friend You Got"

Aristotle's view about human beings as political animals has practical implications. Aristotle's theory explains that Ender isn't happy because he has no friends. Ender, unlike Peter, longs for friends, especially for companionship with Valentine. Ender's depression increases when he believes he has no friends and that he's like Peter. He especially does not wish to live in the way that Nietzsche defines life—as the relentless task of submitting others to his will. This need for friendship clearly sets Aristotle's beliefs about happiness apart from Nietzsche's.

Where Nietzsche dreamed of a superman able to exert his will on others, Aristotle believed having friends is noble, "for we praise those who love their friends."[26] Aristotle, speaking almost directly to Ender's situation, advises, "without friends no one would choose to live, though he had all other goods."[27]

With these thoughts about friendship in mind, we can read Ender's lengthy hesitation in the castle turret room at the End of the World as a suggestion that he has given up on life. When he later comes to realize that he's trapped at the End of the World, "and he realized the sour taste that had come to him ... It was despair."[28] Graff enlists Valentine to try and bring him back from leave, which the I.F. "meant ... to last only a few days. But you see, he doesn't want to go on," Graff tells her.[29] As Valentine talks to Ender, she realizes "they had spent his ambition. He really did not want to leave the sun-warmed waters of this bowl."[30] Then what motivates Ender to pick himself up once more, go to Command School, and eventually to defeat the buggers? Only one answer can satisfy: friendship.

Ender's love for his sister is the biggest motivator, of course, but he has developed other friends whom he empathizes with as well, despite Graff's best attempts to prevent it. In fact, Ender's military success hinges just on that fact: "We had to have a commander with so much empathy that he would think like the buggers."[31] The essential difference between Ender and Peter is revealed in Ender's conversation with his sister on the raft:

"You don't understand," Ender said.
"Yes, I do."
"No you don't. I don't want to beat Peter."
"Then what do you want?"
"I want him to love me."[32]

Ender's greatest wish is to be loved—by Valentine, by Graff, Alai, Petra, Bean, Dink, even Peter. Ender is neither a bugger nor a god—despite Card's skillful attempt to portray him as a Nietzschean superman—but a human being after all. As Aristotle would agree, Ender is human partly because he needs friends. Unlike the buggers, his relationship with his command is not that of extending his single mind or his will over all. He depends on them to exercise their own intuition throughout the games. Unlike Peter, he can only find happiness when he has friends. His reward comes at the end of the book when he's finally able to leave the I.F. behind to be with the one person he's always loved, Valentine. This love, this friendship, is virtually the only thing that makes Ender a likable character in the end. Card writes in a way to make us believe that Graff can create a superman in the mold cast by Nietzsche. In fact, though, the real heart of the story lies in the truth about human nature that Aristotle realized long ago: that friendship is necessary for human life and human beings are political animals, not solitary supermen.

Notes

1. Orson Scott Card, *Ender's Game* (New York: TOR Books, 1991), 1.
2. Ibid.
3. Ibid., xiv.
4. Ibid., 27.
5. Ibid., 34.
6. Ibid., 35.
7. Ibid.
8. Friedrich Nietzsche, *The Antichrist*, trans. H.L. Mencken, http://www.gutenberg.org/files/19322/19322-h/19322-h.htm, accessed October 1, 2012.
9. Card, *Ender's Game*, 298.
10. For an in-depth look at Valentine's virtual influence as Demosthenes, see Ken Sayles' chapter in this volume.
11. Card, *Ender's Game*, 277.
12. Friedrich Nietzsche, *Beyond Good and Evil* in *Basic Writings of Nietzsche*, ed. Walter Kaufman (New York: Modern Library, 1992), 393.
13. Card, *Ender's Game*, 212.
14. Nietzsche, *The Antichrist*, §2.
15. Card, *Ender's Game*, 219.
16. Ibid., 223.
17. Nietzsche, *The Antichrist*, §57.
18. Card, *Ender's Game*, 48.
19. Ibid., 44.
20. Ibid., 282.
21. Ibid., xxiv–xxv.
22. Aristotle, *The Politics and the Constitution of Athens*, ed. Stephen Everson, trans. Jonathan Barnes (Cambridge: Cambridge University Press, 1996), 13.

23. Card, *Ender's Game*, 125.
24. Aristotle, *The Politics and the Constitution of Athens*, 13.
25. For a philosophical look at Ender's relationship with the hive-queen, see Brett Patterson's chapter in this book.
26. Aristotle, *Nicomachean Ethics*, trans. Robert C. Bartlett and Susan D. Collins (Chicago: The University of Chicago Press, 2012), 164.
27. Ibid., 163.
28. Card, *Ender's Game*, 141.
29. Ibid., 233.
30. Ibid., 240.
31. Ibid., 298.
32. Ibid., 242.

Part Four

WAR
KILL OR BE KILLED

CHAPTER 12

"I *Destroy* Them"
Ender, Good Intentions, and Moral Responsibility

Lance Belluomini

In *Ender's Game*, Orson Scott Card envisions a world where children are much more mature than they used to be—they're reflective, observant, and intellectual. In fact, they're portrayed as more capable and intelligent than the adult characters. It comes as no surprise that it's the adults who place the burden of saving the world and protecting the future onto the children, who aren't supposed to have any such responsibility in the first place.

But should we hold Ender morally responsible for his killings of Stilson, Bonzo, and the entire alien race of intelligent buggers? After all, Ender's just a child. He's only six years old when he kills Stilson; nine when he kills Bonzo; and just eleven when he ends the lives of several billion buggers. Ironically, it's children who are the most morally responsible agents in Card's world. The three Wiggin siblings—Ender, Peter, and Valentine—are moral creatures, capable of controlling their actions and well aware of what they're doing, even if they don't do the right thing every time. If this is true, then they should be subject to moral blame or praise for their deeds, at least in their fictional context. Card, in fact, challenges the reader to ask whether Ender is morally responsible for the terrible consequences of his actions.

We could interpret Card's moral view as an author as saying that intentions alone determine what we are responsible for. This interpretation is supported by the explicit creed that Ender adopts after saving

Ender's Game and Philosophy: The Logic Gate Is Down, First Edition. Edited by Kevin S. Decker.
© 2013 John Wiley & Sons, Inc. Published 2013 by John Wiley & Sons, Inc.

humanity as Speaker for the Dead: "Speakers for the Dead held as their only doctrine that good or evil exist entirely in human motive, and not at all in the act."[1] Throughout *Ender's Game*, Card seems to argue for a morality that judges praise and blame in terms of good and bad intentions. He does this by continually deflecting our focus away from the consequences of Ender's violence. For example, Card doesn't inform us of Stilson's and Bonzo's deaths until after the fact, encouraging us to judge Ender's actions not on their fatal effects, but on his intent.

For Card, the connection between intention and moral responsibility is clear. If you act out of good intentions, then you can't be held morally responsible for any bad results because good intentions always give you the right reasons for acting. Card thinks that a person may do wrong without being held responsible for it. For example, Ender visits intense violence on other children without bearing any moral responsibility for those acts. He can beat Bonzo to a bloody pulp, yet not be blameworthy because of his deliberation to do something good—in this case, defend himself. Also, Card views being a good person and having good intentions as connected: good intentions make you a good person, even if you do some morally dubious things. Throughout *Ender's Game*, characters who know Ender well speak of his good intentions and say he's a good person. Early in the book, Graff says to Major Anderson, "He's clean. Right to the heart. He's good."[2] And after we learn that Bonzo and Stilson are dead, Graff assures us that "Ender Wiggin isn't a killer. He just wins—thoroughly."[3] So Ender can inflict harm, even kill other children, and yet remain a good person.

But does this all make sense? Card seems to think the rightness or wrongness of an act and responsibility for it are two different things. For example, Ender isn't held responsible (morally or legally) for his killings of Stilson, Bonzo, and the buggers because Ender doesn't intend to kill them. Instead, Card wants us to sympathize with Ender, and see him more as the victim.

In this chapter, we'll address two questions. First, are Ender's killings of Stilson and Bonzo morally permissible? He destroys them both and robs their families of them. Could this ever be morally permissible? Second, is Ender morally responsible for the consequences of his actions? Ender blames himself for the destruction of the buggers, but would he have done the same thing if he had known it was all for real? Perhaps by allowing the I.F. to train him for this purpose, he had always intended to do it. Of course, Ender isn't the only one involved here: maybe the International Fleet Command is responsible for the consequences of Ender's actions. After all, they unquestionably manipulate and structure Ender's surroundings, and clearly, it's the I.F. that intends for the buggers to die—even if Ender doesn't.[4]

"He Didn't Just Beat Him. He Beat Him Deep"

In one of the first scenes in the book, Stilson and other bullies taunt Ender for being a "Third." Wanting to avoid an unfair fight, Ender says to Stilson, "You mean it takes this many of you to fight one Third?"[5] When the other kids let go of him, Ender unexpectedly kicks Stilson in the chest, leveling him to the ground. Ender reasons that if he wins decisively, then he won't be attacked again by Stilson or other bullies in the future—this would be a way for him to forestall vengeance. What happens next is disturbing: Ender viciously kicks Stilson's motionless body in the ribs and the crotch, and Stilson starts to cry. After intimidating the other kids by telling them what he does to people who try to hurt him, Ender delivers a final blow—a bloody kick to Stilson's face. Unwittingly, Ender (as his name suggests) "ends" Stilson's life.

You might agree that Ender's killing of Stilson doesn't amount to murder, since he didn't intend to kill him. But couldn't a jury have at least found him guilty of manslaughter? We need to be careful here, for killing someone can sometimes be justifiable, as in the case of self-defense. We all have the right to defend ourselves from serious harm or from being killed, and doing so could result in us killing another person.

Let's try to make philosophical progress on whether Ender's killing of Stilson is morally permissible. According to St. Thomas Aquinas (1225–1274), killing in self-defense may not be morally wrong if certain conditions are met. Aquinas introduced what's now known as the "Doctrine of Double Effect" (or DDE).[6] The DDE shows that there can be two different results of acting with deadly force to save your own life: saving your own life (an effect that's intended) and the second, or "double effect" of causing serious harm to, or perhaps killing an attacker. This second result was not intended, but it might have been foreseen.[7]

More generally, the DDE says that acting with good intentions can have both good and bad effects. A lot depends on the relationship between the intention and the bad effects, since it's impermissible, according to the DDE, to actually *intend* to do something bad. Ender's self-defense against Stilson resulted in several other consequences besides protecting himself. As he told Graff, Ender also wanted to prevent Stilson and other bullies from ever taunting or attacking him again, for example. What does the DDE say about Ender's case?

The DDE recommends our actions as morally permissible if four conditions are met: (1) the intended act has to be *good in itself*, so it can't be intrinsically evil (like murder); (2) the person who's acting has to *intend only the good effect*, so for them a bad consequence, even if foreseen, is an unintended side effect; (3) the good effect has to be *produced directly by the action*, not by the bad effect. If the opposite were true, then we'd really be using a bad means to a good end, which is prohibited. Finally, (4) the good effect must *balance out* the bad effect. This provides a sufficient reason for permitting the evil result to occur.

Even if we agree there's nothing wrong with Ender defending himself against Stilson, his choice still fails to meet the last three rules of the DDE. While he acts for the good of self-defense, he also intends to inflict *excessive* harm on Stilson, to "take him out of the picture" as it were. Ender also intends another good consequence—discouraging other bullies—but again, he uses more violence than necessary. In the end, his brutal beating of Stilson in self-defense is not in proportion to the end he intends. To prevent further attacks from bullies like Stilson, Ender only needs to successfully defend himself. Ender does seem to recognize this, but ignores it: "Ender knew the unspoken rules of manly warfare, even though he was only six. It was forbidden to strike the opponent who lay helpless on the ground; only an animal would do that."[8]

So, using the DDE, Ender's method of self-defense wasn't morally justified. Ender himself realizes this, perhaps in the guilt that he feels afterward. Aquinas offers wisdom in this case when he writes, "An act that is prompted by a good intention can become illicit if it is not proportionate to the end intended. This is why it is not allowed to use more force than necessary to defend one's life."[9]

When Aquinas mulls over moral responsibility in his *Summa Theologica*, he distinguishes between bad consequences that are foreseen and those that are unforeseen. Those that are foreseen *must* be taken into account, so Aquinas would say that Ender can certainly be held morally responsible for killing Stilson. Added to this, certain kinds of *unforeseen* bad consequences need to be taken into account. There are two categories of unforeseen bad consequences: ones that usually follow from actions of a certain kind. (Think of the blow to Stilson's noggin; head wounds can be fatal.) There are also bad consequences that follow our choices accidentally, like the death of the Giant after Ender attacks his eye in the virtual free play scenario.

According to Aquinas, the deaths of Stilson and Bonzo belong with the first type of unforeseen consequences. Ender's moral responsibility rests on the fact that the unpremeditated killings naturally follow all the same from the excessively harmful tactics he uses. Ender should've recognized this before acting. Aquinas would conclude that these bad consequences were not excusable.

It's important to point out that Aquinas is not a *consequentialist*. In other words, he doesn't think that a right action is made right solely by the good consequences it brings about. But he does think that consequences play a role in the evaluation of human actions. For Aquinas, acts that are good might be bad in certain situations if their consequences are bad overall. But producing good consequences can't make a wrong act right—the end does not justify the means. Acting from "good intention" matters most. Ultimately, Aquinas thinks that for something to be good, it must be good in every respect; for something to be bad, conversely, just one defect will suffice.[10]

"I Didn't Want to Hurt Him!"

At Battle School, Ender makes enemies because of his successes as a commander. He's also far superior to everyone—more intelligent, creative, and combative. After Dragon Army defeats Salamander Army as a result of Bonzo's ineptitude, Ender adds insult to injury when he tells Major Anderson, "I thought you were going to put us against an army that could match us in a fair fight."[11] Ender infuriates Bonzo when he refuses his ceremonial surrender and asks Bean to publicly announce what the Salamander commander should have done to win the battle.

As a result, Bonzo intends to murder Ender in the Battle School showers. Ender calls on his honor to trick Bonzo into fighting him in one-on-one combat. "Your father would be proud of you," Ender goads him. "He would love to see you now, come to fight a naked boy in the shower, smaller than you, and you brought six friends."[12] When Bonzo attacks, Ender twists in Bonzo's grasp and heads his nose. After having delivered that blow, Ender realizes that he could have escaped, but again he had to win the match decisively. So he treats him the same way as Stilson, and Bonzo simply collapses.

Can Ender's killing of Bonzo be morally permissible? Clearly, Bonzo lets it be known in Battle School that he intends to murder Ender, and Ender knows this. If you know someone is out to kill you and they make an attempt, acting in self-defense certainly seems permitted. Of course, one of the foreseen yet unintended consequences that can happen is that you kill the attacker in your act of self-defense. After Ender delivers the initial stunning blow to Bonzo, he thinks, "The only way to end things completely was to hurt Bonzo enough that his fear was stronger than his hate."[13] Ender decides to beat Bonzo "deep," but this seems contradictory, since as the confrontation ends, he tells Dink, crying, "I didn't want to hurt him! Why didn't he just leave me alone?"[14]

How does Ender's self-defense against Bonzo hold up to the Doctrine of Double Effect? It meets the first three of the conditions about intended versus foreseen consequences, but does it represent a *proportionately good response* to balance the unintended killing? I think we have to say that, as with Stilson, Ender's response is excessive. Ender could have freely walked away after the initial blow, having defended himself and won the fight. Leaving and reporting the incident to Graff and the other I.F. generals would seem to have been the proportional response. Yet, Ender has good reason to believe that the adults have no intent to help him—ever. As we learn from Graff's comment to Major Pace, "Ender Wiggin must believe that no matter what happens, no adult will ever, ever step in to help him in any way."[15] It's likely that Ender realizes this, given Graff's prediction, "If we transfer Bonzo ahead of schedule, [Ender] will know that we saved him."[16] Even if Ender knew this, and his reluctance to seek help from the I.F. is warranted, this still isn't enough to exonerate him. The bad effects of his act outweigh his intended good ends.

So those who still want to insist, with Card, that Ender's deadly actions are justified won't be able to rely on the insight of the DDE for help. But while the Doctrine of Double Effect carries intuitive appeal, it isn't free from objections. One solid criticism of the DDE is based on the contemporary philosopher Harry Frankfurt's distinction between *kinds* of intentions. Frankfurt thinks we have not only *first-order desires* (or intentions), but we also possess the capacity to form *second-order intentions*.[17] First-order intentions are employed on a daily basis for determining our choices—for instance, our intention to eat something from the fridge *or* the pantry, or to quit smoking. A second-order intention is an *intention about an intention*. Ender has first-order intentions to do significant harm to other children in certain circumstances; as we've seen, this intention is morally problematic because it violates the DDE. But he also wants (at the second order) to *not have that intention* to use excessive violence. This may explain why he tells Dink that he didn't want to hurt Bonzo.

Frankfurt might argue that Ender's second-order intention to restrain himself when fighting in self-defense represents his true intention. So while his first-order intentions are morally problematic, his second-order ones are not. This would allow us to concede that Ender can do wrong but remain a good person. Notice that this would lend support to Card's view of Ender's moral character.

But, you might reply, isn't Ender still responsible for *acting* on his first-order intention even though his second-order intention is good? To this we could say that Ender's intent to "destroy" others is not something his settled second-order intentions could have responded to. His first-order intentions were provoked in a way outside of his control and not reflective of his moral character. He didn't act freely. This implies that only second-order intentions can ground our ability to make free and responsible choices. Putting it differently, Ender is not responsible for choices that he didn't freely choose. The DDE presumes the opposite, so it doesn't apply in this case.

But it's not clear what we really mean when we say we're *only* responsible for what our second-order intentions are, even when we fail to act on them. Instead, it seems right that we ought to hold Ender accountable for inflicting excessive harm based on his first-order intentions. Doesn't he have control over *all* his intentions? Doesn't everyone? If someone were to steal something on the basis of a first-order intention, wouldn't we all agree that person should be held accountable for that action, even if in their heart of hearts, they want to be a better person?

So we've established that Ender has immorally harmed both Bonzo and Stilson. Simply having the right intentions wasn't enough, since

Ender should have foreseen that grievous harm or death were the likely consequences of his choice about how to defend himself. So Ender is morally responsible for the terrible consequences that result, despite Major Anderson's opinion that Ender isn't a killer. Near the end of the book, Ender *sounds* like a killer when he admits to Valentine, "I *destroy* them. I make it impossible for them to ever hurt me again. I grind them and grind them until they don't exist."[18] With this, it certainly seems as though Ender acknowledges he has had bad intentions. But still, Card insists this is false.

"All His Crimes Weighed Heavy on Him"

Card writes as if we're morally responsible for an action depending on what's happening in our mind (what I intend and what I foresee). In one sense this is true: we do tend to excuse people who act badly while deranged or forgivably ignorant of the relevant facts. But someone can't escape blame simply by choosing to think well of their own intentions. For example, a woman who commits adultery might tell herself that what she's doing isn't really cheating because there are no feelings of love involved. It's not a breach of trust, it's just a meaningless physical act. This woman is *rationalizing* her intentions rather than giving an honest account of them. And suppose for the sake of argument that the woman is not rationalizing her intention, that she isn't deliberately deceiving herself about her intention not to cheat. What would we say then? Well, her intention doesn't get her off the hook even if she's not deceiving herself.

G.E.M. Anscombe (1919–2001) calls this situation "double-think about double effect."[19] Double-think occurs when we act even though we're *unclear* about our intentions or when we deliberately deceive ourselves about our intention, as the adulterous woman in the example.[20] Now consider Ender's intentions. No matter how Card might try to defend Ender, we can say that either (a) Ender is deceived about his true intentions or (b) Ender is not deceived, and his intentions are genuinely wrong. It certainly seems that when Ender is doing something "wrong," he is deceived about his true intentions.

Card's thinking about intention seems to be too narrow, for two related reasons. He thinks that intentions are private states of mind by which we can justify our actions simply by thinking about them in a certain way. When Ender protests to Dink after his fight with Bonzo, "I didn't want to hurt him!" we see Card explaining Ender's intention in a way that Card wishes—a way that justifies Ender's violence. While Ender doesn't intend to kill Bonzo during his excessively violent attack, he still intends to inflict enough harm so that Bonzo fears him more than hates him. Contrary to what Ender tells Dink, he *did* intend to harm Bonzo.

Intentions are reliably linked to actions. This is why NBA referees don't need to be mind-readers in order to call intentional fouls. If a player shoves or grabs another player to stop the clock or prevent a basket, no reasoning on the player's part can make him innocent of the foul. For his part, Card too easily separates intention and action. For example, there's Graff's comment to Ender's parents about the fight with Stilson, "It isn't what he did Mrs. Wiggin. It's why."[21] Here, Card has Graff excusing Ender from blame, implying that Ender's act is morally permissible. Ender explains that he didn't want to hurt Stilson and Bonzo. Card's message is clear: Ender doesn't intend or have a desire to harm them.[22] But intention is about action as well. Ender's excessively gruesome acts indicate he intends to carry out precisely those acts.

Is Ender equally responsible for killing off an entire species? Most readers feel that Ender was tricked by Graff and Rackham into killing the buggers. When Ender realizes that he's played a principle role in destroying not only the Formic army but also their queens and children, he's horrified. He says "I didn't want to kill them all. I didn't want to kill anybody! I'm not a killer! You didn't want me, you bastards, you wanted Peter, but you made me do it, you tricked me into it."[23] Card unquestionably takes Ender's side. On his official site, Ender's creator says, "Though I assign responsibility for the near destruction of the hive-queen (and Ender takes it up on himself) I do not assign blame, because I don't consider there to be any blame. You can't be held responsible for not knowing what you could not know at the time of a crucial decision."[24]

But is this excuse available to Ender? He knew that one day he was going to kill the buggers, since he had been preparing himself for what the I.F. saw as the inevitable Third Invasion while at Battle School. Graff gives Ender the choice of whether to attend, so he could've said "no" to remain on earth and lead a happy life. Instead, he felt compelled to try and help stop the next bugger attack. Graff convinces

Ender that "individual human beings are tools that the others use to help us all survive."[25] He allows Graff to take him and train him to be a commanding genius like Mazer Rackham—to be an important "tool" that will lead them in war and be humanity's savior. Since ignorance can't be his excuse, all this indicates that Ender bears at least some responsibility, but perhaps not full responsibility, for the xenocide. Of course, instead of feeling like a savior or hero, Ender ends up feeling guilty for the bugger genocide. He takes responsibility for stealing their future from them.

As we mentioned earlier, the popular interpretation is that Ender isn't at fault. After all, he was only 11 years old and had been under the influence of the Battle School administrators since the age of six. Surely at that age he couldn't have been expected to foresee the terrible consequences of his actions. In addition, he didn't know that the battle simulation was real. Imagine you're playing *Call of Duty* online and you find out that every player you killed in the game with a frag grenade was killed in real life. Would you be tried for the crimes? No, because a large part of the law is based on being able to reasonably foresee consequences. Aquinas would agree here: for him, an agent can't be held morally responsible for choosing to act in a way that she didn't know would likely have bad consequences. In Ender's situation, he couldn't have known that his actions were causing harm at all.

While these are reasons for thinking we can't assign *full* moral responsibility to Ender, we should agree that he bears some responsibility for the xenocide. He was a willing tool—he lets the system pull him through, and he doesn't stand up to stop it.[26] Up to the point at which he destroys them in his simulator field, the buggers were monsters in his mind, and he wanted them dead as much as the next person.

"Nevertheless, It's Still You Doing Those Things"[27]

Despite Ender's culpability, the appeal of *Ender's Game* is undeniable. We know why it's popular with readers. It captures our imagination in its themes of aliens attacking Earth, the government's program to train special kids in an effort to defeat the aliens, and the kids' high-tech playing at laser-tag games in zero gravity. Others are drawn to it because of Ender's character. They identify with Ender because they like to think they're as special as he is—that, perhaps, their suffering has made them special. But when we seriously reflect on Ender's character traits and what he does to others, what is there to like? Ender kills. As he himself admits, he grinds people until they don't exist anymore. It seems that Card insists that Ender is a good person who commits wrongful acts, but isn't to blame for them. How can this be? Given his intentions and what he should've foreseen, we've made a case that Ender is morally responsible for the terrible consequences of his actions toward Stilson and Bonzo, and that he bears partial responsibility for the bugger genocide. This implies that Ender isn't a moral exemplar—he's not a good role model. Ender would vouch for us on this after all, as he would say about what he does to others—"I make it impossible for them to ever hurt me again."[28]

Notes

1. Orson Scott Card, *Ender's Game* (New York: TOR Books, 1991), 39.
2. Ibid., 36.
3. Ibid., 226.
4. For more on the connection between the manipulation of Ender and the development of his violent streak, see Jeremy Proulx's chapter in this book.
5. Card, *Ender's Game*, 7.
6. Thomas Aquinas, *The Summa Theologica of St. Thomas Aquinas*, translated by Fathers of the English Dominican Province (London: Burns Oates and Washburn, 1920), Question 64, article 7. Aquinas also argues here that a person can't be held morally responsible for choosing to perform an act that she didn't know was likely to have bad consequences.
7. Not all philosophers think that personal self-defense is moral. Augustine (354–430 CE) said it's better to suffer harm than to inflict it. He argued that if you're attacked, you're obligated to turn the other cheek and die, because personal self-defense is immoral. Only if someone attacks your neighbor's cheek are you permitted to retaliate. Using force is justified only if it's a selfless act when you're helping others. One's life is not an end in itself, to be defended righteously for its own sake, but a means to some higher end, to be sacrificed or preserved as is required by our moral duty to serve others. Augustine discusses this idea and the morality of killing in self-defense in his dialogue *On Free Choice of the Will*, translated by Thomas Williams (Indianapolis: Hackett, 1993), 6–9.

8. Card, *Ender's Game*, 7.
9. Thomas Aquinas, *Summa Theologica*, Question 64, article 7.
10. Ibid., Question 18, article 4.
11. Card, *Ender's Game*, 194.
12. Ibid., 208.
13. Ibid., 211.
14. Ibid., 213.
15. Ibid., 202.
16. Ibid.
17. See Harry Frankfurt, "Freedom of the Will and The Concept of a Person," *Journal of Philosophy*, January 1971: 5–20.
18. Card, *Ender's Game*, 238.
19. G.E.M. Anscombe, "War and Murder," in *The Collected Philosophical Papers of G.E.M. Anscombe*, Volume 3 (Oxford: Blackwell, 1981), 58.
20. This is a problem for the Doctrine of Double Effect according to Anscombe. However, she doesn't think it's a reason to reject the distinction between intended and foreseen consequences.
21. Card, *Ender's Game*, 19.
22. An alternative charitable way of interpreting what Card might be saying is this: While in the midst of fighting Stilson and Bonzo he desires or intends harm, this is not a stable desire or intention. In other words, the desire or intent to harm is not an enduring part of Ender's psychology or character. The result would be that good people (people who routinely act on good desires and intentions) may do bad things (act on a bad desire or intention in a specific but isolated situation), but we wouldn't assign blame to them for doing something we believe is uncharacteristic of them. If this is really Card's view he could condemn Ender's actions on both cases, but say either (a) Ender should not be held morally responsible or (b) this act should not affect our moral evaluation of Ender as a person.
23. Card, *Ender's Game*, 297.
24. Card mentioned this in a response to a question posed by Matt Kauffman at "The Hatrack River"—the official site of Orson Scott Card, http://www.hatrack.com/research/questions/q0114.shtml, March 28, 2003, accessed February 4, 2013.
25. Card, *Ender's Game*, 35.
26. For more about Ender's responsibility to not simply let things happen to him, see Greg Littmann's chapter in this volume.
27. This is a quote taken from an interview with Card where he was discussing how the terrible things that happen in war are the burden that soldiers bear. The full interview can be found on the audiobook version of Card's *Shadows in Flight*, Macmillan Audio, January 17, 2012.
28. Card, *Ender's Game*, 238.

CHAPTER 13

Ender's Beginning and the Just War

James L. Cook[1]

Andrew "Ender" Wiggin spends most of *Ender's Game* in one of three schools—first, a run-of-the-mill elementary school on Earth, then Battle School on a space station, and finally the International Fleet's Command School in a hollowed-out asteroid. Given the portion of his life spent at military schools, it's striking that Ender and his peers apparently never study *military ethics*. This would be less surprising if there weren't any traditional principles and canonical texts on the subject. But in fact there are. More to the point, the ethical lessons Ender and his peers might have learned are so *obviously* relevant to operations against the buggers that you can't help but ask how the I.F.'s leadership could have failed to teach military ethics at all, unless they did so intentionally (which itself is morally dubious). Let's look closely at some highlights of Western thinking on the ethics of war and analyze Ender's education and actions in light of those moral traditions.

"The More You Obey, the More Power They Have Over You"

In talking about the ethics of war in the West, there's a just war *tradition* and then there's just war *theory*. Both are commonly abbreviated JWT. Over time the just war tradition has staked out a

Ender's Game and Philosophy: The Logic Gate Is Down, First Edition. Edited by Kevin S. Decker.
© 2013 John Wiley & Sons, Inc. Published 2013 by John Wiley & Sons, Inc.

middle ground between the idea that employing force is always immoral (or *pacifism*) and the idea that a nation can go to war (and do what it likes in war) whenever it's convenient (or *realism*). Just war *theory* looks at how the interlocking ethical principles we've inherited about conflict can be applied and refined.

The first thing Ender might have learned about JWT is that it contains two sets of principles that retain their old Latin names. One set, the *jus ad bellum*, prescribes the way to go to war justly; the other set, the *jus in bello*, advocates how to fight justly once we're at war. In addition, Ender and his peers might have studied two relatively new fields: one of these, *jus post bellum*, deals with postwar ethics, or how victors should establish a just peace.[2] As things turn out, the I.F. has little use for these sorts of principles because the buggers have apparently been wiped out; only in the last few pages does Ender discover there might be a way to revive the buggers as a species. In sequels to *Ender's Game*, though, Ender is very intent on restoring bugger civilization, in effect following *post bellum* principles.[3] Another new field, the *jus ante bellum*, emphasizes the need to teach the JWT to policy makers and military members, especially officers charged with walking the moral tightrope between obedience and moral autonomy.[4] For the officer, there are no "moral holidays" in war, no chance to take the Nuremberg Trials defense and plead "I was just following orders." The military leader must perceive and evaluate moral alternatives, then choose rightly no matter the pressures. For that reason the I.F. had a serious obligation to teach students like Ender the *ad bellum* and *in bello* principles, and to discuss the difficult moral problems that a military officer might confront in wartime. In thinking about what Ender and his fellow trainees might have learned and how it would have been relevant to the events of the novel, we'll look at these first two categories of just war principles.

"I Don't Have Murder in My Heart"

Seven principles have emerged as especially important in the ethics of *going* to war.

The first is *just cause*, the classic case of which is defense of the homeland or the righting of a past wrong. Ender's generation finds the case for war against the buggers to be unquestionably just. Such a war seems purely defensive: after all, it's an effort to preserve humanity and its way of life. Even though the buggers had not actually attacked Earth during Ender's lifetime they *had* launched two invasions of human space before and they *could* attack again in even greater force.

With its background of preventive defense, the military action in *Ender's Game* anticipated a vigorous debate in military ethics sparked by the March 2003 invasion of Iraq. When a US-led coalition of nations demanded Saddam Hussein relinquish power, then attacked Iraq after Saddam's refusal, a number of rationales were offered. The electrifying *casus belli*, or reason for going to war, was that Saddam might have weapons of mass destruction—nuclear, chemical, and biological—and might employ them against the United States and other nations or provide the weapons to terrorists. Yet there was almost no believable proof that such an attack was to be expected. An imminent attack gives a good reason for what some call *preemptive* war—war initiated to knock the wind out of an enemy who clearly is about to attack.

Card was forward-looking enough in the late 1970s to point out what many in the United States wouldn't realize until a generation later—that acting ethically according to *ad bellum* principles depends in large part on what we *do* know and on what we *can* know, on the difference between preemption and prevention. Truly preemptive wars have always been seen as essentially defensive and so morally permissible, because one side *knew* the enemy would attack if they didn't act first. Preventive wars, on the other hand, depend on a willingness to roll the moral dice, since we can't be sure if or when the potential enemy will attack.

Prevention is ethically more troubling than preemption. Longtime allies and fellow NATO members such as France[5] and Germany followed the United States to war in Afghanistan after 9/11/2001, yet refused to join military operations against Saddam's Iraq less than two years later. Why? Because they weren't convinced that circumstances warranted preemption of imminent Iraqi aggression and they were unwilling to engage in prevention. And they didn't buy the US administration's new "theory" of prevention as found in the United States' 2002 *National Security Strategy*, Section 1, among other places.[6]

The International Fleet's war on the buggers provides an interesting case study in the difference between preemption and prevention. As *Ender's Game* opens, the buggers remain a chronic threat. But the attack Ender will lead turns out to be at best preventive and at worst, totally unnecessary. Ender's gambit is fought many light years away from human civilization, and the Formics seem to have attacked in the first place only because they didn't realize that humans were a sentient species. But Ender doesn't know he's training for anything other than a defensive war to repel the Third Invasion (at least the other possibilities don't dawn on him until the end of the novel, by which time it's too late). Beyond the divergence between preemption and prevention, there's been a vigorous debate over the "moral equality of combatants." Can soldiers, at least those at relatively low ranks, ever *know enough* to be judged as moral agents as part of a war effort?[7] That is, can Ender or his peers be expected to *know* that the buggers might actually pose no threat, or to *know* that there might be a way to communicate with them and so avoid war? Is he morally culpable for fighting a war—and committing xenocide—that might have been unnecessary to humanity's survival?

Even those fighting for a just cause can have the wrong intention, like carrying the fighting beyond self-defense to enlarge their territory or seek revenge unjustly. Card emphasizes the role of right intention, the second *ad bellum* principle, when Ender questions his own intentions in two one-on-one fights with bullies. Of course Ender wants to survive each confrontation, but he wants something more as well—to win so decisively that he won't have to fight the bullies and their gangs in the future. In both cases, his intention was to win decisively rather than to end their lives, even though he does kill them. Or was that his intention, really?

Could it be that he's as vicious as his brother Peter, ready to kill gratuitously as well as in self-defense? This echoes a debate between two thinkers in the just war tradition. St. Augustine of Hippo (354–430 CE) allowed that Christians could fight and kill for the Roman Empire, the official religion of which had become Christianity under Constantine. But to kill for *individual* self-defense would be a sin. By contrast, St. Thomas Aquinas (1225–1274 CE) believed that killing a person in self-defense was morally permissible so long as killing is the *only* way for the victim to survive.[8] Of course, killing to preserve Christians and Christianity is also allowable, according to St. Thomas. The disagreement between Augustine and Thomas emphasizes the difficulty in applying principles such as just cause and right intention. What causes may we do violence for? Can I kill to preserve my life or that of others, or must deadly force serve some higher purpose if it is to be moral?

The Moral Equivalent of War

The need for proper authority is the third *jus ad bellum* regulation. This means that only a nation's legitimate leaders may start a war. The nations of Earth in Ender's future time are at peace largely because the world's leaders have decided that defensive war against the buggers trumps all other considerations. The presence of a common enemy has forced humanity to sideline less urgent matters, at least as long as the threat remains.

But the authorities are also keeping a secret. A human invasion of the bugger worlds is underway; there is no bugger force en route to Earth, or at least not so far as anyone knows. Does the fact that citizens are ignorant of the real situation undermine their political and military leaders' justification to undertake a war?

By implicitly raising this question Card once again seems to have had foreknowledge. In 1999, a NATO-based coalition undertook an air war over Kosovo without approval of the UN Security Council. As the Kosovo Commission paradoxically observed, the air war was "illegal but legitimate." The invasion of Iraq in 2003 proved more problematic. Once again the UN Security Council had not endorsed the invasion. But unlike the case of Kosovo—and very like the final war against the buggers in *Ender's Game*—many politicians, journalists, scholars, and citizens questioned whether the US administration had lied about the alleged threat that Iraq posed.

Would the United States or Ender's Earth have launched an invasion if people had known the real state of affairs? Presumably not. It was hard enough for the United States to scrape together a "coalition of the willing" even when many around the world were convinced that Iraq had weapons of mass destruction. The Warsaw Pact of Ender's generation might well have dissolved its alliances without a bugger threat, leaving Earth with too few resources to launch an invasion. Whether in Ender's world or our own, we might reasonably interpret the *ad bellum* principle to imply that proper authority remains proper only if it doesn't deceive those it represents. But that's merely one possible interpretation. Card urges reflection on this important principle of the JWT by asking who may legitimately start military action and how much they have to tell their fellow citizens.

Under the *jus ad bellum*, peace is the only just goal for a war. But Ender's handlers rarely discuss the aftermath of the coming war: what will the buggers' world look like after war? No one knows. How about the state of a postwar Earth, assuming the humans are victorious? An interesting twist that applies here is in the difference Thomas Aquinas finds between mere peace and "concord."[9] Thomas emphasizes that the proper goal of a just war can't simply be putting an end to hostilities. Action may have stopped between opposing sides only to see the victors do unspeakable acts, like slaughtering or enslaving the vanquished population. This means that the just combatant must seek something far more robust than a mere end to hostilities. The peace achieved must be at least as good as the *status quo* before the beginning of war, and the just combatant should actually strive for something much better. But how could Earth achieve a better peace following a xenocide?

A fifth principle is that of *last resort*: a nation must never go to war when non-violent means might achieve the same objective. The last resort rule normally requires that extensive diplomatic interactions have failed before war is declared. Tragically, the humans of Card's novel can't communicate verbally with the buggers. So how would they apply the principle of last resort?[10] The I.F. presumes there is *nothing* they can do but go to war even if the buggers are not attacking. Yet it seems as though the hive queen *is* attempting to communicate with Ender, even if he doesn't realize it throughout a significant portion of the novel. In this odd situation the reader might find an allegorical representation of real-life human affairs. How often have peoples gone to war because they failed to understand that the other side didn't perceive, let alone understand their attempt to communicate?

This is particularly tragic because so much rides on taking this principle seriously, including Ender's peace of mind. Near the end of the novel, Ender faces a horrible possibility: what if the buggers had never intended to attack humans again? Or worse: what if the buggers were a wholly peaceful race who wouldn't have attacked at all if they'd understood that humans were intelligent? Perhaps the buggers actually respected the rule made famous by the Prussian philosopher Immanuel Kant (1724–1804): "Act in such a way that you treat humanity, whether in your own person or in the person of another, always at the same time as an end and never simply as a means." Kant had a wide enough view of the dignity of persons to cover not just humans but all rational beings. "Rational nature exists as an end in itself," he claimed.[11]

A Waste of Brief Mortality

In part because war can have such a negative impact on the dignity of people, another principle claims that, before going to war, we must reckon the probable goods and harms that are likely to result. This is the *ad bellum* principle of "proportionality of ends." If the balance of harm is greater than the good likely to be produced, the war would be immoral and shouldn't be undertaken. Throughout much of *Ender's Game* this principle seems easy to respect, because if the buggers pose a threat to the existence of all humanity, then to fight them is simply to survive. Laying down arms is to cease to exist. But as the novel comes to a close, with Ender we have to question the proportionality of the war. Did it accomplish more good than evil? If the buggers were never a threat or were no longer a threat, the answer is clearly "no." And what about the fact that the buggers were not just militarily neutralized but wiped out as a species? Does xenocide count as good or bad? By prompting us to ask these questions, Card raises a general problem in ethics. Should we avoid moral reasoning that is based on predictions of good or bad consequences? Should we stick with rules such as, "Don't ever use indiscriminate weapons such as the Little Doctor (or nuclear bombs) because they make non-combatants targets?"

Thinking about consequences also raises the question of whether *success at war* seems likely; this is the final *ad bellum* principle. The lead character of Shakespeare's *Henry V* eloquently captures the destructiveness of war, its uncertainty and wildness, when he admonishes his advisor:

> Therefore take heed how you impawn our person,
> How you awake our sleeping sword of war:
> We charge you, in the name of God, take heed;
> For never two such kingdoms did contend
> Without much fall of blood; whose guiltless drops
> Are every one a woe, a sore complaint
> 'Gainst him whose wrong gives edge unto the swords
> That make such waste in brief mortality.[12]

Henry knows war against France will be horrible and can only guess whether England would succeed in such a conflict. In fact he must guess twice—first whether more good or bad will be the result (proportionality), and then whether his first guess was probably right (reasonable hope of success). If he feels shaky on the second guess, then perhaps it makes more sense to be subjugated than to fight, lose, and then be subjugated anyway. "Better dead than red"? Not really, says this principle of reasonable hope of success; that is, if your country is going to be destroyed and end up red (metaphorically speaking) anyway.

Ender's Game plays with this principle in an interesting way. At first it appears the buggers can't even recognize human beings as worthy of survival. To them, humans are worthless drones, and killing them is not like destroying sentient life such as a hive queen. In this light it makes no sense to question whether any war against the buggers will likely be successful; humans must either fight or else be totally destroyed. But given what we've already said about the hive queen's efforts to communicate with Ender, perhaps it was the humans who unfairly demonized the buggers and wrongly concluded that it was impossible to communicate with them. In the terms set out in the sequel *Speaker for the Dead*, humans might have treated the buggers as *varelse*, or totally alien, when in fact we should have treated them as *ramen*, or creatures who are very different than us, but who can be reasoned with.[13]

The *ramen/varelse* distinction reflects another ancient aspect of the just war tradition. The Roman senator and orator Cicero (106–43 BC) proudly recalled that generations of Romans long before him had been wary of dehumanizing their real and potential foes. As a result, they had dropped the traditional and pejorative term for enemy, the Latin *perduellis*, and instead had begun to use the term for a stranger, *hostis*.[14] Just as we might suspect a stranger's motives but come to trust her in the end, so too we might maintain or forge peace with potential or current enemies if they are not wholly "other." The key is not to beg the question by adopting the wrong assumptions. Many years later St. Ambrose of Milan (c. 337–397 CE) pointed to the same linguistic shift from *perduellis* to *hostis* as an example of the attitude the Christian combatant should adopt and nurture.

"At Least You Have Some Survival Instinct Left"

Perhaps because it acknowledges that once war is declared all sorts of necessities may be demanded of the warring sides, just war theory has only two principles of how war is to be conducted, or *jus in bello*. Non-combatant immunity (also known as the principle of discrimination) demands that only combatants can be military targets. Non-combatants—civilians and those who can no longer fight, such as prisoners of war and the severely wounded—may never be targeted. This principle clearly shows that destroying the Formics' home planet can be nothing other than the grossest possible violation unless it's been verified in advance that *every* bugger is somehow a combatant. Or so it would seem.

But the situation is even more complex, since the principle of immunity is in constant tension with the other major *in bello* principle, the proportionality of means.

This says we can only use the minimum amount of force necessary to accomplish the objective. It includes a ban on means that are *"mala in se"*—wicked in themselves. Raping POWs to demoralize the enemy would be considered a *malum in se*, for example. What about weapons of mass destruction such as the Little Doctor? Presumably these weapons are not evil in themselves. The worst we can say is that they *could* be used indiscriminately, but they also *could* be employed correctly, as Ender does when his target is exclusively military. His final use of the Little Doctor against the bugger home planet poses an interesting dilemma. If we assume the numerically superior bugger fleet will utterly destroy the human forces unless Ender attacks the home planet with the Little Doctor, and if we also assume that if they're then unopposed, the buggers will destroy humanity, then we have a sort of moral zero-sum game. One race or the other, it seems, will inevitably be destroyed. So is it worse to allow my own race to be wiped out or to wipe out the enemy's race? The Doctrine of Double Effect (DDE) examines whether it's morally acceptable to do something bad that you can *foresee* but don't *intend*.[15] For its own part, *Ender's Game* and its sequels reject the either/or approach. Ender overcomes barriers to communication and starts out on a path toward a rapprochement that can allow the buggers and humanity to coexist—if the Formics as a race can be reestablished.

Given all this, it seems odd that just war theory and the tradition weren't taught to Ender. US service academies present just war principles and puzzles to all their cadets and midshipmen. And the US military's commander-in-chief, President Obama, has studied them

in an "attempt to apply the 'just war' theories of Christian philosophers to a brutal modern conflict" against terrorism.[16] "A student of
writings on war by Augustine and Thomas Aquinas," the *New York
Times* reports, "[Obama] believes that he should take moral responsibility for such actions" as drone strikes on suspected al Qaeda
terrorists in Afghanistan, Pakistan, Yemen, and elsewhere. If Ender
had known more about the *in bello* principle of non-combatant
immunity, for instance, perhaps he would have hesitated before
obliterating the buggers' home planet. It is hard to say what his ultimate decision, even in the context of JWT, might have been. This is
because there are limits to what book learning can determine, and
because the JWT doesn't tell us how to resolve the tensions among
its own principles that inevitably arise. So although Ender and his
peers might have been better off knowing more about military
ethics, that knowledge alone would not have guaranteed a happier
ending for the novel. In fact, the book's dark tone says something
important about the study of military ethics in real life. Card writes
in a way to show us how hard it can be to know the basic facts that
make moral judgments about war possible at all, let alone act
ethically on our knowledge and convictions within a chain of
command. Card implicitly keeps us asking two important and ven-
erable questions: can unnecessary wars be avoided? Can wars and
the ways they're fought ever be moral?

Ender's Game teaches powerful lessons for students of just war
theory and the just war tradition because it asks questions that
matter to everyone, from national decision-makers all the way
down to individual soldiers. Genocide and xenocide are extreme in
their *quantity* of killing, but not necessarily in their moral *magnitude*. For the individual soldier, massacring a number of villages at
My Lai or targeting a single non-combatant out of anger or frustration could be as bad as participating in the destruction of an
entire race. In either case, numerous studies suggest an individual
can be overwhelmed by the evil of the act.[17] St. Augustine insists
that even after fighting justly, the moral soldier must never be jubi-
lant, but instead mourn the dead. "I've lived too long with pain,"
Ender tells his beloved sister Valentine on the penultimate page of
Ender's Game. "I won't know who I am without it." We should
take comfort in the fact of Ender's discomfort. It's proof that he's
at least redeemable.[18]

Notes

1. The views expressed are solely the author's and do not reflect the views of the US Department of Defense.
2. Brian Orend, *The Morality of War* (Peterborough, Ontario: Broadview Press, 2006), 95–111.
3. See especially Card, *Speaker for the Dead* (New York: TOR Books, 1986).
4. Roger Wertheimer, "The Morality of Military Ethics Education," in Roger Wertheimer, ed., *Empowering Our Military Conscience* (Farnham, UK: Ashgate, 2010), 159–195.
5. See http://www.nato.int/cps/en/natolive/topics_52044.htm (accessed September 20, 2012) regarding the status of France's membership in NATO after 1966.
6. The White House, National Security Strategy 2002. http://georgewbush-whitehouse.archives.gov/nsc/nss/2002/, accessed May 30, 2012.
7. The sides of this debate can be examined in: Jeff McMahan, "Collectivist Defenses of the Moral Equality of Combatants," *The Journal of Military Ethics* 6:1 (2007): 50–59; Dan Zupan, "The Logic of Community, Ignorance, and the Presumption of Moral Equality: A Soldier's Story," *The Journal of Military Ethics* 6:1 (2007): 41–49.
8. St. Thomas Aquinas, *Summa Theologiae* II.2. Q. 64.7. http://www.newadvent.org/summa/3064.htm#article7, accessed May 30, 2012.
9. Ibid., II.2. Q. 29.1. http://www.newadvent.org/summa/3064.htm#article7, accessed May 30, 2012.
10. For further meditations on whether humanity really had failed in its attempts to communicate with the Formics or not, see Cole Bowman's chapter in this volume.
11. Immanuel Kant, *Grounding for the Metaphysic of Morals*, 3rd edn, trans. James W. Ellington (Indianapolis: Hackett, 1993), 36.
12. William Shakespeare, *Henry V* act I, scene 2, http://shakespeare.mit.edu/henryv/henryv.1.2.html, accessed September 20, 2012.
13. Card, *Speaker for the Dead*, 34.
14. *De Officiis*, excerpted in Reichberg, Gregory M., Henrik Syse, and Endre Begby, eds., *The Ethics of War: Classic and Contemporary Readings* (Malden, MA: Blackwell, 2006), 52.
15. Lance Belluomini's chapter in this book is a detailed look at the Doctrine of Double Effect.
16. Jo Becker and Scott Shane, "Secret 'Kill List' Proves a Test of Obama's Principles and Will," *The New York Times*, May 29, 2012, http://www.nytimes.com/2012/05/29/world/obamas-leadership-in-war-on-al-qaeda.html?_r=1&src=me&ref=general, accessed May 30, 2012.

17. See Jonathan Shay, *Achilles in Vietnam: Combat Trauma and the Undoing of Character* (New York: Simon and Schuster, 1995), 72–75; Dave Grossman, *On Killing: The Psychological Cost of Learning to Kill in War and Society* (Boston: Back Bay Books, 2009), 219–231; Michael Bilton and Kevin Sim, *Four Hours in My Lai* (New York: Penguin, 1993), 284–314.
18. The author wishes to thank Dr. Kevin Decker, volume editor, for *greatly* improving every aspect of this text.

CHAPTER 14

"You Had to Be a Weapon, Ender ... *We* Aimed You"

Moral Responsibility in *Ender's Game*

Danielle Wylie

At the climax of *Ender's Game*, we see Ender exhausted and at wit's end. He is facing a simulated battle that he thinks could only have been designed to break him, to make him finally fail at the endless tests that the International Fleet has been putting him through. Ender knows that his only option for winning the battle—destroying an entire planet—is an unreasonable strategy that would lead the Fleet to remove him as their potential commander. His decision to pursue that strategy anyway seems to be motivated by his desire for just that result, as he finally feels too exhausted and too abused to care anymore. He believes that the strategy will reveal that he would be "too dangerous," a loose cannon, and so he'll be released from his training.[1] Ender thinks, though, that his commands are only being carried out in a simulation, not in a real battle with real lives (both human and bugger) at stake.

Ender thinks that he is only playing against a simulation. He's not trying to show his superiors what he would do if the simulation were real, so he has no reason to consider the costs of actually attacking the planet. These costs don't enter into his thinking, because he doesn't foresee them as real consequences of his actions. His disgust and guilt after learning the truth support Graff's claim that Ender couldn't have attacked the planet unless he was tricked into doing it. Now ordinarily, we'd say we shouldn't hold someone responsible for

Ender's Game and Philosophy: The Logic Gate Is Down, First Edition. Edited by Kevin S. Decker.
© 2013 John Wiley & Sons, Inc. Published 2013 by John Wiley & Sons, Inc.

their behavior when they've been deceived like this. However, Ender feels guilty, and his reactions in the rest of the book and in its sequels suggest that people *do* hold him responsible. More importantly, Ender holds himself responsible, or at least he feels guilty. This is not such a bad thing as Graff describes the situation: Earth's governments see Ender as a hero to be praised and rewarded with the highest honors.[2] Later, however, humanity *blames* Ender for what he has done, labeling him the "Xenocide" for his destruction of an entire sentient species.

We might feel uneasy with both reactions. The initial praise seems inappropriate, as Ender was tricked into doing something that he would not stand by afterward. For the same reason, blaming Ender for something that he didn't intend to do seems wrong as well. Those who thought that the bugger world ought to have been destroyed could praise Ender for his strategic genius, but not for his decision. On the other hand, those who think he was in the wrong may think that Ender was too uncritical of his training or too engrossed in his desire to win, leading him to miss the signs that something was amiss. But public opinion in the sequels, beginning with *Speaker for the Dead*, is that Ender is to blame for something much worse than simply not paying attention.

We might think that if *anyone* is to be praised or blamed for the attack, it ought to be those who were responsible for carrying out the *trick*, including Graff and Mazer Rackham. Rackham tells Ender, "You had to be a weapon, Ender. Like a gun, like the Little Doctor, functioning perfectly but not knowing what you were aimed at. We aimed you. We're responsible. If there was something wrong, we did it."[3] But neither Graff nor Rackham authorized the use of the Little Doctor against the planet, and Rackham even seems to discourage Ender when he asks about the possibility of using it. Ender's decision caused the destruction of the planet, and it seems Graff and Rackham were careful not to force Ender into making it.

Sorting out the mess of who is actually responsible for what is difficult–we feel conflicted about the whole thing, just as Ender does. In this chapter, Aristotle (384–322 BC) will help us make sense of responsibility and voluntary action as we consider whether a person can be responsible for something that he or she didn't cause. We'll also look at why we should care about whether a fictional character is responsible and consider an alternative notion of responsibility that explains Ender's post-xenocide actions as Speaker for the Dead.

Involuntary Bugger-Slaughter

Being morally responsible means that you're worthy of either praise or blame for your actions.[4] Despite their disagreements, philosophers agree on two conditions for moral responsibility. In order to be responsible for my actions, first, I must have the right sort of *control* over my actions,[5] and second, I have to have the right sort of *knowledge* about what I'm doing. These ideas date back two thousand years to Aristotle's *Nicomachean Ethics*. Aristotle's moral philosophy is focused on the virtues that are required for living a good life. Virtues are states of character, ways of behaving, dispositions to do the right things in the right ways.[6] Virtues go beyond just performing the right actions, they also involve the feelings we have toward those actions. For instance, having the virtue of courage doesn't just mean doing dangerous things. Going into a battle that you have no chance of winning, just because you're feeling very confident, isn't courageous at all; it's rash and stupid.[7] That kind of rashness is a bad motive for entering a battle. The decision to fight in the battle isn't the whole story: motives (and acting voluntarily on them) are also important in Aristotle's thinking. If we're to judge someone like Ender in order to determine whether he's virtuous, we need to know whether he acts voluntarily and whether he's responsible (blameworthy or praiseworthy) for his actions.

Aristotle explains that we should praise and blame people only for their *voluntary* choices. So actions should not be forced or coerced or done out of ignorance.[8] These are commonly called the "control condition" and the "knowledge condition" for being morally responsible. When a person is not in control of his actions, according to Aristotle, he contributes *nothing* to motivating the action, "as if he were to be carried somewhere by a wind."[9] For instance, when Ender and Alai throw a frozen Launchie at the older boys attacking them in the battleroom, the thrown Launchie collides with the boys as if he were a stone, that is, entirely involuntarily. Ender and Alai provide the impetus, and the Launchie does nothing to alter his trajectory. But some acts that *seem* involuntary, like giving up your wallet at gunpoint, are "mixed" cases for Aristotle. For him, these are more like voluntary actions than involuntary actions. After all, held at gunpoint, you *do* have the option to give up your life. In some cases you might be blamed for not doing so (imagine, for instance, a case in which your wallet contains nuclear codes that would allow your attacker to destroy the world). While a person might be found blameworthy or praiseworthy in a mixed case (depending on the circumstances), Aristotle also allows us to pardon people because they only played a partial role in the consequences they brought about.

Then there's the knowledge condition. The ignorance that invalidates the knowledge condition can take a number of forms. You might be ignorant of who you are—in the sense of playing a role—as seems to be the case when Ender is oblivious to the fact that he's the Commander of the I.F. forces fighting the buggers. You might also be ignorant of the potential consequences of your actions, as might be true for Ender when he accidentally kills Stilson when trying to stop his bullying. Aristotle also includes ignorance of *how* we might perform an action, as when we say someone "doesn't know his own strength." During the shuttle flight to the Battle School, a boy continually reaches over Ender's seat to hit him on the head. Ender pulls on the boy's outstretched arm, but he doesn't realize his strength in null gravity or how much force he's applying with that strength. As a result, he breaks the boy's arm. All of these incidents have this in common: Ender is ignorant of some fact that, if he had known it, might have kept him from acting as he did.

How do these two conditions come into play in the climactic confrontation with the buggers? Well, in order to find Ender responsible for destroying the bugger home world, we have to be able to show that he meets both of Aristotle's conditions for voluntary action. In other words, Ender has to have the right sort of *control* and the right sort of *knowledge*. But determining this isn't as easy as it might seem. Although Ender isn't literally acted on by an external force (the control condition), he doesn't have good alternatives to the choice that he makes. This sounds like one of Aristotle's "mixed cases," like giving up the wallet. There are a number of reasons to believe that Ender doesn't have good alternatives to his choice: Ender thinks that he is only playing a simulation and that the I.F. has set up an impossible battle for him to lose. He's exhausted and socially isolated. He's sick of playing the game, and he sees a way out. Ender thinks that the game itself has become unfair, as no fair tactics could allow him to win. His options appeared to be twofold: he can let himself be beaten unfairly, or he can win against the game unfairly by doing what the buggers never did: attacking civilians, destroying a planet, and eliminating an entire species. Ender guesses that taking the latter option will finally free him from the games. He thinks to himself, "If I break this rule, they'll never let me be a commander. It would be too dangerous. I'll never have to play a game again. And that is victory."[10] Under circumstances like these, Ender's choice seems to be forced in the way that coercive choices are forced. There's no good option aside from beating the "simulation" by detonating the Little Doctor.

While there are good reasons to believe that Ender's action is like the mixed cases that Aristotle discusses, we can also make a more convincing argument that Ender didn't act voluntarily using the knowledge condition. Clearly, Ender is ignorant of the fact that he's actually guiding an I.F. force in the Third Invasion. He's confused and then dismayed to hear cheers in the room that are too enthusiastic to be reactions to his winning a mere game. Despite this, Ender still doesn't put the pieces together right away—Mazer Rackham has to explicitly disavow that he was Ender's enemy and that Wiggin was fighting the actual buggers. Even then, Ender thinks that some joke is being played; he can't believe that the tests are over and the war itself has been won.

Why It's Not Okay to Let Rich Kids Drown

Now that we've established what moral responsibility is and some conditions for being responsible, we can contrast moral responsibility with causal responsibility. I am *causally responsible* for an action simply if I caused it. Whether a person is causally responsible for something and whether she is morally responsible for that same thing are separate questions. Accidents are usually cases in which a person causes an action without being morally responsible. So we wouldn't blame someone for a car accident if he was being a careful driver and hit an icy patch, just as we wouldn't blame someone for breaking a chair if she had the misfortune to sit on it when a screw worked itself loose.

Is the reverse possible? Could I be morally responsible for something without being causally responsible? Consider a case developed by James Rachels, in which a character named Smith would gain a large inheritance if only his six-year-old cousin wasn't in the way.[11] Jones is in the same situation. Smith drowns his cousin in the bath and makes it look like an accident, while Jones sees that his cousin is (conveniently) already drowning and does nothing to save him. Smith acts in a way that causes the death of his cousin. Jones, on the other hand, merely lets his cousin die. In the most simple sense of causal responsibility, Smith is causally responsible for his cousin's drowning while Jones is not. However, there seems to be no difference in *moral* responsibility—Jones seems just as blameworthy as Smith. This suggests that we can attribute moral responsibility without causal responsibility, or that someone can be responsible for failing to act.

Responsibility for *failing* to act in the right way might not seem to fit well with Aristotle's conditions, particularly the control condition. But this is only true at first glance. Remember that Aristotle thinks that being out of control requires being moved entirely by external forces, as if pushed by the wind. This might be applied to omissions in two different ways. On the one hand, the control condition might dictate that Jones truly *isn't* responsible for the drowning of his cousin, as Jones didn't initiate the events that led to it. On the other hand, we could say that Jones is responsible for his cousin's drowning because (in addition to meeting the knowledge condition), external forces didn't *stop* him from intervening. If he had decided to save his cousin, he could have done so, and so he had control over his actions. Including omissions within our understanding of the control condition seems to better explain our intuitions in situations like the Smith and Jones cases.

"You Tricked Me Into It"

If we're responsible for omissions in at least some cases, then this can help us think clearly about the role that Graff and Rackham play in the Third Invasion. Graff and Rackham are causally responsible for a number of things, most important of which was lying to Ender that he's playing a simulation or playing against Rackham and putting him in command of a real fleet. Now, they might defend themselves against these charges since Ender had been placed in charge before and he led brilliantly, and he was explicitly told not to use the Little Doctor. When Ender asks about using the weapon against an entire planet, Rackham's face goes rigid and he responds, "Ender, the buggers never deliberately attacked a civilian population in either invasion. You decide whether it would be wise to adopt a strategy that would invite reprisals."[12] This warning, weak as it is, certainly implies that Ender ought to not deliberately attack the bugger homeworld. Graff and Rackham could point to both the control and knowledge conditions to reject responsibility, claiming that they didn't have control over Ender's attack, or that they didn't know what Ender was going to do. However, evidence from the text shows that not only did the men have the ability to stop the xenocidal strategy, but that they knew it was going to happen.

When the control condition is understood to include voluntary omissions, we can see how Graff and Rackham might also be responsible. If someone might be responsible for failing to act, unless stopped by outside forces, then clearly no such forces stopped Graff and Rackham from *preventing* the attack. As long as they knew what Ender was doing and had at least a short time before he detonated the Little Doctor, they could have removed him bodily from his computer and reversed the command. So the control condition is met. If the knowledge condition is also fulfilled, that is, if Graff and Rackham could have reasonably foreseen Ender's action just as Jones could have foreseen the death of his cousin, then they meet both conditions, and they bear responsibility for their actions.

In fact, there's an overabundance of evidence that both Rackham and Graff knew what Ender was doing before he detonated the Little Doctor. If we only consider the events of the final battle, Ender clearly thinks that Rackham knows the strategy while Ender is still in the early stages of formulating it. Ender thinks, "The enemy sees now ... Surely Mazer sees what I'm doing. Or perhaps Mazer cannot believe that I would do it. Well, so much the better for me."[13] Unless Ender's wrong about Rackham's ability to perceive military strategies, it seems Rackham knew in time to stop the attack. Given that the Second Invasion showed that Rackham seems to be a genius at understanding his enemies, it seems unlikely that Ender's wrong here.

In fact, if we look farther back, Graff and Rackham already knew that they needed Ender to use the Little Doctor against the planet. The I.F. should have known that their fleet was much too small to take on the bugger fleet in the traditional fashion. After all, Rackham won the Second Invasion because he went for the core of the bugger fleet that invaded Earth, destroying the queen while the rest of the buggers fell with her. Knowing that such a feat was possible, and by betting on the buggers to keep the majority of their queens on their homeworld, the International Fleet could send out their force, outnumbered "a thousand to one" by Ender's estimate, and still have some hope of victory.

The I.F. also had good reason to think that Ender would make the decision to destroy the bugger homeworld. Both Graff and Rackham had already seen Ender in situations analogous to the Third Invasion scenario both in and out of the battleroom. Each time, Ender reacts in ways that clue us into the likelihood that he would make the decision to destroy the planet. In battles, he's willing to do things to win that might seem dishonorable. In the battle against Griffin and Tiger Armies, his soldiers, outnumbered and unable to inflict damage on the enemy, bypass their armies and trigger their gate. Not only is Ender willing to do something that is not in the spirit of the game, but he also shows that he already has the strategy of "get past the enemy and attack their base" in his repertoire.

Out of the battleroom, Graff and the other I.F. officers see that Ender is capable of using great force to end a conflict before his enemy can retaliate. When Ender's only six years old, he responds to Stilson's bullying so violently that Stilson doesn't survive. While his death wasn't Ender's intention, Ender clearly *was* intending to use excessive force. He thinks, "I have to win this now, and for all time, or I'll fight it every day and it will get worse and worse."[14] He intentionally breaks the "unspoken rules of manly warfare" in this scene in the name of preventing further attacks. This pattern's repeated with Bonzo: as with Stilson, Ender strikes hard, and Bonzo does not survive. Regardless of whether we think that Ender was justified in these attacks, they give Graff and Rackham good evidence that Ender is capable of using overwhelming force to prevent retaliation, which is exactly what they need to do to win the Third Invasion.

Despite knowing how Ender will act when he feels threatened, Graff and Rackham still trick Ender into acting rather than honestly presenting the real threat from the buggers. After all, when confronted by the bullies, the potential harm to Ender was up-close and personal, and in retaliating, only one opponent would be harmed (and not intentionally destroyed) as a result. As far as Graff and Rackham knew, Ender's motivation and strategy might not extend to the destruction of an entire species. Ender is not often in scenarios where he knows that his actions will cause real damage: most of his fights are merely games using computer programs or flash suits. In these game scenarios, Ender is willing to do whatever it takes to win. He "kills" the giant in the game on his desk. He's willing to disable himself by freezing his flash-suit legs. As long as Ender thinks of the battle as a game where no one actually gets hurt, he enacts strategies that allow him to win. In the end, Rackham and Graff have good reasons to think that if they make Ender think that the battle is a game, he'll attack the planet, and they do not stop him from doing this. They meet the knowledge condition long before they enter the final battle, and they meet the control condition by failing to step in at a point before the planet is attacked and annihilated.

"The Real Education Was the Game"

As readers who are particularly fond of humans and Earth, we might think that Graff and Rackham are praiseworthy for their actions, and that Ender would have been praiseworthy for choosing to do what he did if he knew the stakes. Or, like the humans in the sequels to *Ender's Game*, we might think that one or more of the characters is blameworthy for the monstrous crime of xenocide. However, the issues we've raised suggest that matters are more complicated than they might seem at first, and assigning responsibility is a tricky business. We might wonder, though, why we should even bother caring about who's responsible for an event that's entirely fictional, one that seems totally outlandish given that we've never encountered aliens or built a spaceship that can be used in combat or carry humans into deep space.

Some of the reasons why we might care about Ender and whether he's responsible are the same reasons that philosophers use seemingly outlandish "thought experiments," or hypothetical case studies. James Rachels' drowning case discussed earlier is fairly realistic, but philosophers have been known to discuss teletransportation,[15] or scientists who spend their entire lives locked in rooms where they can't see colors,[16] or (my favorite) seeds that float in through the window and take root in couches until they grow into people.[17] One reason we might care about these cases is that, to be consistent, our beliefs about ethics should extend to any possible case that could arise; they shouldn't just be "retro-fitted" to cases that have already occurred. Another reason is that we have stronger feelings about whether our beliefs are true once we see they how they work in different cases. Philosophers are often surprised to find that a widely accepted principle is turned on its head when a thought experiment leads us to think about its implications. We might initially think that killing someone is worse than letting someone die, until we vividly imagine Smith and Jones with their nephews and we see that there aren't any important differences between the two cases. *Ender's Game* should lead us to re-examine our moral thinking, too; as we've seen, it's necessary to re-evaluate the commonly held belief that you have to directly cause some event in order to be morally responsible for it.

And sometimes the cases have to be outlandish to contain the features we need, to eliminate unnecessary complications, and to keep us from being swayed by judgments we've already made about more ordinary cases.[18] Looking closely at a situation that occurs in a work of fiction affords us distance *and* more intimacy, benefits that we rarely have in evaluating real cases. We gain some *distance* when we don't have to deal with the "messy" facts of real life. We don't personally have a stake in Ender's life or how his actions will affect politics on his version of Earth, facts that could lead to distortions of our evaluations of the case. At the same time, we gain an *intimate* look at the motives behind Ender's actions. We get this through the omniscient narrator, something we never have when evaluating the motives of others in non-fictional settings. We have more time to learn about the case throughout the course of the novel than we do when we read or hear about a case on the news. This lengthy exposure gives us a chance to be won over by characters. By contrast, we might be biased against real people or find that we don't understand them sufficiently. All of these factors taken together enable us to really imagine the case and all of the relevant factors for determining responsibility, which in turn makes us more sensitive to these factors when they do come up in real life.

"I'll Tell Your Story to My People, So That Perhaps in Time They Can Forgive You ..."

One final note: sometimes, we mean something entirely different than what this chapter has emphasized when we use the term "responsibility." Sometimes, even when we think that we're not to blame for something, we "take responsibility" and make sure that things are set to rights (or as close as we can get to fixing the situation, anyway). For instance, you might trip, entirely by accident, bump into a stranger and spill his coffee. In such a case, you might take responsibility for the situation, even though no one would think that you're blame-worthy. In this case, taking responsibility doesn't mean taking the *blame*, but rather doing something to help the situation, like buying the stranger a new cup of coffee. Ender seems to appreciate this notion, as we see in his work as the Speaker for the Dead. Even though he's not to blame for the destruction of the buggers, he does what he can to try to make things right. This is best illustrated in Ender's explanation of his decision to visit the bugger colony: "I know the buggers better than any other living soul, and maybe if I go there I can understand them better. I stole their future from them; I can only begin to repay by seeing what I can learn from their past."[19]

Notes

1. Orson Scott Card, *Ender's Game* (New York: TOR Books, 1991), 293.
2. You might get the feeling, however, that Ender is starting to be blamed almost immediately after the attack. A particularly revealing moment comes when Ender is on Eros, when we see that people have started to refer to what he's done as "his murders," when murder is commonly understood to be a term not just for killing, but rather for an *unjust* or *blameworthy* killing. At the time, those people still explicitly excuse him because he is just a child, but we can see how this tendency to excuse might be forgotten and fade away over time. There are interesting issues to consider regarding whether Ender's status as a child does excuse him from responsibility, but we will leave those issues aside here.
3. Card, *Ender's Game*, 298.
4. Another important notion of responsibility is *legal* responsibility, which is sometimes confused for moral responsibility. Legal responsibility depends entirely upon the nature of a given legal system; one is legally responsible now for driving on the wrong side of the road, which was not part of the law in eras without cars. We will not consider Ender or anyone else's legal responsibility, if only because we do not know enough about the legal system in Ender's world to determine what that system would dictate about the status of minors, the powers of the International Fleet, and so on.

5. Can we have responsibility if we are determined by our psychology or biology to do what we do? This problem of free will is an interesting one, but it isn't any more troublesome in *Ender's Game* than in any other case, so let's set it aside.

6. Aristotle, *The Nicomachean Ethics* (New York: Oxford University Press, 2009), 29.

7. Ibid., 49–51.

8. Ibid., 38–40.

9. Ibid., 39.

10. Card, *Ender's Game*, 293.

11. James Rachels, "Active and Passive Euthanasia," *The New England Journal of Medicine*, Vol. 292 (1975): 78–80.

12. Card, *Ender's Game*, 290.

13. Ibid., 294.

14. Ibid., 7.

15. Derek Parfit, *Reasons and Persons* (New York: Oxford University Press, 1986).

16. Frank Jackson, "Epiphenomenal Qualia," *The Philosophical Quarterly*, 32 (1982): 127–136.

17. Judith Jarvis Thomson, "A Defense of Abortion," *Philosophy & Public Affairs*, Vol. 1 (1971): 47–66.

18. This is one of the advantages of Thomson's "people seeds" case and the others in her article. The oddness of these cases allows us to separate them from our pre-formed judgments about abortion in order to give Thomson's case a fair trial.

19. Card, *Ender's Game*, 314.

CHAPTER 15

The Unspoken Rules of Manly Warfare

Just War Theory in *Ender's Game*

Kody W. Cooper

Ender knew the unspoken rules of manly warfare, even though he was only six. It was forbidden to strike the opponent who lay helpless on the ground; only an animal would do that.[1]

When Ender Wiggin is faced with an immediate threat to his life and bodily integrity at the hands of Stilson and his gang, he reasons, "I have to win this now, and for all time, or I'll fight it every day and it will get worse and worse."[2] As the I.F. authorities permit private threats and acts of violence against his person, Ender reasons the same way during his Battle School training. Each time he acts in self-defense, Ender feels deep remorse for harming another person, and fears he is becoming like his ruthless brother Peter. Ender also recognizes when the games he is forced to play are set up on dishonorable terms. At these times, Ender decides it's justified to cheat—and his act of "cheating" in the final "game" amounts to an act of xenocide that will haunt him forever.

Ender's tortured conscience is an illustration of the moral importance of following principles of just war theory—the "unspoken rules of manly warfare"—and their apparent tension with the demands of war and survival. This chapter is about the ethics of conflict in Ender's various games—his *battles* and *wars*. It asks, was justice served in the Third Invasion and destruction of the bugger worlds, the event that came to be called the xenocide?

Ender's Game and Philosophy: The Logic Gate Is Down, First Edition. Edited by Kevin S. Decker.
© 2013 John Wiley & Sons, Inc. Published 2013 by John Wiley & Sons, Inc.

Peace Is the End of War

Someone who thinks he loves war is always wrong, because war destroys everything it touches.[3]

Ender hates war. As Ender's lieutenant and closest friend Bean puts it, Ender "hates it so much that he'll do anything to win and put an end to it."[4] Why is war itself so hateful? Because it's the kind of thing that destroys all that it touches. As the Civil War general William Tecumseh Sherman famously put it, *war is hell*. Its flames rend families, friendships, and cities; its fires raze the landscape and everything we hold dear to the ground.

So why isn't Ender a pacifist then? Ender's life is actually a testimony to the just war axiom that all people desire peace. In just war thinking, peace is a harmony or order *within a person* and *between persons*. In the terms set out by classical thinkers from Aristotle (384–322 BC) to St. Augustine (354–430 AD), *internal* peace consists in governing our passions by reason, while peace *between* persons requires a just political or social order as demanded by reason. Ender always sought peace, from his childhood command to his adolescent position governing the colony of Shakespeare, from his itinerant speaking for the dead to his marriage on Lusitania. Even when Ender made war on his enemies, this was *as a means* to the end of peace. Ender's life seems to give witness to the truth of an axiom of St. Augustine's: all men wish to have peace. From this axiom, Augustine derived a key principle of just war theory: peace is the end sought for by war.[5]

This thought is never far from the minds of even those people who delight in belligerence, like Ender's bullies. Their belligerent souls desire victory, and victory establishes peace. In truth, the "hawkish" person in a state of peace wants to establish a peace that is *more advantageous* to him. Stilson, Bernard, and Bonzo all sought to establish a "peace" that would honor them, while Ender was shamed.

Ender's life is a quest for a just peace. Before and after the war, Ender sought both inner peace and peaceful order in the lives of the individuals and communities he touched. He also learned from an early age that everyone has the potential to do horrible things and rupture peace. Peter, Bonzo, and others who bully Ender are so many case studies of the human tendency to act according to passion that's not governed by reason, that is, to do evil.[6] Since evil acts always rupture inner and social harmony, and since there are always persons willing to commit evil acts for their own advantage, it follows that the establishment and maintenance of a just peace requires measures to stop evil persons. Ender's not a pacifist … but *not* because he doesn't seek peace. Rather, it is because he believes war is one among several reasonable measures that people can use to protect the peace. But when is going to war justified? There are several rules that we can use to tell if going to war is a reasonable course of action or not.

The Rules of the Game

Ender didn't like games where the rules could be anything.[7]

In the tradition of just war theory, there are five principles that lay out the requirements of *jus ad bellum*, or how to go to war in an ethical way. They include just cause, legitimate authority, right intention, probability of success, and last resort. Once these conditions are met, there are two principles that guide soldiers and strategists in war, or *jus in bello*: discrimination and proportionality. The just war theorist can apply these principles to assess the justice or injustice of the acts of individuals and communities in conflicts.

Let's look at the five requirements for going-to-war.[8] First, there's *just cause*. If peace is always the end of war, then the goal of just wars is to end unjust disturbances or repel threats to peace. The unjust acts that just wars oppose are "without right" because they threaten or destroy the rights of others, and so attacking a foe can only be justified if the enemy is first at fault. The kinds of injustice that war addresses include defense against active aggression or conquest, and Ender's battles tend to target this sort of injustice.

Just cause has to be accompanied by *legitimate authority*. An authority is a person or group of persons who have charge of the common good or the peace of a community. The Formic Wars provide good illustrations of the principles of just cause and legitimate authority. Humanity was initially the victim of the unjust aggression of the buggers. Since the most basic right of individuals and communities is the right to life, the peoples of Earth were justified in defending themselves with military force from subjugation or annihilation at the pincers of the buggers. After beating back the invaders' attempted

colonization of Earth in the Scathing of China, the world united under
the Hegemony and International Fleet. The peoples of earth *authorized* these groups to defend earth from alien aggression. They became
the legitimate military authority for the duration of the Bugger Wars,
including the Second and Third invasions.

Right intention is the third requirement for going-to-war to be just.
In having the right intention, we seek to secure or advance the good
of peace and to avoid evil. Here's where the just war requirements can
begin to become complicated: it's possible that a legitimate authority
could have just cause to go to war, but still have wicked intentions.
Bad intentions are incompatible with advancing goodness and peace.
The intentions of the Hegemony and the I.F. would be wicked if they
intended, say, to enslave and subjugate the Formics. Such an intention
would be framed by lust for power and domination rather than
establishing a just peace. We'll return to the idea of right intention in
considering the justice of the Third Invasion below.

A *reasonable probability of success* is required for a just declara-
tion of war. It would be unjust for a government to throw its citizens,
willy-nilly, into an unwinnable war, just as it would be unjust to send
citizens to war under incompetent commanders. A reasonable probability of success requires *excellent commanders*. Clearly, the I.F.'s
recruitment of Ender to command the Third Invasion fleet is an
attempt to increase the probability of success.

Colonel Graff thought Ender would greatly increase humanity's
chances because Ender's temperament and genius are key factors in
what makes for excellent commanders. The great philosopher of war
Sunzi (c. 6th century BC) pointed out that being skilled at making war
requires the commander to know his or her enemy.[9] To know your
enemy, you have to look at the world through his eyes, to understand
his wants, desires, and needs. Ender came to understand that, in order
to do this, you must *love* your enemy. Ender was both loving enough
to know his enemies and ruthless enough to defeat them. Ender was
"half Peter and half Valentine": empathy and ruthlessness attained a
delicate balance in his soul.[10] His empathy and compassion garnered
the trust and devotion of his lieutenants and allowed him to think like
his enemies and anticipate their actions. His ruthlessness drove him to
defeat his opponents in ways they couldn't recover from.

In the Second Invasion, which took place 80 years before Ender was
born, the probability of success was low. The human fleet was vastly

outnumbered, outgunned, and technologically inferior. But, because of
the genius shown by Mazer Rackham at the Battle of Saturn, the
Formics were defeated again. Faced with such overwhelming odds, just
war thinking would have recommended a diplomatic course of action
to establish peace and avoid a second bugger invasion. The trouble was
that human beings couldn't find a way to communicate with the
Formics. The prospect of human space being stormed by a bellicose and
intelligent, but uncommunicative, species led the I.F. to the conclusion
that war was effectively the *last resort*—the final requirement for the
justice of going-to-war. When communication seems impossible, even a
low probability of success does not forestall military action, because
war is the last resort in the face of annihilation.

Was the Third Invasion a war of last resort? Ender's sister Valentine,
writing under the pen name Demosthenes, gave the label *varelse* to
aggressive, intelligent species with whom we can't communicate. Just war
ethics confirms Valentine's reasoning that defensive war against *varelse* is
justified. Of course, it turned out that the hive-queen was in the process
of establishing philotic, mind-to-mind communication with Ender.
Communication with the Formics wasn't impossible after all. This doesn't
mean that humanity didn't have initial just cause, though. The Formic
hive-queens didn't consider *their own* responsibility to make war as a last
resort since they failed to exhaust all paths for communicating *before*
attacking the natives of Earth, whom they thought to be mere dumb animals. The hive-queens clearly bore the initial fault. However, it's an open
question whether humanity made sufficient effort to establish communi-
cations before or during the Third Invasion. Was the preemptive strike
force (which Ender would unknowingly command) a truly last resort?
Ender's command increased the probability of success of the invasion.
Did it meet the other requirements of going-to-war: just cause, legitimate
authority, and right intention? Let's postpone answers to these questions
until we can assess the justice of the Third Invasion with the full armory
of just war theory, including the principles of justice-in-war.

Playing by the Rules

*Life is precious. Sentient life is more precious. But when one
sentient group threatens the survival of another, then the threatened group has the right to protect themselves.*[11]

After the requirements of going-to-war have been satisfied, there are two principles of *jus in bello* that govern how the war must be waged. These are *discrimination* and *proportionality*. In the light of this part of just war theory, the adage, "all's fair in love and war" is false. Why is that?

The reason can be found in a basic axiom of just war theory: sentient life is precious. Sentient creatures, beings capable of perception and consciousness, are very different from bugs. In the tradition of just war theory, all beings with reason and will—all persons—are possessed of an intrinsic dignity and due respect. In this respect, just war theory draws on the moral perspective of natural law theory, which holds that all persons have the natural powers of reason and will in order to know and love truth, beauty, and goodness. Since non-rational beings don't have these powers, these goals are not available to them. But, since all persons *can* reach for these transcendent goals, they can't be made into mere tools for the use of other persons.

Given their powers of reason and free will, persons are capable of acting well or poorly, uprightly or wrongly. They're susceptible to being *praised, blamed*, and *found innocent*. With these ideas in mind, it makes sense that the first requirement of justice-in-war would be discrimination between *guilty* combatants and *innocent* non-combatants.

There are notable examples from both our own history and Ender's fictional universe of the failure of discrimination. The first is World War II, when the United States dropped two nuclear bombs on Japan. The second occurred in Ender's near-future world: a nuclear weapon was dropped on Mecca during the "Islamic civil wars." Use of wide-scale weapons like these is an example of *injustice*-in-war, since the bombs indiscriminately kill innocent non-combatants—*and that was the point of dropping them*. Intentionally targeting and destroying innocent lives is always an offense to human dignity—it's always unjust. It can't even be justified by saying that the intention behind these efforts was peace, because intentionally targeting innocents is wrong in itself.[12]

The principle of discrimination can be coupled with the principle of *proportionality*. Here, the degree of force used to achieve a particular objective should be proportionate to the value and importance of the goal sought; that is, the good sought should outweigh the evils foreseen. The weapon Ender uses on the home world of the Formics, the Molecular Detachment or M.D. Device, can obliterate entire planets at a time. Using it would fail to be just-in-war *if* the evil it inflicts is disproportionate to the goal of ending the war and reestablishing peace. Whether the I.F.'s response is proportional or not is a key point that we'll return to in the final section.

The Justice of Ender's Games

Ender Wiggin must believe that no matter what happens, no adult will ever, ever step in to help him in any way.[13]

So, are Ender's conflicts just? At first blush, Ender's battles with bullies don't seem to count as *wars* because his engagements with Stilson, Peter, Bernard, and Bonzo don't appear to be conflicts between persons with legitimate political or military authority. But on closer examination, they don't seem to be merely private interpersonal conflicts either.

After all, Graff deliberately sought to keep Ender in a hostile situation at Battle School by *withholding protection* from his enemies, and vice-versa. Because of this, the I.F. seriously diluted its authority. After all, the most basic duty of authority is to protect the people under its care from private acts of violence; as a result, Graff would later be put on trial for the I.F.'s actions. Ender was thrown into what Thomas Hobbes (1588–1679) and other philosophers called a "state of nature": a warlike condition void of lawful authority. In the state of nature, each individual has the right to protect her own life by use of force. Considered in this light, Ender's battles *can* be discussed in terms of just war principles because they're conflicts between individuals with personal authority to defend themselves in a warlike condition.

Ender's strategy is always to use devastating force to incapacitate the enemy. Ender is constantly confronted by bullies who attack him dishonorably and usually with a gang in tow. But each time Ender completely incapacitates the enemy. Ender's choice to do this wasn't motivated by lust for power, blood, or personal glory. He acted the way he did so that he wouldn't have to fight again. There's a strong case that Ender's going-to-war was just in each of his battles against bullies. He was attacked in a condition in which he had authority because the I.F. was derelict. Ender intended not any disordered end, but a just peace. Counter-attack had reasonable chance of success. And, Ender always exhausted measures of diplomacy and cunning—coercive force was his last resort.

As regards justice-in-war, Ender *discriminates* as much as he can. For example, when he's surrounded by Bonzo's gang in the bathroom, he quickly discerns that only Bonzo has murder in his heart. But if we ask whether the good Ender sought in his counter-attacks was *proportionate* to the evil foreseen, we run into a problem. While Ender didn't deliberately seek to use fatal force, his retaliation killed Stilson and Bonzo. Surely Ender could have established peace without the complete and utter destruction of his opponents, and Ender recognized this when he was racked by feelings of guilt after learning about their deaths. The principles of just war accused him, in conscience. As to Ender's actual guilt or *blameworthiness*, it seems to be diminished given his intention to stop his opponent (not kill him) *and* the injustice done to him by the I.F. when they withheld protection. It seems that a strong use of force *was* proportionate to the good of personal safety, since Ender couldn't rely on the protection of the I.F.

Ender's Last Game: The Justice of the Third Invasion

"I killed them all, didn't I?" Ender asked.
"All who?" asked Graff. "The buggers? That was the idea."
Mazer leaned in close. "That's what the war was for."
"All their queens. So I killed all their children, all of everything."[14]

To assess the justice of the Third Invasion, we first have to ask exactly who has the moral responsibility for the invasion. This requires tracing back the reasons for why Ender attacked the bugger home planet in the first place.

At Battle School, Ender's real enemy was the I.F. administration. They constantly harrowed Ender with more and more difficult tasks—isolation, rapid promotion to commander, placing green soldiers in his army, and demanding more than one battle a day without notice. And all along, they demanded nothing less than perfection. It was in these conditions that Ender began to spend hours studying the old vids of the first two bugger invasions to learn new tactics. When Ender got transferred to Command School and was placed under the tutelage of Rackham, he continued his close study of Formic tactics. Ender sought to know his enemy.

In the last phase of his training, Ender thought he was fighting Mazer Rackham in a simulation. All along, the authorities planned to deceive Ender into thinking this while he was actually commanding the Third Invasion against the buggers. Graff and his fellow officers were in ultimate control of the "simulator" and could have counter-manded Ender's commands at any time. So it seems the moral respon-sibility for the Third Invasion rests on the adult authorities and, by extension, the citizens of Earth. The fact that all the peoples of Earth had given authority to the Hegemon and the I.F. accounts for this collective responsibility. As Mazer and Graff said, "*We* aimed you. We're responsible. If there was something wrong, we did it."[15]

In fact, by lying to Ender and the other young commanders, the injustice of the I.F.'s methods was made clear well before the destruc-tion of the bugger worlds. The same principles that require respect for human dignity in war apply to an authority's treatment of its *own* citizens during wartime. Clearly, the I.F. did a grave injustice to Ender and his lieutenants because systematic deception and manipulation is an offense to human dignity, and duly respecting someone requires telling him or her the truth.

This doesn't necessarily mean that the Third Invasion failed the just war test. Launching a preemptive fleet against the bugger worlds was justifiable *in principle*. The buggers' repeated acts of injustice and the perceived communication barriers gave humanity just cause. The Hegemony and the I.F. were authorized to protect humanity. If the intention of the invasion was establishing a just peace, then the invasion could also be said to have the right intention. Steps may have been taken to increase the probability of success, including improvement of technology and training excellent commanders. It's conceivable that such an invasion could be a last resort to forestall annihilation.

However, the actual Third Invasion is riddled with injustices other than the manipulation of Ender and his fellow soldiers. The invasion simply fails to meet the requirements of right intention, last resort, discrimination, and proportionality. Mazer Rackham believed, with some good evidence, that bugger workers were not individually endowed with reason and will, but merely drones of the hive-queens, the mind and will of the hive. While he was ultimately wrong about the workers and drones, he was correct that the hive-queens were rational creatures.[16] So the principles of *right intention* and *last resort* demanded that the I.F. create a plan to try and contact the queens when the fleet reached the homeworld. Beings with reason and will would, all other things being equal, be able to communicate. Such a plan seems necessary if *all* rational life is precious. It's true that humans vainly tried various means of communication during the first two bugger wars, but this wasn't a good enough reason to *give up* any attempt to communicate in favor of a plan of annihilation.

So the I.F. intended to annihilate the buggers. Yet the right intention of a just peace would have required humans to see if coexistence was possible. The hive-queens' own failure in this regard should not have been repeated. Since coexistence was possible, use of the M.D. device was not a genuine last resort.

Using it also violated the principles of justice-in-war. The M.D. device nearly wiped out the Formics. But the principles of *discrimination* and *proportionality* require that we find out if there might be members of the hive who were innocent. Given the lapse of 80 years since the previous bugger invasion, humanity should have considered if the absence of bugger invasions was evidence of *repentance* on their part. Only then could humanity have known whether the hive-queens and their workers were utterly *varelse* or not. Without this knowledge, it was a grave act of injustice for the authorities to permit the xenocide. It was in no way clear that peaceful coexistence between humans and hive queens was impossible or even unlikely.

When Ender's "virtual" fleet was outnumbered a thousand to one at the bugger homeworld, he believed this to be another dishonorable cheat on the part of the teachers. So he decided to thwart them by blowing up the planet with the M.D. device. Ender personally sought peace in this last battle with his teachers since he assumed he would be washed out of Command School. The guilt that he carried after he learned the truth was not his *own* guilt. To be properly guilty of xenocide, Ender would have had to know what his superiors knew and also share their intentions. Ender carried the sins of *the I.F. and humanity* for the injustices done to the Formics.

Ender would eventually find and speak with the last remaining hive-queen on the planet Shakespeare. Based on his conversation with her, he wrote *The Hive Queen*, a book telling the true story of the

Formic leaders' regret and repentance for their original hostility; he also helped restore the Formic species by finding a new world for the last hive queen. In the end, it was the force exercised on his conscience by the principles of just war that led Ender to seek to remedy the injustices done to the Formic race on humanity's behalf, and so establish a lasting peace.[17]

Notes

1. Orson Scott Card, *Ender's Game* (New York: TOR Books, 1991), 7.
2. Ibid.
3. Card, *Shadows in Flight* (New York: Tor Books, 2011), 81.
4. Ibid., 80.
5. See Augustine, *City of God*, trans. Henry Bettenson (Penguin Classics, 2003), Book 19, Chapter 12.
6. For a philosophical account of "the evil that men do," see Jeremy Proulx's chapter in this book.
7. Card, *Ender's Game*, 261.
8. For more reading on the principles of classical just war theory, see Thomas Aquinas, *Summa Theologiae*, trans. Dominican Fathers (Christian Classics, 1981), II–II, Question 40.
9. See *The Art of War*, trans. John Minford (Penguin Classics, 2009), and Morgan Deane's chapter on Chinese military philosophy in this volume.
10. Card, *Ender's Game*, 24.
11. Card, *Children of the Mind* (New York: Tor Books, 1997), 322.
12. In this regard, dropping civilian-targeting nuclear bombs can be assessed by the ethics of the "Doctrine of Double Effect"; see Lance Belluomini's chapter in this volume for more.
13. Card, *Ender's Game*, 202.
14. Ibid., 297.
15. Ibid., 298.
16. Spoiler alert! Notably, it was eventually discovered by Bean and his children that hive drones and workers are *not* devoid of reason and will. See Card, *Shadows in Flight* (New York: Tor Books, 2012).
17. I would like to thank Zach Mikkelson, Devin Rose, and John Praeuner for helpful comments on an earlier version of this chapter.

Part Five

HEGEMON

THE TERRIBLE THINGS ARE ONLY ABOUT TO BEGIN

CHAPTER 16

Locke and Demosthenes
Virtually Dominating the World

Kenneth Wayne Sayles III

What if children ran the world? *Ender's Game* answers this question by having Peter and Valentine Wiggin use their world's online nets to get weighty political influence. Peter, whose goal is to seize control of the world by guiding political debates through fabricated online personalities, convinces Valentine to help him in this task. Gradually, they build influence and attract followers. The world at large doesn't know that it's being swayed and manipulated by two *children*, thinking them instead two adult political adversaries. Later, Peter and Valentine use their influence to set the stage for a world takeover after their brother Ender successfully annihilates the buggers.

As a computer security professional and fledgling philosopher, I find it scary that people could anonymously gain this much influence. While Peter's and Valentine's achievement doesn't seem possible right now, I think that anonymous virtual politics are a real possibility in the future. We're living in a world where more and more trust is placed in information sources on the Web, more of our personal information is stored online, and children are raised to embrace technology and the Internet. The Internet is now used to gain influence, and society is already creating the potential for anonymous virtual politics just like those in *Ender's Game*. From the perspectives of philosophy and computer security, I want to show that the dangers of anonymous virtual politics parallel some of the conditions that the philosopher and social critic Hannah Arendt recognized as essential

Ender's Game and Philosophy: The Logic Gate Is Down, First Edition. Edited by Kevin S. Decker.
© 2013 John Wiley & Sons, Inc. Published 2013 by John Wiley & Sons, Inc.

for *totalitarianism*, a political scenario in which the state has absolute authority over all aspects of human life.[1]

A Child's Rise to Power

At 12, Peter is extremely intelligent and ambitious, and he has a brilliant and terrifying plan. A student of history, he tells Valentine, "There are times when the world is rearranging itself, and at times like that, the right words can change the world."[2] Hitler, he says, "... got to power on words, on the right words at the right time."[3] As his plan unfolds, he says, "Val, *we* can say the words that everyone else will be saying two weeks later."[4] Valentine points out that Peter is only 12, but he replies, "Not on the nets I'm not. On the nets I can name myself anything I want, and so can you."[5] Valentine manages to get their father to allow them his citizen's access to the nets so they won't be identified as minors. They begin studying the various debates and political issues on the net. They also participate in online debates using disposable identities to learn how to write in a mature way; as a result, they begin to attract online attention.

After much preparation, Peter becomes "Locke" and Valentine becomes "Demosthenes." Demosthenes is a paranoid personality, while Locke is more moderate and reasonable. Their online personas are the opposite of their own personalities, just part of the deception to ensure people don't make a connection between their virtual and real-life selves. This practice isn't new: in the freshly minted United States, Alexander Hamilton, James Madison, and John Jay wrote *The Federalist Papers* under the pseudonym Publius. Peter and Valentine carefully craft the debates of their online personalities and create memorable phrases similar to today's sound bites and catch phrases. Peter tracks the occurrence of these phrases and, discovering that others on the net are using them in major debates, he cries, "We're being read ... The ideas are seeping out."[6] He's excited that "nobody quotes us by name, yet, but they're discussing the points we raise. We're helping set the agenda. We're getting there."[7] After some time, Demosthenes is asked to produce a weekly column on a newsnet. Later, Locke's asked to produce a weekly column to rebut Demosthenes' opinions. Peter remarks, "Not bad for two kids who've only got about eight pubic hairs between them."[8] They even see their influence at home when they learn that their father looked for Demosthenes in the international debates.

Peter and Valentine earn money from their online writing, get invited to important discussions, and learn more than the average citizen about political matters. And they continue to build the influence of Locke and Demosthenes, in a public arena in which "influence *is* power."[9] Demosthenes is even asked to join the President's Council on Education for the Future! When Ender defeats the buggers, Peter's "Locke" puts forth a proposal that ends an erupting war and power grab on Earth. Much more develops from this in Card's subsequent Ender novels, but let's stay with our focus on the children's rise to power through the nets, a premise both intriguing and alarming.

"Every Citizen Started Equal, on the Nets"

The Internet is extraordinarily similar to the virtual structure that Card prophetically describes in *Ender's Game*. In both, there are political discussion forums, news sites, and anonymity is possible to some degree. The Internet also plays an increasing role in real-life politics. Jeremy W. Peters, writing about an Obama political campaign's YouTube video, says, "The Obama campaign's efforts underscore the importance that political campaigns now attach to Web video and the role the medium will probably play in the coming election ... online video is vital in the way campaigns communicate with and persuade voters."[10] Outside of politics, we have Internet celebrities, such as Philip DeFranco. At the time of this writing, he has 2,157,529 subscribers to his YouTube videos and has had 964,291,788 views.[11] Whether or not these viewers and subscribers agree with DeFranco, it's clear he's at least being heard on the Internet. President Obama and DeFranco are just using a fairly new medium to reach out to people personally. Their efforts can be likened to meeting with people at a convention center, though this "convention center" contains more people than a brick-and-mortar one ever could! Although politicians and opinion-makers are, like Valentine and Peter, gaining influence through the real-life Internet, perhaps we don't have to be worried in their cases because they're *openly* reaching out to people. Their efforts can often be verified by an objective third-party on the Internet, or by registering for security certificates to lend more credibility to their identity. The larger danger, though, is that people will gain power over the opinions of others *anonymously*.

The potential problems stem from two important moral ideas: identity and responsibility. While each person has a unique *physical* identity in the real world, a person can have multiple *virtual* identities in their explorations of the Internet. People can use these virtual identities to shop, play online video games, or chat with others. And they don't necessarily need an exclusive "one-to-one" connection between their physical and virtual identities. Interestingly, a "real" Locke, John Locke (1632–1704), is famed for a theory of identity. He stated,

> When we see anything to be in any place in any instant of time, we are sure (be it what it will) that it is that very thing, and not another which at that same time exists in another place, how like and undistinguishable soever it may be in all other respects: and in this consists identity, when the ideas it is attributed to vary not at all from what they were that moment wherein we consider their former existence, and to which we compare the present.[12]

What Locke determined was that identity required a consistency across time and space to allow us to trust that we're dealing with the same *identical* person, and by extension, the views of a person. Even twins have unique identities because they physically occupy different positions in space and have different experiences. However, today's computer users can establish a more than one-to-one correspondence between a physical person and multiple virtual identities at the same time. It's no wonder that some users can abuse virtual identities!

While virtual identities can be used to provide safe and anonymous Internet interaction with others, virtual anonymity has also led to personal information being stolen, websites being defaced, and misinformation running rampant.[13] Identity theft, where someone obtains information relating to a person's physical identity and uses it to impersonate them in the virtual world, is an abuse most people are familiar with. TransUnion, one of the three large credit monitoring agencies, claims that "identity theft is the fastest growing crime in America."[14] Incidents of identity theft include cases in which a person may have stolen or hacked another person's virtual identity.[15] According to Surfnetkids, a clearinghouse of information for helping kids surf the net safely,

> Online identity thieves can compromise your online safety by using your email address. Lots of different websites will sell your email

address to spammers and phishers, who will then hassle you with spam emails and will also try to break into your accounts and get your personal information, which they then use to steal your identity and suck you dry.[16]

Most of us know that a big part of information security is protecting personal information so the risk of identity theft is lowered. Despite this, it's impossible to completely secure anything unless you simply never use it!

As we've developed the Internet into an open forum similar to Card's "nets," we've also made crime like identity theft easier. It's nearly impossible for the average web surfer to know who he or she is dealing with in a virtual setting, and this situation parallels *Ender's Game*. The thought that we now have the means to both gain and exercise influence through anonymous virtual identities, like Peter and Valentine did, is shocking. What if an evil person gets this kind of influence or simply steals it from another? If influence can be developed through a virtual identity with no direct ties to a physical identity, then this is entirely possible. This potential hazard brings to mind the "Ring of Gyges" in the *Republic* of Plato (429–347 BC). This mythical ring made its wearer invisible to others. Glaucon, Plato's older brother and, like him, a student of Socrates, claimed that with such a ring, "no man would keep his hands off what was not his own when he could safely take what he liked out of the market, or go into houses and sleep with anyone at his pleasure, or kill or release from prison whom he would, and in all respects be like a god among men."[17] Glaucon thinks that people only stay honest out of fear of reprisal from society; if people can't be caught or punished, then they will do whatever they want (who else thought of Kevin Bacon in the movie *Hollow Man* just now?). After much to and fro in the dialogue, Socrates argues that "justice in her own nature has been shown to be the best for the soul in her own nature. Let a man do what is just, whether he have the Ring of Gyges or not."[18] Socrates' point is that doing the right thing is better for a person's overall happiness than doing the wrong thing. Even if a person could get away with using the ring, eventually that pattern of wrongdoing would destroy him.

Anonymous virtual identities certainly parallel the Ring of Gyges in that they allow users to hide their online actions, but there aren't grounds for widespread worry *yet* since an anonymous entity on the

Internet isn't likely to develop enough credibility to obtain significant power. The Internet provides anonymity to a certain degree, but professionals and hackers have tools and techniques that can trace a person's true physical identity behind their online persona. For the sake of argument though, let's assume that true anonymity like that which Peter and Valentine employ is possible. Would we be likely to find an anonymous source believable enough to allow it to gain influence and power?[19] With the rise of Internet entities like "Anonymous," we're heading down a dangerous road where such things are likely.

"[He] Knew How to Exploit Fear in His Writing"

"Anonymous" is a hacker group that's gained attention in the news through its unique approach to social concerns; they are self-styled "Hacktivists." According to the Anonymous Analytics website, "Anonymous is a decentralized network of individuals focused on promoting access to information, free speech, and transparency ... To this end, we use our unique skill sets to expose companies that practice poor corporate governance and are involved in large-scale fraudulent activities."[20] *Time Magazine* recognized Anonymous as an influential person in 2011. According to Doug Aamoth of *Time*:

> Anonymous has been called many things ... but the so-called group is really more of a way of life than something that's easily definable. Anonymous has changed the way the world thinks about hacking by turning it into a form of social activism ... Despite having no central leadership, Anonymous has seen its reputation grow, thanks to the nature of its anyone-can-join mentality. Did Anonymous members really threaten a Mexican drug cartel? Did they really take down the PlayStation Network? That's the power and peril of an organization as inherently disorganized as Anonymous.[21]

Anonymous is an Internet entity very much like Locke and Demosthenes in the sense that average users are listening to Anonymous without knowing whose views Anonymous represents. What's more troubling is that it's impossible to know exactly what Anonymous has accomplished because there's no central leadership, no clear agenda or consistency. Of course, one of the key ideas behind Peter's and Valentine's development of Locke and Demosthenes was collaboration to make certain that their views were clear and easily recognized. Because of this, Locke and Demosthenes had consistent political platforms that net users could rally behind. Valentine contrasted them, saying: "Demosthenes began to develop as a fairly paranoid anti-Russian writer ... [but] Locke followed her moderate, empathic strategies."[22] What is the difference between them and Anonymous, you ask?

People are willing to grant credibility to Internet entities if they recognize them as representing actual people, which is easier when we can clearly tie a virtual identity to a recognizable *physical* identity, such as with President Obama or Philip DeFranco. I don't think we can make this connection as easily for *wholly* virtual identities such as Anonymous, or for social networking friends we've never met in person. However, virtual identities that develop over time and show consistency in beliefs, seem more "real" to us; we're willing to make this leap, just as Card's net users did with Locke and Demosthenes.

Consider John Locke's view that "to find wherein personal identity consists, we must consider what person stands for; which, I think, is a thinking intelligent being, that has reason and reflection, and can consider itself as itself, the same thinking thing, in different times and places."[23] In other words, a personal identity should be identifiable across different times and places. Being able to connect aspects of that identity in various instances is the ground for having faith that this identity *represents* a real person. This faith is called for on the Internet, as a person has multiple options to create a consistent virtual identity, among them email addresses, social networking pages, and blogs. Yet a consistent anonymous virtual identity that's never directly connected to a personal physical identity is *also* possible. This raises an alarming parallel with political totalitarianism, in which the exercise of power on people is made anonymous by equating it with the operations of "the state," and no particular individual. Totalitarian governments are historically untrustworthy. Could we ever trust a wholly anonymous entity as much as a person though? I'm not sure, but to look further at the tendencies that anonymous virtual politics might have toward totalitarianism, let's discuss political philosopher Hannah Arendt's views.

New Friend Request from Hannah Arendt

Hannah Arendt (1906–1975) described the conditions necessary for a totalitarian regime to develop in *The Origins of Totalitarianism* and continued this discussion in *The Human Condition*. Arendt, who thought that the key to human flourishing was the *vita activa*, or "active life," noted that, "The fact that man is capable of action means that the unexpected can be expected from him, that he is able to perform what is infinitely improbable."[24] In other words, a person's ability to take action means that any action is possible—the sky's the limit! But Arendt also believed that anonymity was the *enemy* of meaningful action. She stated, "Action without a name, [without] a 'who' attached to it, is meaningless."[25] What Arendt means is that an anonymous act is not as socially impactful as one that can be traced back to a specific person or group. For example if we hear that a $2,000 donation was made to charity, we say that it's a nice thought, but it becomes more meaningful if we know who made that donation and that they gave up a month's wages for it. Also, we must know who's responsible for an action so that we aren't deceived or manipulated. If there isn't a "who" attached to an action, how can we hold anyone accountable if something goes wrong?

It's difficult to really know what Anonymous has accomplished and how important those actions are because we don't know who Anonymous is. In the Enderverse, Peter and Valentine were able to portray two intelligent-sounding political personalities on the net, and net users had no idea they were listening to children. In today's environment, the *virtual* political blogger you are reading and supporting could be anyone: an intelligent, well-read activist; a terrorist; a psychopath; a young prodigy. This situation presents a problem because you have no idea if the "person" you are agreeing or disagreeing with is *really* that person. You can't connect her actions to a *physical* identity, and you can't hold someone directly accountable if things go wrong (or right, as the Anonymous example shows). As Arendt points out, anonymity is a precursor to totalitarianism because you never really know what's going on or who's running the show! According to Arendt, "The forms of totalitarian organization ... are designed to translate the propaganda lies of the movement, woven around a central fiction ... into a functioning reality, to build up, even under non-totalitarian circumstances, a society whose members act and react according to the rules of a fictitious world."[26] The powers behind totalitarian governments create a false reality using propaganda, intimidation, and violence to establish a world where the citizens live according to rules without question. It's easy to see how anonymity can help in the establishment of totalitarianism: if the propaganda doesn't work, the leaders can simply blame it on others. There's no accountability with anonymity so by staying faceless, leaders can always progress toward their goals by taking credit when it suits them and denying responsibility when it doesn't. While Arendt might have approved of the democratic potential of the Internet, she would have had serious concerns about people using anonymous virtual politics because of the danger of granting power to an unknown entity.

"We'll Be Too Entrenched to Suffer Much Loss"

The Internet resembles a true democracy in the sense that anyone with the technology can use the Internet, share opinions, and vote on issues.[27] Anonymous has claimed to want to protect this aspect of the Internet, and Arendt would support this open communication. *Deathandtaxes* blogger Andrew Belonsky interprets Anonymous's message as, "'We are tired of corporate interests controlling the internet and silencing the people's rights to spread information, but more importantly, the right to SHARE with one another.' The collective are exercising ... Hannah Arendt's ideal concept of power."[28] And as Arendt wrote, "The fundamental deprivation of human rights is manifested first and above all in the deprivation of a place in the world which makes opinions significant and actions effective ... They are deprived, not of the right to freedom, but of the right to action; not of the right to think whatever they please, but of the right to opinion."[29] In other words, a totalitarian regime finds roots where there are fewer places for humans to act and think freely. The Internet is a place where humans can exercise freedom with few political boundaries to restrict them. But as Arendt notes, "It has frequently been pointed out that totalitarian movements use and abuse democratic freedoms in order to abolish them."[30] This danger is genuinely present in the Internet.

As a novice philosopher, I appreciate the many information sources, blogs, social networking, and other opportunities the Internet provides us; in my case, it allows me to be a philosopher in my spare time.

But it's as a full-time computer security professional that I also clearly see the dangers Arendt warned against. With anonymity, it's much easier to be deceived by others to suit their interests. An anonymous entity can pretend to be whatever is most useful to its aims.

It's a disheartening prediction of the future that as technologically advanced as the world of *Ender's Game* is, net users there were willing to put an incredible degree of trust in totally unknown sources. The net users that followed Locke and Demosthenes were naïve and foolhardy. They had no idea they were listening to children, and it didn't occur to them to seriously question who they were actually reading and following. Some instruction in Socratic reasoning may have helped them be less vulnerable to this deception! But the Hegemony seems to have taken advantage of this ignorance by allowing Peter and Valentine to continue writing as Locke and Demosthenes to prevent the collapse of vibrant public opinion on Earth.

Consider another possibility. What if the Hegemony had blocked Peter and Valentine's access, turning the influential Locke and Demosthenes personalities to their own ends? By usurping each virtual personality's tone, word preferences, and writing style, it's likely that they could have deceived the net users for a long time. How would Locke and Demosthenes' followers know that they were being led by different people? As Arendt pointed out, "The question therefore is not so much whether we are the masters or the slaves of our machines, but whether machines still serve the world and its things, or if, on the contrary, they and the automatic motion of their processes have begun to rule and even destroy world and things."[31] I contend that if we don't guard against anonymous virtual identities on the Internet and limit how much trust we place in them, we're leaving ourselves open to abuse. While the Internet itself may not end up ruling us, it could certainly enable and facilitate an anonymous entity to do just that. We must ensure that the Internet continues to benefit, not harm us.

The Heart of the Matter

The thread running through this chapter is that there's a larger problem than anonymity with virtual politics: it's how to maintain freedom in both worlds. The Internet is a useful tool to exercise our freedoms through sharing ideas, exploring new interests, and educating ourselves. Arendt firmly believed that these forums are crucial to expanding our capabilities and making it more difficult for totalitarianism to take hold in our society. But, there are clear dangers, both on and off the Internet, like identity theft, scams, and deliberate misinformation. Some people may agree that groups like Anonymous have accomplished some good, but their methods, their goals, and their consistency are all controversial. And, there is no accountability if Anonymous causes harm! As much as we might admire Socrates' idealism, Glaucon's view does have merit since, like the possessor of the Ring of Gyges, anonymous entities can't be held responsible for their actions or mistakes. With such a tool as an anonymous virtual identity, an unscrupulous person or group of people can gain widespread political influence and turn it toward nefarious, perhaps totalitarian, aims. Peter and Valentine used virtual identities on the net to end Earth's dangerous political situation in *Ender's Game*, but of course, that's only fiction. In the real world, we have to accept that such power could be used for the wrong ends, and it's clear that a virtual political crisis could occur through our own Internet. So let's keep this question in mind: how much trust should we place in *virtual* people when we can never know which *real* people are controlling them?[32]

Notes

1. "Totalitarianism," Wikipedia, the free encyclopedia, http://en.wikipedia. org/wiki/Totalitarianism, accessed June 10, 2012.
2. Orson Scott Card, *Ender's Game* (New York: TOR Books, 1991), 91.
3. Ibid., 93.
4. Ibid., 129.
5. Ibid., 92.
6. Ibid., 135.
7. Ibid., 96.
8. Ibid., 98.
9. Ibid., 161.
10. Jeremy W. Peters, "With Video, Obama Looks to Expand Campaign's Reach Through Social Media" (Mar. 14, 2012), http://www.nytimes. com/2012/03/15/us/politics/with-youtube-video-obama-looks-to-expand-social-media-reach.html, accessed May 29, 2012.
11. Philip DeFranco, The Philip DeFranco Show, http://www.youtube.com/user/sxephil, accessed September 9, 2012.

12. John Locke, *An Essay Concerning Human Understanding* (New York: Barnes & Noble, Inc., 2004), 259.
13. Anonymity doesn't necessarily have to be malicious. Some people use anonymity to join discussion forums in which they haven't developed trust in other users; anonymity can help them stay safe by not betraying personal information that others may misuse. One way to create anonymity on the Internet is through disposable email addresses or anonymizing tools.
14. "Identity Theft Facts | TransUnion," http://www.transunion.com/personal-credit/identity-theft-and-fraud/identity-theft-facts.page, accessed June 3, 2012.
15. Hacking is when someone exploits weaknesses in a computer program or system to cause unexpected behavior, which allows obtaining sensitive information, stealing money, etc. More information about hacking can be found at Hacker (computer security), Wikipedia, the free encyclopedia, http://en.wikipedia.org/wiki/Hacker_(computer_security), accessed June 16, 2012.
16. Surfnetkids, "Online Safety Concerns with Social Networking: Internet Safety," http://www.surfnetkids.com/go/safety/432/online-safety-concerns-with-social-networking/, accessed June 9, 2012. Note: Phishers are attackers who use spam emails to trick users into providing personal information, such as social security numbers and passwords.
17. Plato, *Republic* (New York: Barnes & Noble Classics, 2004), 42.
18. Ibid., 341.
19. I do want to note though that certain high military officials knew the true identity of Locke and Demosthenes and what Peter and Valentine were doing. They chose to keep these facts secret, a fact about which we'll talk very soon.
20. Anonymous Analytics: Acquiring information through unconventional means, http://anonanalytics.com/; accessed June 16, 2012.
21. Doug Aamoth, "Time Person of the Year, People Who Mattered: Anonymous," (Dec. 14, 2011), http://www.time.com/time/specials/packages/article/0,28804,2101745_2102309_2102294,00.html, accessed June 3, 2012.
22. Card, *Ender's Game*, 97.
23. Locke, *An Essay Concerning Human Understanding*, 265.
24. Hannah Arendt, *The Human Condition*, 2nd edn (Chicago: The University of Chicago Press, 1998), 178.
25. Ibid., 180–181.
26. Hannah Arendt, *The Origins of Totalitarianism* (New York: Harcourt, Inc., 1994), 364.
27. In some developing countries, the Internet may not be as widespread as in more developed countries. People everywhere may not have the same

physical capability to access the Internet, and some users may restrict *virtual* access to certain areas. But, the Internet structure itself is open to anyone to explore and set up his/her own *virtual* areas.

28. Andrew Belonsky, "Operation Payback, Wikileaks and Hannah Arendt's Power: A Perfect Union?," *Deathandtaxes*, http://www.deathandtaxesmag. com/40235/operation-payback-wikileaks-and-hannah-arendts-power-a-perfect-union/, accessed June 10, 2012.

29. Arendt, *The Origins of Totalitarianism*, 296.

30. Ibid., 312.

31. Arendt, *The Human Condition*, 151.

32. I would like to thank Erika, Brenda, and Kevin Decker for providing feedback on earlier versions of this essay and helping me to organize my competing thoughts!

CHAPTER 17

Ender's Dilemma

Realism, Neoliberalism, and the Politics of Power

Ted Henry Brown and Christie L. Maloyed

The world is always a democracy in times of flux,
and the man with the best voice will win.

—Peter Wiggin

What child hasn't dreamed of ruling the world? Of having power over siblings, parents, classmates, and teachers? Of being thought of as more than just an ignorant and immature kid? What makes the dreams of the Wiggin children so remarkable is that despite their youth, their dreams aren't the fanciful reveries of children; they're all in positions to wield real power. At the tender age of nine, Ender's given command of his own army in Battle School, and is placed in charge of the International Fleet only two years later. Peter and Valentine are under the age of 13 when they begin their opinion-shaping careers on the nets. Despite being children whose true identities were hidden, and who were never elected into positions of authority, the Wiggins influence the fate of the inter-galactic system simply with their voices. Their understanding of the politics of war rivals that of politicians and commanders generations older than them.

Written during the United States' Cold War with the Soviet Union, Orson Scott Card's novel is an exploration of political power. The Cold War focused tremendous energy on building the biggest weapons with the longest range and the highest sophistication. The assumption that the side with the most firepower had the most political power

Ender's Game and Philosophy: The Logic Gate Is Down, First Edition. Edited by Kevin S. Decker.
© 2013 John Wiley & Sons, Inc. Published 2013 by John Wiley & Sons, Inc.

fueled the war. But as the Wiggin children show, power doesn't necessarily lie in technology or troop numbers. The power to persuade can be just as potent as detonating the Little Doctor.

Survival of the Fittest

When *Ender's Game* opens, the buggers are preparing to attack the Earth for a third time, or at least that's what the I.F. would have the citizens of Earth believe. There are only two options: wait for the Third Invasion to destroy the planet or launch a preemptive attack directly against the buggers and permanently eliminate the enemy. The formation of the Hegemony and the International Fleet clearly illustrates that Earth has opted to attack the buggers at their home world, but all the while a far more subtle battle is being waged for control on Earth.

To understand political power it's necessary to comprehend why individuals and entire nations make the choices they do. When should we expect countries to choose preemptive, rather than defensive action? When is it possible to reach a truce or compromise? And when is military conflict the best solution?[1] Specialists in political philosophy, political science, and international relations have tried to answer these questions and predict the future course of events by first understanding the reasons behind our actions. Two influential approaches to understanding the intentions behind human behavior are known as *realism* and *liberalism*.

For realists, power is everything and it's assumed that people are motivated primarily by their own self-interest. As the realist Thomas Hobbes (1588–1679) explained, without government, humans live in a state of nature in which man is in a constant struggle to survive and life is "solitary, poor, nasty, brutish, and short."[2] In order to avoid this war of "all against all," individuals create a society to gain protection through superior numbers. Realist thought can thus be reduced to the belief that gaining power is necessary for survival and whoever has the most power is the most likely to survive.

Self-interest and the will to survive govern relationships between individuals, and, according to the realists, relations between countries. As international relations theorist Hans Morgenthau explains, "International politics, like all politics, is a struggle for power."[3] Every country, and in the case of *Ender's Game* every species, must try to gain the most power—as defined by material, military, and economic advantage—or risk being overtaken by other countries (or species) willing to stop at nothing to ensure their own survival. Colonel Graff embodies the realist philosophy in thinking that humans are motivated by their most primal self-interest: "Humanity doesn't want to die. As a species, we have evolved to survive."[4] Within the realist's world, there is no room for moral principles because survival is the primary concern. As Graff later attempts to convince Ender, "When it comes down to it, though, the real decision is inevitable: if one of us has to be destroyed, let's make damn sure we're the ones alive at the end."[5] Defining the universe in such basic terms, however, only partially explains the actions of Ender, Peter, and Valentine.

Why Can't We Be Friends?

While the I.F. fights for the survival of the human race, the countries on Earth are united against the buggers. The positions of Hegemon, Polemarch, and Strategos evolved as a means to ensure that political infighting wouldn't constrain the resources and ability to fight the buggers. The question remains, though, would the Hegemon be strong enough to ensure peace on Earth once the threat of the buggers had subsided, or would the age-old tensions between countries resurface and engulf the efforts of the International Fleet? As Dink Meeker, a Battle School comrade, explains to Ender, "As long as people are afraid of the buggers, the I.F. can stay in power, and as long as the I.F. is in power, certain countries can keep their hegemony. But keep watching the vids, Ender. People will catch onto this game pretty soon, and there'll be a civil war to end all wars."[6] Peter comes to the same conclusion: "When the bugger wars are over, all that power will vanish, because it's all built on fear of the buggers. And suddenly we'll look around and discover that all the old alliances are gone, dead and gone, except one, the Warsaw Pact."[7] Dink and Peter believe that without an external threat looming on the horizon, societies will return to the realist strategy of scrambling for power in hopes of guaranteeing survival. Even Valentine concludes that the alliance that had come together since the bugger wars began had been a "façade of peace and cooperation."[8] But is the possibility of continued cooperation really so unlikely?

Against the view that power is both necessary and sufficient for survival, liberalism suggests that the nature of the world is not so clearly divided into black and white. Realists think states are likely to move toward conflict when there's an imbalance in the levels of power between them. When an imbalance exists, conflict necessarily emerges as each state struggles to survive and gain power. Liberal political thinkers *also* assume that world politics is fairly anarchic, but they diverge from realists by insisting that states shouldn't be solely or even primarily motivated by their narrow self-interest. If states are willing to forego the quest for absolute power, then it's possible that all or most states could benefit from working together. Associated with thinkers such as John Locke (1632–1704), Immanuel Kant (1724–1804), and later with President Woodrow Wilson, liberalism stresses that humans are capable of working with one another in hopes of achieving more together than they would individually.

Neoliberalism developed in response to the charge that liberalism represented an overly utopian view of the world. This variation on liberalism stressed the importance of institutions and information in facilitating cooperation over conflict. Neoliberals don't view the world as a zero-sum game where a gain for one side always represents a loss for the other. Instead, they say that mutual advantage can be achieved when states work together. Reducing uncertainty about the intentions of other actors in the anarchic world is the key to increasing international security and continued cooperation. Neoliberalism's focus is on developing international organizations providing all states more and better information, and neoliberals believe this kind of communication is paramount in order for cooperation to occur.

Ender's Dilemma

To explain whether cooperation or conflict should be expected between two parties, international relations scholars often try to calculate costs and benefits of either strategy. Among the most famous of their scenarios is the "Prisoner's Dilemma," which starts by presuming two individuals have committed a crime and are being interrogated by the police. The police need a confession in order to convict either of the suspects and so each is placed in separate interrogation rooms. During questioning, each prisoner is given two options: they can remain silent or betray their partner in crime. If both suspects betray each other, both receive jail time. If only one rats out the other, the betrayer is set free and the other suspect is given a jail sentence. If both prisoners refuse to confess, this will force the investigators to charge each suspect with a minor offense with minimal jail time for each. Both prisoners get the best outcome if neither chooses to cooperate with investigators, but this only works if each of them can trust the other to not confess. Given that each prisoner realizes that serving the least amount of jail time is the best outcome, there's a high likelihood that each prisoner will betray the other, resulting in more jail time for both.

The Prisoner's Dilemma gives us several key insights into decisions about cooperation and betrayal (or "defection") generally. The best outcome for both is also the most difficult to achieve, since they're in isolated cells and can't communicate with one another. Because they have limited information, they're both likely to defect. If they were given the chance to communicate with one another, increase their information, and develop a joint strategy, they both would remain silent and suffer a short sentence, but reap larger benefits on the whole. In the case of *Ender's Game*, the humans and buggers face a similar dilemma about whether or not to cooperate with one another or defect, which means fighting a war for survival. If only one side decides to defect (in this case, attack the other), then the aggressor would benefit. If both sides choose the option of defecting, then the resulting war would be costly for both sides. Cooperation leads to minimal damages.

The dilemma for Ender and the I.F. is complicated by the fact that there seems to be no possibility of communication between humans and buggers. Without communication, it might still be possible to foster cooperation when there is a "shadow of the future," or expectations that they'll meet again in the future. As Robert Axelrod explains, "What makes it possible for cooperation to emerge is the fact that the players might meet again."[9] According to Graff, the reason the two sides went to war in the first place was the failure to communicate: "This isn't just a matter of translating from one language to another. They don't have a language at all. We used every means we could think of to communicate with them, but they don't even have the machinery to know we're signaling. And maybe they've been trying to think to us, and they can't understand why we don't respond." As Ender pithily responds, "So the whole war is because we can't talk to each other."[10] Without the ability to communicate, the best strategy that either side can take is the realist position—fight for survival at all costs. Both humans and buggers defect rather than cooperate, leading to massive losses of life on each side. This is the real-world equivalent of jail sentences for each side. It certainly isn't the desirable outcome, but as Graff rightly notes, "If the other fellow can't tell you his story, you can never be sure he isn't trying to kill you."[11]

This problem about communication that overshadows the Third Invasion isn't as much of a problem for the nations on earth. Despite this, the realist and neoliberal debate thrives among those vying for power on Earth as the Third Invasion draws to a close. Peter and Valentine use their online personas of Locke and Demosthenes to perpetuate this debate and promote the assumptions of realism and neoliberalism in order to persuade the masses to their preferred outcomes. While Locke champions the idea of cooperation, Demosthenes emphasizes the probability of conflict.

There are two constant battles being waged: the war for the survival of the human species and the war for continued peace on Earth. One battle requires that Ender succeed. The other battle requires that Peter and Valentine stabilize the tensions between factions on Earth. These intentions are not completely selfless, though, as Peter desires to someday conquer the world. Valentine explains to Ender, if Peter "… had allowed the League to fall apart completely, he'd have to conquer the world piece by piece. As long as the Hegemony exists, he can do it in one lump."[12] As Peter and his online persona of Locke have suggested, the power of the Hegemon should be upheld, even in the absence of the bugger menace, because it ensures that cooperation will continue between countries. If cooperation and communication are the keys to global survival, then the power to persuade is the essential ingredient to wielding political power.

The Power to Persuade

The I.F. finds it laughable when it first discovers two children are behind the identities of Locke and Demosthenes. Given that Valentine and Peter are so young, and because they haven't done any real damage, they're allowed to continue writing without interference. Since "they're still just talking," one I.F. officer reasons, "they have influence, but no power." But as the other officer astutely cautions, "In my experience, influence is power."[13]

How do Peter and Valentine come to command attention and respect on the nets and eventually among news publishers and even government leaders? The Wiggin children are not born into a prominent family, nor are they politically connected. To gain influence, they have to create their own opportunities and build their own networks. Niccolò Machiavelli (1469–1527), a notorious political realist, advised that a person can acquire power either through fortune or ability, but "… rulers maintain themselves better if they owe little to luck."[14] Peter's nothing if not a good Machiavellian. When he first proposes creating online personas to Valentine, he stresses to her that his study of history has revealed the insight that in order to make a difference, a person has to take opportunities that are presented. Despite Valentine's mocking that it's apparently up to a couple of pre-pubescent children to save the world, Peter retorts: "It's not my fault I'm twelve right now. And it's not my fault that right now is when the opportunity is open. Right now is the time when I can shape events."[15] The ability to shape events doesn't necessarily depend on who you know, on being in an elected position, or even on commanding troops. As Peter explains to Valentine, political power merely rests on the ability to persuade others at certain times: "There are times when the world is rearranging itself, and at times like that, the right words can change the world."[16] Much as Machiavelli did in his controversial book *The Prince*, Peter undertakes a study of history, focusing on great leaders and statesmen in order to understand how they came to power. He argues that historians have spent too much time "[quibbling] about cause and effect" and too little time studying actual power. Peter no doubt hopes to have his own name listed alongside those he thinks had "the right voice in the right place": Thomas Paine, Ben Franklin, Bismarck, and Lenin.[17]

Of course, Peter doesn't dismiss the importance of strength and force entirely; far from it. Peter turns to the example of Adolf Hitler in claiming that political power lies in the balance between force and persuasion. "Everybody thinks Hitler got to power because of his armies," Peter explains, "because they were willing to kill, and that's partly true, because in the real world power is always built on the threat of death and dishonor. But mostly he got to power on words—on the right words at the right time."[18]

The different tactics needed to win power initially and to keep power are also one of Machiavelli's interests. While Peter repeatedly emphasizes the importance of delivering the right message to persuade others, *keeping* power often rests on force. Machiavelli was concerned with the relationship between persuasion and force as tools of power, and he thought, "… the people are fickle; it is easy to persuade them about something, but difficult to keep them persuaded. Hence, when they no longer believe in you and your schemes, you must be able to force them to believe."[19] It's not only important to have the right words at the right moment but also to know at which moment force is required.

Even Valentine recognizes the usefulness of this approach after the end of the bugger war. She tells Ender that it's inevitable that Peter will eventually win power. She observes that even though Peter has often been a "destroyer" he also has something of the "builder" in him: "He isn't kind, but he doesn't break every good thing he sees anymore. Once you realize that power will always end up with the sort of people who crave it, I think that there are worse people who could have it than Peter."[20] Valentine's endorsement is less than enthusiastic, and yet she also recognizes the need to balance building and destruction as complementary components of political power. Although this view of power owes a lot to the realist tradition of political thought, it also embraces neoliberal ideas. Peter's goal isn't to destroy his enemies for the sake of his own survival, but to forge alliances and build institutions that will facilitate cooperation.

Fighting for the Future

This model of political power works perfectly well on Earth because communication exists and interactions among rival groups continue to be possible. For the battle with the buggers, however, the ability to influence and persuade can't get off the ground, making physical force more important than political power. Ender, who personally wishes to have as little in common with Peter and his realist mode of thinking as possible, surprisingly adopts a realist position in order to survive. After his fight with Bonzo, Ender despondently realizes that he's the only one responsible for his own survival and that power is ultimately rooted in force: "Peter might be scum, but Peter had been right, always right; the power to cause pain is the only power that matters, the power to kill and destroy, because if you can't kill then you are always subject to those who can, and nothing and no one will ever save you."[21]

This is a disturbing and paradoxical conclusion, given that Ender had displayed gentleness and compassion, especially in contrast with Peter's penchant for cruelty. And yet, Ender agrees with Peter that destruction is necessary. What is even more confusing to Ender is that he realizes in order to destroy his enemies, he has to first understand and even love them.[22] This requires a degree of empathy and understanding. Once Ender stops focusing on the *threat* of the buggers, he finds they have been communicating with him and the war was unnecessary. Card's verdict on realism says that just as long as one group is convinced that another—with a different language and unknown values—are committed to erasing their way of life, then the desire to survive will be used to justify conflict. But as Peter's appearance in the mirror in the Giant's Drink game shows us, perhaps there is truth in the old axiom that "we have seen the enemy and he is us."

Ender realizes after he has committed xenocide that all species wish to survive, and that contrary to the realist position, war's not necessarily the answer when communication fails. This is not to say that conflict should always be avoided. Nor should we presume that all communication is beneficial, in earnest, and without an agenda. Power by persuasion is inherently political. But as Ender learned in governing his own colony in the new world, there are "differences between military and civilian leadership" and the most successful leader governs "by persuasion rather than fiat."[23]

Notes

1. For insight into the military side of such decisions, see the chapters by Kody Cooper and James A. Cook in this volume.
2. Thomas Hobbes, *Leviathan*, ed. Edwin Curley (Indianapolis: Hackett Publishing Company, 1994), 76.
3. Hans Morgenthau, *Politics Among Nations: The Struggle for Power and Peace, Brief Edition* (Boston: McGraw-Hill, 1993), 29.

4. Orson Scott Card, *Ender's Game* (New York: TOR Books, 1991), 35.
5. Ibid., 253.
6. Ibid., 110–111.
7. Ibid., 126.
8. Ibid.
9. Robert Axelrod, *The Evolution of Cooperation* (New York: Basic Books, Inc., 1984), 12.
10. Card, *Ender's Game*, 253.
11. Ibid.
12. Ibid., 311–312.
13. Ibid., 228–229.
14. Niccolò Machiavelli, *The Prince*, ed. Quentin Skinner and Russell Price (Cambridge: Cambridge University Press, 1988), 19.
15. Card, *Ender's Game*, 130–131.
16. Ibid., 128.
17. Ibid.
18. Ibid., 131.
19. Machiavelli, *The Prince*, 21.
20. Card, *Ender's Game*, 239.
21. Ibid., 212.
22. Ibid., 238.
23. Ibid., 315.

CHAPTER 18

People Are Tools

Greg Littmann

Individual human beings are all tools.

—Hyrum Graff

Life's hard when you're the last hope for humanity. Andrew "Ender" Wiggin is beaten up, socially isolated, lied to, spied on, manipulated, and almost murdered. Not only do the adults in his life never try to *help* him, they actively conspire to make sure the kid is friendless, endangered, and unhappy. Colonel Hyrum Graff, principal of the Battle School, takes care to "surround him with enemies all the time," commanding that "his isolation can't be broken. He can never come to believe that anybody will ever help him out. Ever."[1]

Ender does nothing to bring this hellish existence on himself. He's earnest, well meaning, and kind. Graff admits, "He's clean. Right to the heart, he's good."[2] It's true, Ender does tend to kill other children, which is not the sort of behavior we want in our schools, but he strikes only in self-defense and it is hard to blame a child for fighting for his life. How can the adults tolerate such cruelty to a kid, let alone *promote* it?

Ender's Game is a horror story about the demands that can be made on individuals in the name of the greater good. Ender is a child who is treated in a way that, under normal circumstances, would be morally wrong on grounds of cruelty. Obviously, children shouldn't generally be subjected to violence, denied the right to have friends, or tricked

Ender's Game and Philosophy: The Logic Gate Is Down, First Edition. Edited by Kevin S. Decker.
© 2013 John Wiley & Sons, Inc. Published 2013 by John Wiley & Sons, Inc.

into joining the army at the age of six. But Ender lives in very *special* circumstances. As far as humanity can tell, they stand on the brink of extinction at the hands of the alien buggers. Earth needs to quickly produce a commander capable of defeating the bugger fleet. The best way to do this, it turns out, is to make poor Ender's young life a misery.

Ender's Game raises difficult moral questions: when can we harm people for the greater good? When is it okay to mislead them or make decisions on their behalf in the common interest? And are these actions *ever* acceptable? The naïve response would be to answer both questions, "Never," unless people are incompetent to decide for themselves. In reality, things are not so simple, most obviously in times of war. It's impossible, for instance, for a nation to defend itself in wartime without harming the innocent. Even if no civilians are killed and we judge every enemy soldier to be guilty, we still harm these combatants' innocent children every time we take one of their fathers and mothers in battle. Likewise, a nation at war must conduct maneuvers that deceive both the enemy and even their own troops and civilian populations because of the need for secrecy. Nor can a nation at war help making decisions on behalf of other people. Even if a country has no military draft, sometimes civilian populations need to be moved or their supplies rationed whether they like it or not, either for their own safety or for the sake of the war effort.

In fact, as *Ender's Game* should remind us, you can be morally justified in doing *anything* to people, innocent or otherwise, if the consequences serve the greater good. "Consequentialism" is the view that the moral rightness or wrongness of an act depends entirely on its consequences. Simply put, for the consequentialist the ends justify the means. People are tools in that they have no value over and above their ability to bring about the desired consequences. The best-known form of consequentialism is "utilitarianism," which states that the *only* consequence that matters is happiness. In the words of utilitarianism's most famous advocate, English philosopher John Stuart Mill (1806–1873), utilitarianism is the view that "actions are right in proportion as they tend to promote happiness; wrong as they tend to produce the reverse of happiness."[3] Mill argued that happiness must be what is most desirable because happiness is what human beings truly desire. However, he was not advocating a life of selfish hedonism, but just the opposite. Mill believed that it was unreasonable to value your own happiness more than that of anyone else. We must constantly be striving to do whatever will best promote happiness in general, even if this makes our own lives miserable. In fact, one of the common objections to utilitarianism is that it asks too much in demanding that we *never* place our own interests ahead of someone else. Considering the actions of Graff and Ender from Mill's point of view can increase our appreciation for utilitarianism. Both Ender and Graff are driven by the need to serve the greater good, even when this means that they must step over accepted moral boundaries.

Chosen to Save Humanity

John Stuart Mill's early life parallels Ender's surprisingly closely. Like Ender, Mill was a gifted child, subjected to an arduous training program because he had been chosen to save humanity. His father, the historian and radical thinker James Mill, was a passionate advocate of utilitarianism. On utilitarian grounds, James Mill argued that humanity needs democracy, individual liberty, education, rationality, and fewer wealthy parasites living off the sweat of others.

James decided to raise his son John to be the ideal ambassador for utilitarian thought, someone who would reform society by spreading utilitarian ideals. Like Ender, John was given a grueling education to prepare him to be humanity's champion. Ender enrolled in Battle School at the age of six; John began learning Greek at three and was soon being drilled in Latin, poetry, literature, history, and mathematics. At seven, Ender was training Launchies in the battleroom during free play; at eight, John's father made him a schoolmaster to his brothers and sisters. Ender at ten was transferred to Command School to train directly for combat against the buggers; John at 12 was made to study philosophy, politics, and economics to train directly for the war to reform society.

Like Ender, John was forced to be an independent thinker, able to analyze new situations and to come up with his own ideas. Where Ender had to continually find new ways to win his teachers' games, Mill was made to debate with his father and other adults. Both young men were intentionally isolated from other children in order to mold them as perfect tools. Where Ender was isolated in a crowd – a child alone in a bunkroom of children – Mill was kept away from people his own age for fear that they would have a corrupting influence on his intellectual development.

Like Ender, Mill was pushed to the limits of his abilities. He wrote that his father "demanded of me not only the utmost that I could do, but much that I could by no possibility have done."[4] Both boys' early, brilliant successes gave way to despair and apathy. Ender's breakdown occurs after he kills Bonzo Madrid. For three months, Ender languishes doing nothing, until he reconnects with his sister Valentine and the planet Earth and is reminded of what he's fighting for. Mill's breakdown occurred when he was 20 and already a rising radical political writer. His depression sprang from the stresses of his intensive training, which sharpened his mind but neglected his emotional needs. For Mill, it was the joy of literature, poetry, and music that finally roused him from him gloom, rekindling his love of life and his commitment to the utilitarian cause.

Ender was precocious enough to have saved humanity before he turned 13, and being a spare messiah, next devoted himself to saving the *buggers*. John Stuart Mill's quest to save humanity lasted until his death at the age of 67. He championed the abolition of slavery, the interests of the working classes, land reform for poor Irish farmers, and the rights of women. Sitting as the Radical member for Westminster in the House of Commons (1865–1868), he was the first person to make a speech in the house insisting that women should be given the vote.

The Tragedy of *Ender's Game*

Ender's Game is a tragedy in which dedicated individuals like Colonel Graff and Ender Wiggin give their all to do their duty, only to have their efforts and sacrifices bring about almost the worst possible result. However, the most terrible loss in the book isn't Ender's childhood or the lives of the two children he kills, but the near extinction of an intelligent species, the *only* other intelligent species (as far as humanity knows). The extermination of the buggers turns out to have been entirely unnecessary. As Ender learns after committing xenocide, the buggers had only attacked the humans by mistake in the first place, and were ready to establish peaceful contact. Even if we consider only human happiness, the loss of what humans might have learned from the buggers is catastrophic.

But a concern with only human happiness is not in the spirit of Mill's utilitarianism. Since Mill insisted that we should abandon preferential treatment based on race and sex, it's hard to imagine him discriminating against someone just because of their planet of origin. Hive queens are at least as intelligent as human beings and are capable of reasoning. They feel emotions, as Ender learns when he makes telepathic contact with the last surviving pupa and sees the war through the buggers' eyes: "What the hive-queen felt was sadness, a sense of resignation."[5] They even understand familiar moral concepts, as demonstrated when the last hive queen thinks, "The humans did not forgive us."[6] Mill specifically recognized that we owe moral duties to non-humans and advocated greater legal protection for them. As one of the earliest animal welfare activists, he wrote "The reasons for legal intervention in favor of children, apply not less strongly to the case of those unfortunate slaves and victims of the most brutal part of mankind, the lower animals."[7] Though the buggers aren't human, once we recognize that they have moral status, as Ender does, we can see that the tragedy is more terrible still. The buggers lose almost everything.

For a utilitarian, it's clear that Graff and Ender were wrong to act as they did, even though they both devoted their lives to doing the right thing. If Graff had been a less diligent principal of the Battle School, maybe tragedy could have been averted. If only Ender Wiggin had lacked the compassion for others that drove him to fight for humanity, if only he had devoted himself to reading comic books or using his powerful intellect to cheat at cards, then the buggers could have been spared.

However, just because Graff and Ender acted wrongly according to the utilitarian model doesn't mean we need to *blame* them for their actions. As we'll see, given the information they had, they make exactly the choices most likely to bring about the greatest happiness. For the utilitarian, Graff and Ender are both *heroes*. Ender scores better than Graff, though, because he has the moral sense to want to help the buggers as well as the humans.

The Court-Martial of Colonel Hyrum Graff

Graff has been intending to exterminate his enemies all along: "If we can, we'll kill every last one of the buggers."[8] He's delighted when he thinks they've been entirely wiped out. Tears of joy pour down his face as he embraces Ender and thanks God for him. Graff could offer a utilitarian defense of his attitude. As far as he knows, the buggers are a race of bloodthirsty killers, not the sort of species that is likely to bring a lot of happiness into the universe. But Graff never offers a moral defense, instead, avoiding all talk of morality and framing the slaughter of the buggers as a necessary consequence of human psychology: "The real decision is inevitable. If one of us has to be destroyed, let's make damn sure we're the ones alive at the end. Our genes won't let us decide any other way."[9]

Likewise, Graff can offer a good utilitarian defense for treating Ender in the brutal way that he does. Graff just does what he has every reason to believe will bring about the best consequences, and so he's far from being a "monster," as Major Anderson suggests.[10] He doesn't dismiss the significance of Ender's suffering; in fact, it's Graff's compassion for Ender that makes him bitter about his duty. "I hope you had fun, I hope you had a nice, nice time being happy, Ender. It might be the last time in your life. Welcome, little boy. Your dear Uncle Graff has plans for you."[11] However, weighing up the needs of all humanity, Graff decides that the need to meet the threat justifies violating common standards of decency. The ends justify the means, even if in this case that includes the unjust suffering of an innocent child.

That we should not hurt children, or allow them to be hurt by our negligence, is an excellent moral rule in almost all circumstances. Many utilitarians after Mill have believed that we should always obey a rule if following that rule in general would promote happiness. These "rule utilitarians" would condemn Graff for the brutal way he treats kids. On the other hand, Mill, as an "act utilitarian" believed that we should perform whatever action will best promote the greatest happiness, regardless of what general rules we break. Graff even conceives of his ultimate goal in terms of human happiness: "Survival first, then happiness as we can manage it."[12] Humanity can't *win* the war with the buggers under the normal rules, and as far as Graff can tell, losing means extermination.

Again, Graff denies that his actions are being driven by moral judgments. Anderson objects to his methods: "I just don't believe you, and you alone, should decide the fate of the world." Graff replies, "I don't even think it's right for me to decide the fate of Ender Wiggin."[13] This is not true, of course, since it's only Graff's committed belief that it *is* right for him to decide Ender's fate that allows him to overcome his feelings of compassion as he watches the boy suffer.

We can only assume that Graff knows what he's doing in subjecting Ender to this treatment to produce a great military commander. In the real world, Graff's methods would be much more likely to ruin or corrupt sensitive minds than to produce sane, effective, and morally trustworthy generals. However, *Ender's Game* is a science fiction novel, so perhaps Graff has access to futuristic psychological research that backs him up. Mill would certainly like to see that research, because he places an especially high value on individual freedom and would be horrified to see government taking control of people's lives in the name of the public good.

While Mill accepted that the only thing that matters in itself is happiness, he also observed that this end is best served when people have the freedom to run their own lives. He wrote in *On Liberty* (1859): "The only part of the conduct of anyone for which he is amenable to society is that which concerns others. In the part which merely concerns himself, his independence is, of right, absolute."[14] While he acknowledged that this rule might be suspended regarding decisions on behalf of young children, this would only last until they are "capable of being improved by free and equal discussion."[15] As Peter and Valentine demonstrate by conquering the Earth by *blogging*, the Wiggin kids are more than ready to talk to the grown-ups as equals.

Mill recognized that the need for collective self-defense may justify breaking the rule against telling people what to do. He wrote, "the sole end for which mankind are warranted … in interfering with the liberty of action of any of their number is self-protection. That the only purpose for which power can be rightfully exercised over any member of a civilized community … is to prevent harm to others."[16] Ender's refusal or failure to defend Earth might or might not count as "harming" humanity, but the justification for interfering in his life is the same. As bad an idea as it normally is for the government to override someone's liberty, it would be the right thing to do if the whole world were at stake. As Graff puts it, "Human beings are free except when humanity needs them."[17]

What Is Ender's Game?

Ender, like Graff, is willing to break normal standards to achieve the ultimate goal. Rule-breaking to achieve victory is Ender's specialty. Sometimes, he finds a way to win by breaking the standard *strategic* rules, such as when he deliberately freezes the legs of his flash suit to protect himself in the battleroom, or when he reorganizes his Dragon Army into groups of four and makes one in four a human shield. Just as often, Ender wins by breaking the normal *moral* rules.[18] The consummate consequentialist, he understands that normal moral rules don't apply when there is enough at stake.

The first time we see this happen, he's just had his monitor removed and is cornered by a gang of bullies. Ender opens with an appeal to his enemies' honor to fight him one at a time: "You mean it takes this many of you to fight one Third?" Then when the kids holding him release him, he follows up by kicking Stilson, the ringleader, in the sternum, dropping him to the ground. Having won the battle by exploiting his enemy's sense of honor, Ender goes on to throw honor out of the window in order to win the war: "I have to win this now, and for all time, or I'll fight it every day and it will get worse and worse."[19] With that, Ender delivers enough vicious kicks to Stilson's ribs, crotch, and face to kill the other child.

Later, as commander of Dragon Army, Ender applies the same tactics to defeat and kill Bonzo Madrid, rival commander of Salamander Army. Once more, Ender exploits the very rules of honor that he is intending to betray. As with Stilson, Ender shames Bonzo into fighting him one-on-one, taunting him about what his father would think if he could see his son's cowardice. He even shames Bonzo into fighting him naked, since Ender is already naked (though why nobody suggests that they even things up by allowing both combatants to put their pants on, I don't know). Left with only one opponent and now able to use his soapy condition to his advantage, Ender is ready to finish the fight "quickly, and permanently."[20] Having dropped Bonzo with a head-butt to the nose, he again brutally attacks a helpless enemy lying on the ground. Ender kicks Bonzo so hard in the crotch that he kills the child, just as he killed Stilson.

Even in his final victory against the buggers, Ender wins only by breaking normal moral rules. To say that he uses weapons of mass destruction against civilian population centers would be a gross understatement. To win the war, he wipes out an entire world and its intelligent species with the Little Doctor. That he does this by resorting to *kamikaze* tactics is only icing on the cake. He thinks, "If you can cheat, so can I. I won't let you beat me unfairly—I'll beat you unfairly first."[21]

Even if Ender's actions are appropriate given his circumstances, this doesn't mean we have to accept that people in the *real* world should adopt his solutions. As immoral acts go, killing children ranks pretty highly, and even this pales against genocide. We shouldn't suggest that real-world victims of school violence, of which there are very many, should go out and buy themselves a gun. Nor should we conclude that victims of violence should seek safety by inflicting such vicious kicks to the ribs, groin, and face of defeated attackers that nobody will dare to assault them again. Likewise, even if Ender's actions are justified, this doesn't provide grounds for us to seek similar solutions in warfare. As an approach to international relations, the model of "I'll kick you so hard as you lie helpless on the ground that you won't ever dare to fight me again" is spectacularly counterproductive.

In fact, it's *precisely* the fact that Graff's and Ender's actions are morally justified yet *not* templates for general moral rules that makes them so interesting as cases of consequentialist thinking. The morally correct decisions made by Graff and Ender are *exceptions* to the general moral rules, but only because of their escalated stakes. All their feelings of guilt, and in Ender's case, even self-hatred, come from doing the very things that duty quite rightly tells them to do.

Lessons from *Ender's Game*

Ender's Game holds a special place in the long tradition of literary consequentialist nightmares. Many critics of consequentialist and utilitarian morality have tried to use fictional scenarios to demonstrate that these moral theories have outrageous implications. For example, in *Crime and Punishment* (1866), author Fyodor Dostoyevsky has his protagonist Raskolnikov decide on utilitarian principles to murder an old woman. She's a pawnbroker with many people in her debt, and her money could be used to help the poor. He reasons that "on one side we have a stupid, senseless, worthless, spiteful, ailing, horrid old woman, not simply useless but doing actual mischief, who has not an idea what she is living for herself, and who will die in a day or two in any case ... On the other side, fresh young lives thrown away for want of help and by thousands, on every side!"[22]

Similarly, Ursula K. Le Guin shows us, in her short story, "The Ones Who Walk Away From Omelas," a utopian city filled with happy people, only to have us learn their joyful lives are made possible by the suffering of an innocent child locked away forever in darkness, isolation, and filth. The people of this city, Omelas, know about the child's suffering. It is, somehow, the source of their compassionate nature and "makes possible the nobility of their architecture, the poignancy of their music, the profundity of their science."[23] Suggestions that the child should be released are rejected by the citizens on utilitarian grounds—when weighing the happiness of so many against the unhappiness of a single individual, it makes more sense to leave the child to suffer.

In both of these tales we're shown acts that would normally be morally repugnant, but would, at least according to these characters, produce the greatest total happiness. In both cases, the authors want us to conclude that bringing about the greatest total happiness doesn't make these actions at all moral: Dostoyevsky and Le Guin want to show that utilitarianism can't be the right moral standard. *Ender's Game*, though, is different from both *Crime and Punishment* and "The Ones Who Walk Away From Omelas." In *Ender's Game*, the consequences to humanity of sticking by our normal moral rules are clearly so terrible that it would be monstrous *not* to break those rules.

Dostoyevsky's Raskolnikov appeals to utilitarian principles, but he is also a fool with delusions of grandeur and a silly plan. His crime, as you might guess from the novel's title, brings only punishment; it was absurdly optimistic of him to believe that becoming a murderous urban Robin Hood in nineteenth-century St. Petersburg would turn out for the best. Le Guin's Omelas, on the other hand, rubs our moral intuitions the wrong way by being populated with citizens whose psychology is alien to ours. Since it is Le Guin's imaginary city, she's free to decide that all the moral and cultural benefits of living in Omelas (as in "Omelet"?) come from the child's suffering. But no real human beings could be improved morally by knowing that a child is in torment on their behalf. It could never be a boon to real scientists or music lovers to understand that an innocent is being cruelly abused.

In *Ender's Game*, on the other hand, the protagonists are neither fools nor psychologically alien to us, and the stakes they are playing for are so great that there's no individual right that couldn't be violated for the greater good. Any moral theory that implies that individuals have *inalienable* rights, rights that must not be violated under any circumstances, can't accommodate the scenario of *Ender's Game*.

In Graff's case, choosing *not* to treat Ender as a tool would amount to complicity with a bugger genocide of the human race, however unfair this might be for Ender. In fact, Graff could have treated Ender a good deal worse, even tortured him, and still have been morally justified if he had reason to believe that it was the only way he could save humanity. In Ender's case, failure to treat Stilson and Bonzo as tools to spread fear would have meant suicide. By making an example of them, he makes them instruments to serve his ends, and in turn, those ends serve Graff's and humanity's ends. None of this proves that utilitarianism, or any type of consequentialism, is correct. After all, you don't have to think that *only* consequences matter to see that the results of Graff's treatment of Ender outweigh all other moral considerations, even compassion for a child. Likewise, you don't need to be a consequentialist to think that Ender is justified in defending himself with lethal force in personal combat and defending humanity with lethal force in space. All you *need* to accept in order to think Ender justified is that the total consequences in these cases were serious *enough* to outweigh other moral considerations, like the lives of a couple of children and an alien civilization.

However, *Ender's Game* does clearly demonstrate that moral rules almost always have exceptions if circumstances are strange enough. By taking general happiness as the only thing that matters, utilitarians can explain the fact that almost all moral rules have exceptions. Utilitarianism supports a wide variety of general rules that apply in almost all circumstances—rules like "do not kill," "do not lie," and "do not surround children with enemies," but also allows that the rules don't apply in cases where they do not serve the greater good.

One of the things that makes *Ender's Game* such a powerful novel is that Orson Scott Card doesn't flinch from forcing his characters to make hard decisions. There is no easy way out for Graff or Ender. Whatever course of action they take, innocent people will be hurt. It is important that we tell stories like this because *life* is sometimes like this, and to pretend otherwise is dangerously unrealistic. The danger is not that we'll fail to violate normal individual rights or moral standards when we need to. Rather, it's that we'll assume that if we're making the right decision, nobody innocent will get hurt. A similar mistake is to think that if a given course of action would hurt the innocent, then *not* taking that course of action will *not* hurt the innocent. Unfortunately, reality is not that simple.

As citizens in first-world societies, our power to vote means that we are all, in a way, required to play Ender's game to defend humanity. Like Ender, we have this power thrust into our hands whether we want it or not. Like Ender, we need to be extremely careful about the choices we make, examining our moves with great attention and making sure that we are not being trapped by old ways of thinking. As in Ender's case, the price if we fail to be diligent enough could be extinction.

Notes

1. Orson Scott Card, *Ender's Game* (New York: TOR Books, 1991), 38.
2. Ibid., 36.
3. John Stuart Mill, "Utilitarianism," in *Utilitarianism and Other Essays*, ed. Alan Ryan (London: Penguin Classics, 1987), 278.
4. John Stuart Mill, *Autobiography* (London: Penguin Classics, 1990), 28.
5. Card, *Ender's Game*, 320.
6. Ibid.
7. John Stuart Mill, *Principles of Political Economy* (Indianapolis: Hackett Publishing Company, 2004), 291.
8. Card, *Ender's Game*, 254.
9. Ibid., 253.
10. Ibid., 28.
11. Ibid., 155.
12. Mill, *Principles of Political Economy*, 277.
13. Card, *Ender's Game*, 98.
14. John Stuart Mill, "On Liberty," in *On Liberty and The Subjection of Women* (London: Penguin Classics, 2007), 16.
15. Ibid., 17.
16. Ibid., 16.
17. Card, *Ender's Game*, 35.
18. For a different look at Ender's rule breaking in the context of the games he plays, see Brendan Shea's chapter in this volume.
19. Card, *Ender's Game*, 7.
20. Ibid., 209.
21. Ibid., 293.
22. Fyodor Dostoyevsky, *Crime and Punishment*, trans. Constance Garnett (London: Dover Publications, 2001), 53.
23. Ursula K. Le Guin, "The Ones Who Walked Away From Omelas," in *The Winds Twelve Quarters: Stories* (London: William Morrow Paperbacks, 2004), 283.

Convening Authorities of the Court Martial of Colonel Hyrum Graff

Lance Belluomini did his graduate studies in philosophy at the University of California, Berkeley; San Francisco State University; and the University of Nebraska-Lincoln. He has recently contributed chapters to Wiley-Blackwell's *Inception and Philosophy* and *The Walking Dead and Philosophy*. His philosophical interests include ethics and the philosophy of popular culture. Lance doesn't think it's a coincidence that in the new *Ender's Game* movie, an actor named Han Soto plays Colonel Graff's aide, and the actor who plays Colonel Graff played Han Solo.

Cole Bowman is a graduate of Eastern Washington University, where she received baccalaureate degrees in both philosophy and English literature. At this time, she is a graduate school hopeful, and occupies most of her time with writing. Like Demosthenes and Locke, she maintains an active presence on the nets.

Matthew Brophy teaches at High Point University as an Assistant Professor of Philosophy. He enjoys exploring philosophy through science fiction, and has contributed to such popular press volumes as *Avatar and Philosophy* (Wiley-Blackwell, pending) and *Inception and Philosophy* (Open Court). Brophy has also contributed essays to Wiley-Blackwell's series "Philosophy for Everyone" in volumes spanning porn, Christmas, college sex, and serial killers. Though a "Third"

Ender's Game and Philosophy: The Logic Gate Is Down, First Edition. Edited by Kevin S. Decker.
© 2013 John Wiley & Sons, Inc. Published 2013 by John Wiley & Sons, Inc.

child himself, Brophy struggles at winning Angry Birds, so doubts he'd be very adroit at commanding intergalactic starship battles.

Ted Henry Brown is an Assistant Lecturer and Ph.D. candidate in political science at Texas A&M University. His research and teaching interests combine the fields of American political thought, rhetoric, and international relations. Ted discovered *Ender's Game* while in graduate school and the book continues to provide invaluable lessons to him at the beginning and end of every semester when his students begin to swarm like buggers.

Cam Cobb is Assistant Professor of Education at the University of Windsor. He teaches courses in such topics as differentiated learning, issues in education, and curriculum theory. His research interests include special education, parental inclusion, and social justice. While Cam does make use of technology in his teaching, his students never actually get to play "the Giant's Drink."

James L. Cook is Professor and Head of the Department of Philosophy at the US Air Force Academy, a position he has held since US Senate confirmation in 2002. An Air Force Cyber Officer and Foreign Area Officer, he has served at the Pentagon, in NATO, and as Senior Academic Advisor to the National Military Academy of Afghanistan. He speaks and publishes primarily on military ethics and hermeneutics, interests piqued by his years as an officer and Ph.D. student at Heidelberg. Those years also convinced him that a military leader's most valuable weapon is a good Bean.

Kody W. Cooper is a Ph.D. candidate in government at the University of Texas—Austin. Cooper has published in the areas of political philosophy, jurisprudence, and constitutional theory. He has also contributed a chapter to *The Wire and Philosophy* (Open Court, 2013). In his spare time, he offers affordable political counsel to aspiring hegemons and engages in political machinations on the nets under the pseudonym "Hobbes."

Morgan Deane has a BA from Southern Virginia University and an MA in history from Norwich University. In 2009 he separated from the military after serving nine years as an infantry riflemen, squad leader, and intelligence analyst. He is the author of "Preemptive Warfare in the *Book of Mormon* and a defense of the Bush Doctrine," has written articles for the *Encyclopedia of Military Philosophy*, and authored a chapter on East Asia for *World History to 1650*. Currently, he works as an Adjunct Professor of History at Brigham Young University, Idaho, and he is studying Chinese in preparation for a Ph.D. program in East Asian history. In his free time he tries to summon his inner Peter to conquer the world in the game Civilization V.

Kevin S. Decker is Associate Professor of Philosophy and Associate Dean of the College of Arts and Letters at Eastern Washington University. He writes and teaches about American and Continental philosophy, social theory and applied ethics. He's been actively involved in publishing on popular culture and philosophy and is the co-editor (with Jason T. Eberl) of *Star Wars and Philosophy* and *Star Trek and Philosophy* (Open Court), and (with Richard Brown) *Terminator and Philosophy* (Wiley-Blackwell). He has published chapters in similar books on James Bond, Transformers, *The Daily Show*, *Doctor Who*, the films of Stanley Kubrick, and *30 Rock*. And he had a bugger of a time editing this book.

Jeff Ewing is a graduate student in sociology at the University of Oregon, and has published a number of popular culture and philosophy chapters, including chapters in *Terminator and Philosophy* and *Arrested Development and Philosophy*. Jeff wanted to take an Ender-style approach to chapter writing, and divide his chapter into several sections, each written independently by a different person, but he couldn't decide whether to name them "Three-Toed Sloth Army," "Duck-Billed Platypus Army," or the "Goldenpalace.com Monkey Army," so it never quite happened.

Greg Littmann is of no strategic military value. He is Associate Professor at Southern Illinois University Edwardsville, an unfortified university protecting no natural resources. Here, he teaches critical thinking, metaphysics and philosophy of mind, all at low range and at volumes that cause no physical damage. He has published in metaphysics and the philosophy of logic, yet despite the dependence of game theory on logic, has never managed to kill a single person with his work. He has also written 17 chapters for volumes relating philosophy to popular culture, including books on *Big Bang Theory*, *Doctor Who*, *Dune*, *Game of Thrones*, Neil Gaiman, *Planet of the Apes*, Ridley Scott, Sherlock Holmes, *Terminator*, and *The Walking Dead*. Should it be necessary, Greg Littmann is most easily attacked by drop troops from above, armed with lasers if available, though any weapon would suffice.

Christie L. Maloyed is an Assistant Professor of Political Science at the University of Nebraska Kearney. She discovered the writings of Orson Scott Card in graduate school and credits him with having made that experience far more bearable. Having dabbled in various fields of research including American political thought, religion and politics, and politics and popular culture, she hopes to spin her research into a career as prolific as that of Valentine Wiggin.

Jeffery L. Nicholas is Assistant Professor of Philosophy at Providence College and writes on political philosophy, pop culture, and human nature. He edited *Dune and Philosophy* (Open Court) and contributed to *The Big Lebowski and Philosophy* (Blackwell). He believes that philosophers are the original Speakers for the Dead, and hopes one day to have some student write a book explaining his fascination with science fiction.

Brett Chandler Patterson completed degrees at Furman, Duke, and the University of Virginia and has taught at Meredith College, Anderson University, and Francis Marion University. He has written several essays for Wiley-Blackwell's "Philosophy and Pop Culture" series, including essays on *Lost*, *Downton Abbey*, Batman, Iron Man, and Green Lantern. He has used several of Card's novels in the classroom, attended Card's writing workshop, and contributed to *The Authorized Ender Companion*. After having lived with technology these last few years, he hopes that he can find a space away from cellular phones, but he realizes that even in such a place there would be the ansible!

Jeremy Proulx, fresh from philosophy battle school at McMaster University in Hamilton, Canada, went on to become Lecturer in Philosophy at Eastern Michigan University. Proulx writes in the field of classical German philosophy and has published articles and reviews in *Intellectual History Review*, *Kant Studies Online*, and *The British Journal for the History of Philosophy*.

Kenneth Wayne Sayles III earned his MS in computer science in 2004 from the University of Texas at El Paso (UTEP) investigating the effects of computer personalities on users. He has worked in information security since 2006 and holds the following certifications: CISSP; CEH; CEPT; CISA; and CISM. He completed his MA in philosophy in 2010, also from UTEP, after demonstrating how classical social contract theory can be used to better understand the Internet. He began contributing to popular culture and philosophy with a chapter on *The Big Bang Theory*. He found finishing his chapter in this book especially challenging since he wasn't used to writing in zero gravity.

Brendan P. Shea is Assistant Professor of Philosophy at Winona State University, where he teaches courses in the history of philosophy, logic and critical thinking, and the philosophy of science. He enjoys writing and thinking about philosophy and popular culture, and has published articles about the philosophy of *Alice in Wonderland*, J.J. Abrams, *Jeopardy!*, and the *Twilight* books. If he were forced to choose a single philosophy book to share with the buggers, he'd probably choose Plato's *Republic*.

Chad William Timm is an Assistant Professor of Education at Grand View University in Des Moines, Iowa. He has also published chapters in *The Girl with the Dragon Tattoo and Philosophy*, *Hunger Games and Philosophy*, and *Game of Thrones and Philosophy*. When he isn't writing about pop culture and philosophy he spends his time constructing the identity of future teachers in order to help them train future space commanders.

Danielle Wylie is a Ph.D. candidate in philosophy at the University of Wisconsin— Madison. She is currently writing a dissertation on the cognitive processes responsible for moral judgment. While she loves grad school, she imagines that it would be much more fun if it involved battlerooms and flash suits.

Andrew Zimmerman Jones is writer and editor of the About.com Physics Guidesite. He has an undergraduate degree from Wabash

College, where he studied physics, mathematics, and philosophy, later earning a master's degree in mathematics education from Purdue University. He is a member of the National Association of Science Writers, Toastmasters International, and American Mensa. As a teenager, he attended the Indiana Academy for Science, Mathematics, and Humanities, which was much like Battle School, but with gravity.

The Ansible Index

Ender's Game and Philosophy: The Logic Gate Is Down, First Edition. Edited by Kevin S. Decker.
© 2013 John Wiley & Sons, Inc. Published 2013 by John Wiley & Sons, Inc.